GENDER AND INSTI
Welfare, Work and Ci

This important interdisciplinary volume explores what might constitute a feminist approach to institutional design and reshaping. What is the scope, it asks, in contemporary Australian society, for ensuring that institutions acknowledge gender difference and deliver more equitable outcomes? This feminist perspective on institutional design shows how gendered regulatory norms underpin and intersect with all other institutional settings. The leading team of writers discuss topics including: institutions, embodiment and sexual difference; the welfare state; housing policy; household work; republicanism and citizenship; gender-based discrimination. Edited by Moira Gatens and Alison Mackinnon, this book makes a major contribution to debates about the reshaping of our institutions.

Moira Gatens teaches philosophy at the University of Sydney. She is the author of *Feminism and Philosophy: Perpsectives on Difference and Equality* and *Imaginary Bodies: Ethics, Power and Corporeality*. She is currently completing a book on Spinoza with Genevieve Lloyd and is one of six editors of the *Oxford Companion to Australian Feminism*.

Alison Mackinnon is professor of history and women's studies at the University of South Australia, and is also director of the Institute for Social Research and of the newly established Hawke Institute. She has written three books, including the award-winning *Love and Freedom*, published by Cambridge in 1997, and she has jointly edited five others.

RESHAPING AUSTRALIAN INSTITUTIONS

Series editors: Geoffrey Brennan and Francis G. Castles,
Research School of Social Sciences, Australian National
University
Published in association with the Research School of
Social Sciences, Australian National University.

This program of publications arises from the School's
initiative in sponsoring a fundamental rethinking of
Australia's key institutions before the centenary of
Federation in 2001.

Published in this program will be the work of scholars
from the Australian National University and elsewhere
who are researching and writing on the institutions of the
nation. The scope of the program includes the institutions of public governance, intergovernmental relations,
Aboriginal Australia, gender, population, the environment, the economy, business, the labour market, the
welfare state, the city, education, the media, criminal
justice and the Constitution.

Brian Galligan *A Federal Republic*
  0 521 37354 9 hardback   0 521 37746 3 paperback
Patrick Troy (ed.) *Australian Cities*
  0 521 48197 X hardback   0 521 48437 5 paperback
Ian Marsh *Beyond the Two Party System*
  0 521 46223 1 hardback   0 521 46779 9 paperback
Elim Papadakis *Environmental Politics and Institutional
  Change*
  0 521 55407 1 hardback   0 521 55631 7 paperback
Chilla Bulbeck *Living Feminism*
  0 521 46042 5 hardback   0 521 46596 6 paperback
John Uhr *Deliberative Democracy in Australia*
  0 521 62458 4 hardback   0 521 62465 7 paperback
Mitchell Dean and Barry Hindess (eds) *Governing
  Australia*
  0 521 58357 8 hardback   0 521 58671 2 paperback
Nicolas Peterson and Will Sanders (eds) *Citizenship
  and Indigenous Australians*
  0 521 62195 X hardback   0 521 62736 2 paperback
Martin Painter *Collaborative Federalism*
  0 521 59071 X hardback
Julianne Schultz *Reviving the Fourth Estate*
  0 521 62042 2 hardback   0 521 62970 5 paperback
David Peetz *Unions in a Contrary World*
  0 521 63055 X hardback   0 521 63950 6 paperback

GENDER AND INSTITUTIONS

Welfare, Work and Citizenship

EDITED BY

MOIRA GATENS

and

ALISON MACKINNON

CAMBRIDGE
UNIVERSITY PRESS

PUBLISHED BY THE PRESS SYNDICATE OF THE UNIVERSITY OF CAMBRIDGE
The Pitt Building, Trumpington Street, Cambridge, United Kingdom

CAMBRIDGE UNIVERSITY PRESS
The Edinburgh Building, Cambridge CB2 2RU, UK   http://www.cup.cam.ac.uk
40 West 20th Street, New York, NY 10011–4211, USA   http://www.cup.org
10 Stamford Road, Oakleigh, Melbourne 3166, Australia

First published 1998

Printed in Australia by Australian Print Group

Typeset in New Baskerville 10/12 pt

A catalogue record for this book is available from the British Library

National Library of Australia Cataloguing in Publication data

Gender and institutions: welfare, work and citizenship
Bibliography.
Includes index.
ISBN 0 521 63190 4.
ISBN 0 521 63576 4 (pbk).
1. Sexual division of labor. 2. Sex role – Australia. 3.
Sex discrimination against women – Australia. 4. Feminism.
5. Social institutions – Australia. 6 Women – Australia –
Social conditions. 7. Australia – Social life and customs.
I. Gatens, Moira. II. Mackinnon, Alison, 1942–   .
305.420994

ISBN 0 521 63190 4 hardback
ISBN 0 521 63576 4 paperback

Contents

Part I Beyond the Male Breadwinner:
Welfare, housing and household labour

Part II Triumphs and Failures of Feminist Design:
Reshaping the workplace

Figures

Tables

Contributors

CAROL LEE BACCHI, associate professor in politics, University of Adelaide, has published widely in feminist history, politics and social policy. She is currently using social construction and discourse theory to examine meaning construction in policy texts and in the constitution of the field of bioethics.

JANEEN BAXTER is a senior lecturer in sociology, University of Tasmania. Her research interests focus on gender inequality in paid and unpaid work. She is currently involved in a longitudinal study of gender, mobility and career trajectories.

VALERIE BRAITHWAITE is a senior lecturer in psychology, Australian National University, on temporary transfer to the Research School of Social Sciences. Her research interests focus on the micro-macro processes of institutional design, particularly as they relate to institutions of care in the workplace, schools and households.

CHILLA BULBECK is professor of women's studies, University of Adelaide. She has taught social sciences and women's studies for the last two decades and published on aspects of feminism and on women and republicanism in Australia, Korea and France. She was director of the Australian Institute for Women's Research and Policy in 1992–94.

BETTINA CASS, AO, is professor of sociology and social policy and Dean of the Faculty of Arts, University of Sydney. She has been elected a Fellow of the Academy of Social Sciences in Australia. Her research and writing cover Australian and comparative social policies. She is particularly interested in exploring policies concerned with social justice.

LENORE COLTHEART, formerly senior lecturer in politics at the University of Adelaide, is now Publishing Editor for the National Archives of Australia in Canberra. She is currently writing a biography of Australian feminist Jessie Street.

JOAN EVELINE teaches organisational and labour studies at the University of Western Australia. With a research background in women's issues, her studies of women and work have probed the shaping of male advantage in management, mining, politics, tertiary education and approaches to citizenship.

MOIRA GATENS is associate professor of philosophy at the University of Sydney. She has written widely in the areas of feminist philosophy and social and political theory. She is also an editor of the *Oxford Companion to Australian Feminism.*

ALISON MACKINNON is professor of history and women's studies, director of the Institute for Social Research and the newly established Hawke Institute, part of the Bob Hawke Prime Ministerial Centre at the University of South Australia. She has written widely on the history of women's education, on feminist approaches to demographic change and on women and computerisation.

DEBORAH MITCHELL is a Fellow in the Research School of Social Sciences in the Australian National University. Her primary research interests are the impact of globalisation on the welfare state, women's labour force participation and the comparative analysis of welfare state institutions in OECD countries.

Preface

Like all anthologies, this one has a history. Each chapter was written especially for this volume and together they reflect the type of research conducted by feminist scholars working in the 'gender strand' of the Reshaping Australian Institutions project, an initiative of the Research School of Social Sciences at the Australian National University. In addition to the 'gender strand', Reshaping Australian Institutions identified the following institutions as central to contemporary Australian society: the labour market, the welfare state, the economy, the city, civil society, the institutions of population and of governnance. As its full title would suggest – Reshaping Australian Institutions: Towards and Beyond 2001 – the project is ambitious and forward-looking. From the beginning, the RAI project endeavoured to create a context in which theoreticians and practitioners, academics and representatives of various governmental agencies, could exchange ideas and engage in mutual constructive criticism. The project as a whole is concerned to understand institutions, their design, the outcomes they achieve, and their openness, as well as their resilience, to intentional re-design or re-shaping.

In broad terms, participants in the Reshaping Australian Institutions project understand institutions as complex organisations governed by regulatory norms that give rise to stable and recurring patterns of action (see Goodin 1996: 1–43). However, to acknowledge that institutional structures constrain and determine the behaviour of social actors is not to deny that human agency can be an effective motor for institutional reshaping. The late twentieth century is a key moment to consider the meaning and importance of social and political institutions along with the scope that such institutions provide for intentional change. A search for fresh directions seems particularly apposite at a time when major political systems have collapsed, when grand narratives describing social life are under challenge and when boundaries between the roles of men and women are unstable. The restructuring of the national economy in the wake of the globalisation of capital adds an urgency to the study of the institutional mechanisms which attempt to regulate relations between the market, the state, and citizens (see Edwards and Magarey 1995).

A theoretical approach which attempts to explain the macro structures of social life (for, example, the labour market) at the same time as it allows scope for individual and group agency (for example, initiatives such as affirmative action and equal employment opportunity which are designed to create more equitable outcomes for women and other disadvantaged groups) should be attractive to feminist theorists. Yet many of the contributors to this volume found that the theories of institutional design and re-design which were being employed by researchers in the other strands were problematic from a feminist perspective. Part of the problem may well stem from the widespread assumption that one can analyse gender as one 'strand' among others. Sexual difference permeates all institutional settings and is central to the normative force and power of all social institutions. As all the papers in this volume show, gendered regulatory norms intersect with, shape, and provide the underpinning for all other institutional settings. A clear point of consensus that has emerged in this volume is the broad interpretation of the term 'institution' which feminists bring to the theorisation of institutions. The family, marriage, and heterosexuality, are likely to be seen by feminists as the fundamental institutions which structure patriarchal social, political and economic relations.

Feminists in a range of disciplines are inclined to stress the inter-connectedness of all social institutions. Gendered patterns of social interaction which are developed in the family, for instance, are often confirmed by the norms which govern education, the workplace, and the law. Connection, trust, and co-operation are central values in feminist thinking about institutions. This focus on the interrelatedness of persons affects the manner in which feminists theorise social and political life. For example, it may give rise to a notion of citizenship which highlights *associative* rather than separative conceptions of the individual (see Coltheart and Bulbeck, this volume). This emphasis on *association* contrasts sharply with a dominant strand of institutional design theory, namely, the 'rational actor' or 'rational choice' approach. This latter line of thinking lends itself to the economic rationalist perspective that is so influential in the policy decisions of the present (and the immediate past) Australian governments. Needless to say, many feminists have argued that the 'abstract individual' or the 'rational actor', central to much contemporary political and economic theory, is not an abstraction at all but rather is a notion which tracks masculine traits and lifestyles (see Pateman, 1988, Ferber and Nelson 1993, Nelson, 1996, and Gatens, this volume). Many of the essays in this volume attempt to show how assumptions about the sexual 'neutrality' of social actors contributes to women's disadvantage in a range of institutional settings, including housing, employment, and tertiary education.

The contributors to this volume are a disparate crew. Our disciplines include political science, history, economics, philosophy, social policy, psychology, sociology and women's studies. Our participation in the project has been uneven. Some contributors hold fixed-term positions at the Research School of Social Sciences at the Australian National University, others were seconded from various universities for one or two semesters especially to contribute to this project. The conceptual tools of each and the fields of study of each vary widely but we all share a central concern with feminist theory and a desire to understand and change women's position in the key institutions of contemporary Australian society. As well as working individually within our disciplines, some of us formed an interdisciplinary collective within the Reshaping Australian Institutions project. Our discussions frequently highlighted the different commitments of our various disciplines. This was often amusing, sometimes frustrating, but ultimately rewarding and enriching. Our different researches converge on the questions: What would constitute a feminist approach to institutional design and reshaping? What is the scope, in present Australian society, for ensuring our institutions deliver more equitable outcomes for those whom they are supposed to serve? The experience of participating in the gender strand of the project has been challenging. We have not had the luxury of sufficient time together, nor the breadth of representation that we would have liked in order to develop an adequate feminist perspective on institutional design. Certain key elements are unfortunately missing. Several of the chapters gesture towards the important role played by legal institutions, but there is no essay specifically devoted to this topic (however, see Thornton 1995). We regret, too, the lack of an essay dedicated to the influence of contemporary Australian institutions on indigenous peoples' lives (however, see Flick 1990, Wanganeen 1990 and Daly 1995). Each contributor to this volume attempts to identify the elements of a feminist approach to reshaping institutions within the realm of her expertise. This research has been enhanced by the experience of crossing boundaries, of stretching both our imaginations and our disciplinary frameworks. It is in this interdisciplinary spirit that we offer this volume. We will be very pleased if these essays act to stimulate debate around the reshaping of Australian institutions.

Of course, this volume does not stand alone. It may be read alongside two recent feminist collections which traverse neighbouring terrain. *Women in a Restructuring Australia* (1995), edited by Anne Edwards and

Susan Magarey, maps specific aspects of the restructuring of the economy and the state in the context of the globalisation of capital. Belinda Probert's essay (in Edwards and Magarey) provides an excellent introduction to the significance for Australian women of globalisation. Margaret Thornton's *Public and Private: Feminist Legal Debates* (1995) raises problems central to the public/private dichotomy from the perspective of feminist legal theory. Laura Bennett's essay on enterprise bargaining (in Thornton) warns that the loss of the few institutional mechanisms that act to counterbalance the power of employers will result in a deepening of the economic disadvantage suffered by women. Taken together these two edited collections cover a broad spectrum of social and legislative change from which particular insights for feminist demands to reshape contemporary institutions may be drawn. We see our anthology as complementing existing literature in this important area. Such research seems even more urgent now than in the early- to mid-1990s. Many of the initiatives of the Hawke, and then Keating, Labor government which sought to reshape Australian legal, labour market, constitutional and educational institutions now face an uncertain future. The restructuring strategies put in place by Labor, along with the planned initiatives leading up to the year 2001, have now taken on new directions or been abandoned. The issues of republicanism, the reconciliation of indigenous and non-indigenous Australians, and a desire to achieve equity for all Australians, cannot be assumed to be central to the present government's agenda. We believe that this makes the themes central to this volume more, rather than less, important.

This collection opens with an introductory chapter followed by three focussed sections which deal respectively with welfare, the workplace and citizenship. Chapter 1 engages with an influential strand of institutional design theory based on the rational actor model. Moira Gatens argues that the modelling assumptions of this approach are inappropriate to many women's lives and fail to capture the pervasive nature of the norms which govern the family and gender. Embodied individuals are institutionally constrained by normative expectations about sexual difference. Feminist approaches to 'universalist' or 'abstract' institutional arrangements endeavour to show that such arrangements affect embodied individuals differently. Attempts to reshape institutions in order to promote equity must take account of these embodied differences between men and women, as well as racial, ethnic and class differences amongst women. Part One addresses issues which flow from assuming the male breadwinner model as a basis for organising the Australian welfare state. The erosion of that model has major implications for a range of linked policies on income transfer and entitlements. Deborah Mitchell examines alternative models, such as the Swedish-style individual welfare state and argues that it is not necessarily the answer for Australia. Mitchell's chapter outlines the broad parameters of our shifting policy base and its implications.

In the following chapter, Bettina Cass focusses on an often neglected aspect of welfare state analysis. Housing, and the distribution and redistribution of capital and assets through domestic housing policies, is a dominant form of equity and capital accumulation for most Australians. For women, housing and its location is a key determinant of opportunities to enter and remain in employment, education and training as well as being a real and symbolic source of security. The unequal distribution of affordable housing is particularly noted in women-headed households and for those who have an interrupted or low attachment to the labour market. The male breadwinner model leads to a highly discriminatory set of housing outcomes. Both Cass and Mitchell make clear the cumulative effect of disadvantage in several sectors of the welfare state and the labour market.

In Chapter 4, Janeen Baxter demonstrates that the male breadwinner model that is enshrined in the workplace has its equivalent in the 'private' sphere of the household. The expectation that men would be breadwinners and women housekeepers and carers results in a sharp division of household labour, one which appears intransigent in spite of changing work patterns and policies. Baxter seeks an explanation beyond sex role theory and asks in what way doing housework may be seen as 'doing gender'; and why for some women in contemporary society housework provides a form of satisfaction? Mitchell's chapter may suggest a partial response to this question. Current structural benefits and economic realities, such as the fact that most husbands earn more than their wives, impose 'penalties' on the male partner who attempts to share housework.

Within the Australian state women have been instrumental in achieving important policy changes designed to remove gender-based discrimination. One important site of such design is the Equal Employment Opportunity and Affirmative Action legislation. Legislative attempts to re-design social practices along feminist lines are the subject of Part Two, which addresses change in the workplace which is designed to challenge male advantage. The naming of sexual harassment has been an important aspect of challenging the control and exploitation of women in the workplace. As Valerie Braithwaite points out, these changes are not merely cosmetic. Rather, they involve changing deeply ingrained mores of our culture.

Carol Bacchi addresses the issue of sexual harassment within the university in Chapter 5. The problem, she suggests, lies not in individual male psychology, nor in the aberrant 'lecherous professor', but in the entire structure and curriculum of the university, an institution historically established for men where women remain 'the other' in both organisational and epistemological terms. In the following chapter, Joan Eveline examines three disparate sites where stories of women's supposed unsuitability for certain types of work serves to construct and maintain male advantage in employment.

Valerie Braithwaite's assessment of the Australian Affirmative Action (Equal Employment Opportunity for Women) Act of 1986, in Chapter 7, speaks of both triumph and failure. The act, a piece of 'loose and gentle' legislation contained the potential for mobilising a consensus around equal opportunity for all, an acknowledged core value in Australian society in the 1980s. That opportunity was lost in the implementation, Braithwaite argues, when necessary resources were not directed towards informing and educating the public. Instead, media reports encouraged an attitude of cynicism and fear. Nevertheless Braithwaite suggests that powerful levers for institutional re-design, such as consensus on over-riding principles, empowerment of civil society and institutional redundancy, were embedded in the legislation and provide a model for institutional and cultural change.

The issues addressed in Part Three converge on the concept of citizenship. Throughout the twentieth century Australian women have sought full access to citizenship, a citizenship formulated in their own terms. The concept of citizenship and of the citizen is unstable and historically contingent. Initially many women used the concept of the citizen-mother to gain rights within education, the welfare state and the polity. Paradoxically, on gaining those rights, many acted, and continue to act, in both national and international fora to assist women to gain reproductive autonomy, to argue for quality not quantity in childbearing and for state support for childrearing. Lenore Coltheart in Chapter 8 demonstrates that in the nineteenth century middle-class Western women eagerly adopted new social science principles which sought to ameliorate the conditions which burdened many women and children. However, the notion of separate spheres embedded in positivist thought promoted a contrast between a public, or civil, world of politics and a private, social, world of the home. This contrast encouraged the relegation of women to the newly delineated domain of 'the social'. Women with education and the means to travel nevertheless took their concern for women and children into the international arena, shaping a new form of citizenship: the international 'outdoor parliament'. Global 'associative citizenship', Coltheart argues, was a forerunner of a form of participatory democracy much needed in our own time.

The struggle for reproductive autonomy, for the right to control fertility, was a central plank of the women's movement in the nineteenth century. As Alison Mackinnon argues in Chapter 9, explicit attempts to reshape the population (pronatalist policies, for instance) may be subverted by other policies (on education, for example) which are not specifically designed with such an aim. Where national aims for population growth intrude into the bedroom, public and private become hopelessly entangled. Yet men and women frequently subvert national population aims, re-designing the population in ways deplored by policy-makers. Issues of race and nation complicate any simple story of institutional change. While some women in developed countries appear to control their fertility, broader issues – such as the shape of the work-place, the form of the welfare state or national concerns on population policies – frequently influence outcomes. Conversely, attempts to lower population growth in developing countries by increasing women's educational opportunities often founder on broader cultural issues. Not only does the field of population studies highlight the complexity of institutional change, it also illustrates the impossibility of separating issues of race, class and gender.

In the final chapter, Chilla Bulbeck asks what type of republic do we want as we approach the new century and how can we achieve it? Will it promise a better future for women and for indigenous groups? The outcome will be no different, Bulbeck suggests, unless the process by which it is achieved changes. Focussing on a fundamental strand of feminist thinking, Bulbeck stresses the importance of inclusiveness, of connectedness, of negotiation and reconciliation. The process through which the citizenry reaches consensus is every bit as important as the goal. The response to the 1998 Constitutional Convention demonstrates very clearly the willingness of the Australian public to participate in broad discussion about national goals. As active participants, commen-tators, television viewers, and writers of letters to the editor women (and men) expressed their interest in constitutional reform. Both Mackinnon and Bulbeck acknowledge the importance of recognising differences between women and the ways in which the same institutional structures may affect different women differently.

This volume does not claim to provide solutions to the problems women confront in contemporary Australian society. Nor do we offer a 'blueprint' for the feminist reshaping of our institutions. However, a number of themes recur in these papers and these themes deserve further attention and development. We indicate several paths which 'designing women' might explore in pursuit of a fairer future, a future in which the common themes which have emerged in this anthology – the importance of connection, trust and co-operation – would be valued.

Acknowledgements

This book grew from discussions amongst several participants in the 'Gender Strand' of the Reshaping Australian Institutions: Towards 2001 project at the Research School of Social Sciences, at the Australian National University. We wish to thank the Research School for its hospitality, its stimulating intellectual milieu and the collegial inter-actions of Fellows and Visiting Fellows. If at times those interactions – and some seminars – seemed to us to convey a particularly male view of the world, and of institutional design, that too was part of the impetus which led us to put together this collection and to begin to imagine a more gender-inclusive idea of reshaping institutions.

There were many people at the Research School who encouraged us in this project and shared discussions of our work. We particularly thank John Braithwaite and Geoffrey Brennan, then co-ordinator of the project and School director respectively, for their support throughout. Robert E. Goodin provided generous advice during the project. Frank Castles, current co-ordinator of the Reshaping Australian Institutions project, assisted us in the final steps to publication. Mary Hapel at the Research School stepped in at short notice to undertake the index. We are grateful to the four anonymous readers who gave excellent advice on the manu-script, which we followed wherever it was possible to do so. Kim Castle at the University of Sydney provided expert research assistance. We thank Phillipa McGuinness for her faith in the project during a somewhat protracted process, Jean Cooney for copy editing assistance and the team at Cambridge University Press for their meticulous attention to detail. The editors wish to acknowledge the support of the University of Sydney and the University of South Australia in facilitating the periods of second-ment and leave which enabled us to be part of the project at the ANU.

And of course our major thanks to our contributors for their enthusiasm, their friendship and their patience. Last but by no means least, our thanks to Paul Patton and Malcolm Mackinnon, for whom the 'institutions of daily life' were often significantly reshaped by the demands of this collection.

MOIRA GATENS AND ALISON MACKINNON

CHAPTER 1

Institutions, Embodiment and Sexual Difference

Moira Gatens

Feminist theory, perhaps necessarily, often takes the form of critique. Typically, feminism involves criticising the false 'universalism' of assumptions about human beings found in dominant, or mainstream, social, economic and political theories. Such critical engagements have spawned hybrid theories, such as socialist feminism, liberal feminism, feminist economics and so on. These engagements, though frequently productive, have not been without friction and the relations between progenitors and their hybrid offspring have frequently been unhappy. As many have observed, Australian feminism is remarkable for its critical and forceful engagement with institutions and theories about institutions (see, for example, Watson 1990; Edwards and Magarey 1995). Against this background, it perhaps is not surprising that the term 'femocrat' originates in Australia. In this chapter, it is not my intention to continue the tradition of creating hybrid creatures by attempting to offer a theory of 'feminist institutional design'. Feminists have learnt to be cautious of this style of theorising, a style that has been described as 'add women and stir'. Inevitably, women figure in these theories as something less than the ideal. Feminist critique has shown, time and again, that mainstream theories fail to attend to the difference that sexual difference makes to the manner in which individuals inhabit, act within and are treated by, the institutions which structure our lives (see, for example, Okin (1989) on Rawls' influential theory of justice; Pateman (1988) on contractual society; Ferber and Nelson (1993) on neo-classical economics, and Thornton 1995 on the law). In short, feminists have shown that sexual and racial differences are embodied differences that have far-reaching effects on the way individuals are able to engage with institutions. To acknowledge embodied difference in this way does not amount to the abandonment of any attempt to engage with those theories which, in any

1

given period, come to dominate ways of thinking about social and political life. If feminist theory is to have any impact on dominant theories and policies then such engagement is not so much a choice as a necessity.

This chapter attempts to open a conversation between feminists and those working with the model of the 'rational actor', or 'rational choice', central to some forms of institutional design theory – a conversation in which it is hoped that each can learn something about the other and in so doing may come to appreciate some of what is at stake in each approach. Such engagement has a twofold dividend. First, some approaches to institutional design have much to learn from feminist theory: a critical feminist analysis can show that assumptions central to rational actor versions of theories of institutional design unwittingly obscure the specificity of women's social situation. Second, the dominance of the rational actor approach in public policy contexts may help to highlight how and why our institutions are so resistant to reshaping, including feminist attempts at reshaping.

This chapter is in four parts. First, I consider the institution of the family and argue that gender should be understood as a cluster of norms which regulate the formation of dichotomously sexed subjects. The family is the single most important institution which constructs and shapes the behaviour of both sexes. The family produces sexed individuals with particular sorts of sex-appropriate preferences and tastes which are carried over into other institutional settings (for example, the labour market) where these preferences are reinforced and, in case of deviance from social norms, 'corrected'. Second, I assess the commitments of the modelling devices typical of rational actor approaches to institutional design and argue that such models conceal rather than clarify the manner in which the sex of the social actor plays a determining role in the options for action open to that actor. As I will show, this is largely achieved through the operation of gender as a 'norm of partiality', which functions to conceal the structural privilege accorded to men in various social settings. Focussing on the distinction between endogenous and exogenous preference-formation deepens this analysis.

The third section tackles the moral dilemmas that always accompany attempts to reshape or redesign traditional institutions. The reshaping of the institution of the family elicits particularly strong reactions: vitriolic moralising as well as overt violence.[1] The final section attempts to bring together the various strands of the chapter by signalling possible future directions for feminist research into institutional reshaping.

The institution of the family: gender as a 'norm of partiality'

In *The Theory of Institutional Design*, Robert Goodin notes the recent interest among historians, sociologists, economists, political scientists and social theorists in 'new institutionalism'; a term which, he cautions, describes 'not one thing but many' (Goodin 1996: 2). What emerges from 'new institutionalism' is not so much a uniform methodology as 'a reminder of the various contextual settings within which social action is set' (1996: 19). In other words, 'new institutionalism' stresses that the actions and projects of individuals and groups are constrained by the various institutions within which such actions are performed. Jennings (1993) has noted there are several points of similarity between aspects of the 'new institutionalism' and some feminist theories. Such similarities permit a prima facie belief that a profitable dialogue between the two could take place. Like 'new institutionalist' theories, feminist theories argue that individuals are formed in culture through various institutions, governed by norms, which constrain forms of behaviour and restrict options for action. 'New institutionalism', like feminism, stresses the agency of social actors, as well as the structures within which they act. Both approaches understand institutions to be the historical outcome of past human action as well as the frame through which present human actions are rendered socially meaningful. Human beings both construct and are constructed by a variety of institutions, some of which, over time, come to be seen as second nature – as just the way things are – rather than as the result of the iteration of conventions (Offe 1995). The family, along with the gender norms which govern it, is perhaps the best example of an institution which is seen as natural – timeless and ahistorical – rather than the result of a long social and political evolution. Social and political theorists rarely fail to list the family as a core institution. However, such acknowledgement rarely extends to a critical analysis or appraisal of the family. Rather, the family, and all too often women, tend to be left to one side. Social and political theorists – whether of a liberal or socialist bent, whether consequentialist or deontologically inclined – tend to focus on those institutions that are deemed 'public'.[2] Institutional design theorists, unfortunately, often do not break with this tendency.

Along with others, (Eisenstadt 1968; Huntington 1968; Weimer 1995; Goodin 1996) I will understand a social institution as a stable, valued, recurring pattern of behaviour that co-ordinates and constrains the behaviour of individuals in their social interactions. By generating shared expectations for norms of behaviour, institutions release individuals from the cognitive and affective burden of constantly processing large amounts of information. Such a broad definition is suitable for analysing the family as an institution – organised around sex-specific roles and normative expectations – which provides the ground and stability for all social actors in all contexts. Rather than concealing the family under the cloak of the 'private' sphere, it will be treated as a social institution that is essential to understanding social action in all contexts. I take this to be *the* central point of feminist theory: every social actor is sexed in a way that *determines* the differential normative constraints under which she or he acts. Furthermore, these norms *strongly predispose* sexed actors to form sex-specific tastes and preferences. If one accepts this proposition then one cannot have as the centre-piece of one's theories or models a notion of the 'rational actor' or 'the abstract individual', since every actor or individual is constrained and formed through either a masculine gender norm or a feminine gender norm. (Of course, there are deviations – but such deviations attract harsh penalties and *all* our institutions have mechanisms which seek to 'correct' these non-normative cases.) This view extends Simone de Beauvoir's famous maxim, 'one is not born but rather becomes a woman' (1949), to include 'one is not born but rather becomes a man'. Recognising the family as a *social* institution, which interpenetrates all other institutions, strips (public) man of his mantle of 'neutrality' or 'universality' and exposes him – no less than (private) woman – as a socially constructed sexed subject. Insofar as institutional design theories incorporate rational actor and rational choice models in their analyses, they fail to note the difference made by sexual difference to the motivations for action of embodied men and women. Moreover, these models fail to note that identical institutional constraints may have different effects on the actions of men and women.

For the purposes of this chapter, I will posit gender as a set of regulatory norms which are diachronically perpetuated by the institution of the family (and marriage) and synchronically reinforced (and, if necessary, 'corrected') by all the other institutions that interpenetrate the family (for instance, educational institutions, the labour market, the welfare system, the legal system.) Gender, understood as a set of regulatory norms, functions to constrain the forms of conduct of men and women as well as restricting their options for social action. Below I will argue that although both sexes are constrained by these norms, it is men who, by and large, benefit from these constraints. Traditional social and political theory encourages the view that only women have a gender whereas men are taken to embody the position of the neutral social actor. This conflation of the masculine position with the 'universal' is aided by the standard relegation of women and relations between the sexes to the private sphere of the family. Treating the family as a fully *social* institution will help to make its inter-dependence on all other institutions visible. Here, I will insist upon two genders – masculine and feminine – which are formed in, and perpetuated through, the institution of the family. Both men's and women's options for action are constrained by gender norms which function differentially to make sexual difference socially meaningful.

Gender norms should be understood as 'norms of partiality', that is, norms which perpetuate a *status quo* of inequality by promoting the interests of the party (or group) favoured by the inequality (see Ullmann-Margalit 1977: 173). Although Ullmann-Margalit does not mention gender in her study of norms, it is nevertheless a paradigm case of the norm of partiality that she sketches. (Interestingly, the example of a norm of partiality that she does use is private property – a norm that is historically utterly intertwined with gender norms. On this, see Shanley 1989.) Gender norms support a status quo in which one party is placed in a position of advantage and power in relation to the other party and this situation is itself presented as the 'natural order of things' rather than as an exercise of power. (Ullmann-Margalit 1977: 189). A similar point has been made in the context of sexual difference by Catharine MacKinnon. She has argued that '[t]o one-sidedly measure one group's differences against a standard set by the other incarnates partial standards' (MacKinnon 1987: 44). MacKinnon's point is that gender is not a mark of simple difference but rather of domination. As such, she argues that the hierarchical relation between men and women is not a contingent but rather a *constitutive* feature of gender difference. As Ullmann-Margalit observes, to be effective norms must be impartially and universally applied. The cost of the advantage derived from norms of partiality is that the favoured party is bound by them too. For example, a law that states that 'both the rich and the poor are forbidden to sleep under bridges', applies to *all* persons. Of course such an impartial and universal norm, considered in the context of the norm of partiality of private property, will affect the poor rather than the rich. However, gender norms impart an added advantage to the favoured party that one does not usually find in norms of partiality. As Ullmann-Margalit states,

> . . . if one could issue norms by which one need not abide oneself, it would seem to be an ideal means of domination and coercion. It would be to enjoy the best of two worlds: not to suffer the costs associated with the exercise of direct and personal power, and yet not to be bound and restrained by one's own legislation. (1977: 189–190)

Gender norms construct specific forms of human embodiment as socially meaningful. Hence, it is possible to 'impartially' apply norms which nevertheless impact differentially on embodied men and women (for example, laws prohibiting *any person* to procure an abortion; the normative expectation that child care is a private, rather than a corporate, matter; the laws of provocation and self-defence). When social inequality is associated with *embodied* differences – for example, sexual and racial differences – norms may be 'universally' applied without such 'universality' affecting all classes, or types of person. These particular cases of norms of partiality are precisely of the kind, as Ullmann-Margalit notes, that offer the 'ideal means of domination and coercion'.

These 'universal' and 'impartial' norms have both diachronic and synchronic dimensions. The historical exclusion of women from citizenship, and women's consequent lack of a subject-position in law,[3] has meant that notions of citizenship and law have developed in a manner which favours men because it is European man who has been taken as the abstract model of 'the citizen', 'the worker' and so on. Notions of citizenship have historically excluded indigenous peoples too. This has led to indigenous peoples suffering a similar 'invisibility' in legal and other institutional settings (see Brennan 1995: 6). Indigenous women suffer a double race/sex burden. These biases have become embedded in our present institutions because past institutions and practices are diachronically continuous with present ones. To admit women to full citizenship under these circumstances amounts to extending them rights insofar as women's tastes, preferences and lifestyles, track those of men. Such bias, if unrecognised, functions synchronically to present advantages enjoyed by men as if such advantages reflect nature's favour.

In general terms, one could say that norms are perpetuated by customs and habits, by various discourses and practices (for example, juridical, medical, educational, economic), and by institutions such as the family, the law, the education system, the welfare system, the labour market. Further, generally speaking, norms involve an exercise of power that may amount to open coercion or may be exercised by more invidious means, for example, through ideology or propaganda.

Although I argue that gender is normative, it is nevertheless important to note that gender norms are very specific sorts of norms. We tend to think of norms as transcendent – they act upon subjects to constrain certain kinds of behaviour. Gender is not a norm of this sort since gender norms are implicated in the very formation of human sexed subjects *who do not pre-exist the norm which constitutes them as sexed.* I am in agreement with theorists such as Foucault (1978), Butler (1990, 1993) and MacKinnon (1987) when I say that lived sexual difference is an effect of gendered norms, not their cause. Alternatively, in institutional design theory terms, this would be to claim that norms of gender are the input of the institution of the family and sexed subjects the output. This view has important consequences since it amounts to the claim that the power relations between the sexes are *intrinsic* to the very formation of sexed subjects. Even formally gender-neutral norms will produce sex-specific effects since gender norms are the ground on which all other norms operate. Embodied individuals cannot be conceived as the 'neutral substance' upon which power acts, but rather may be seen as the living, dynamic products of power relations. This fact is concealed by social theories which take as their object the public sphere and the abstract (that is to say, the masculine,) individual. This sleight of hand is made possible by conceptualising the private sphere as the realm of particularity and the public sphere as the impartial realm of universality. As many theorists have argued, however, a close analysis of the so-called 'impartiality' of the public sphere reveals its partiality. It is a sphere where the 'impartial' position is occupied by a very specific sort of subject: the white, able-bodied, heterosexual, middle-class man (see Benhabib 1987; Young 1990).

The self-conscious inclusion of the family in theorisations of social institutions prohibits this compartmentalisation of human life into discrete public and private parcels. This, in turn, shows the manner in which masculinity historically has been able to present itself as the sex-neutral human norm. Women, in traditional social theory, are assessed and analysed in terms of deviations from, or complements to, a *human* norm which is really the masculine norm. Put differently, although there are two norms of gender – the masculine norm and the feminine norm – in fact, there is one standard which divides into two unequal and complementary components. The abstract individual is presented as universal and impartial but is, in fact, the beneficiary party of a norm of partiality. This is to say that masculinity and femininity are defined interdependently and hierarchically. Masculine mastery assumes feminine submission. Masculine reason assumes feminine affectivity, and so on (see Nelson 1996: 5–19).

Norms of gender involve strong moral and psychological components. Failure to live up to norms of masculinity (if one is a man) or norms of femininity (if one is a woman) is not simply to fail as a 'player' in any given institutional setting, it is to fail as a person – it is to *be* a failure. To deviate from norms of gender is not to commit a bad, or inappropriate, *act*, it is to be a bad, or inappropriate *person*. The strong psychological dimension of gender norms ensures their resilience since sex-specific, socially prescribed behaviours are internalised and self-monitored. The self-esteem of individuals is inevitably linked to their sex as a founding component of their sense of 'self'.

Dilemmas of modelling and preference-formation

Democratic institutions generally claim to be governed by rules that apply equally to all and which provide a non-prejudicial context for social action. Feminist critics have pointed out that the abstract 'individual', 'citizen' or 'rational actor' is implicitly a man who is assumed to be Janus-faced: in the institution of the labour market and that of citizenship he is conceived as an atomistic self-interested actor, whereas in the institution of the family he is conceived as an altruistic and benevolent head of a household (Strassman 1993: 58–59). The manner in which the private individual and the public citizen are conceived in liberal theory both constructs and perpetuates a serious power imbalance between men and women in terms of their agency. If the rules which govern our major social institutions are such that they allow free rein to the operation of the prejudicial and pre-formed status of some social actors, then such rules are undemocratic. An example of such an institution is marriage. Each sex enters the institution of marriage with their status pre-formed (Pateman 1988; Okin 1989). This is not merely socially but also legally sanctioned. A desire to make our institutions more democratic should result in a desire to reshape institutions in such a way that men's historically embedded advantage as well as women's disadvantage are eradicated. Theories about institutional re-shaping, or design, should be interesting to feminists who wish to change institutionally embedded masculine advantage. However, many feminists have been reticent to engage with institutional design theory. This may be explained, in part, by the predominance of game-theoretic models which strike many feminists as unconvincing. These models are seen to obscure or ignore the sex of the social actor as well as reifying the dynamism and the processual nature of social identities and interactions. Many feminist economists and political scientists have argued that conceiving of the rational actor as an isolated individual fails to capture salient features of many women's (and men's!) lives. The experiences of individuals in the family, the educational system, and in the market place will be affected by the race, sex and class of that individual. This, in turn, will affect how that individual interprets her or his interests, forms her or his preferences, and how she or he determines the best means by which to satisfy these preferences.

Of course, all models involve abstracting from complexity and making judgements about the essential features of any given situation – to draw attention to this necessary feature of modelling does not amount to criticism. But this is not at all what is intended. Rather, the criticism is that when the influence of the family and gender norms are ignored, institutional design theory errs in its judgement about an *essential* feature of our social present. Furthermore, the assumption that rational actors act to maximise their self-interest will be misleading if that *self* (and its preferences and interests) is not acknowledged as a *sexed self*, that is, as a 'self' that possesses sex-linked interests.

Sexual difference – which cuts across both race and class differences – is an important indicator of the development of the specific tastes and preferences of social actors. This fact is prejudicial to women's options for social action in a complex sense. Since each social institution is interpenetrated by all the rest, inequity in one institutional context will carry over to all other contexts. For example, market discrimination against women is an important factor in creating women's inferior bargaining power in the family which, in turn, reinforces the vulnerability of women in the market place (see England 1993: 49).

The concentrated analysis of any particular institution in isolation will probably obscure this fact and may make women's social and political subordination to men appear natural. Such intense analysis of particular institutions may be analytically necessary at certain stages of research, but if such analyses do not link up each with the other, then the explanatory power of institutional design theory will be impoverished.

The traditional treatment of the public sphere and the private sphere as distinct is a case in point. The tendency to treat institutions as analytically distinct is responsible for the lack of an adequate analysis of power in rational actor versions of institutional design theory. An adequate theory of power would have to take into account the manner in which the rules which govern institutions inhibit the acquisition and development, as well as the expression, of certain sorts of capacities and preferences. To abstract from the interconnectedness of our social institutions hides the way in which the rules of any particular institution apply differentially to sexed 'players' across all the 'games'. In this case, not only is the deck 'stacked' and the cards 'marked', but the position of the 'banker' is fixed, making the game itself thoroughly undemocratic.

Embodied particular selves have psychological and affective dispositions that feed into their 'rational' calculation (Linder and Peters 1995: 151). The affective aspects of social action are not easily accommodated by game-theoretic models. One should pause to consider the difference that embodying the rational actor as female or male would make in the context of an attempt to model the strategies open to employees in an enterprise bargaining context. One would need to consider that the hours that most women spend attending to household matters and child care is time that they cannot devote to paid work. On the other hand, the hours that men gain by leaving household work and child care to their wives is time that they may choose to devote to their paid work.[4] No doubt this difference between many male and female workers affects their powers of negotiation in an enterprise bargaining context.[5]

I have argued that the gender norms which govern the institution of the family ensure the development of sex-linked preferences. The assumption of the rational actor serves to mask not only the synchronic networks of power that discriminate against women but also the diachronic operation of power through which sex-linked preferences are formed. As England has argued, 'the rationality assumption, *in combination with the assumption of exogenous tastes*, does entail an androcentric bias in that it considers emotion and reason to be radically separate phenomena, an idea tied to notions of gender differentiation in the history of Western thought' (1993: 49, n. 15). A sobering example of the effects of such bias was demonstrated in the infamous North American case, Sears versus Equal Employment Opportunity Commission. The presiding judge rejected the claim that Sears discriminated against its female employees by finding that women simply *preferred* (the lower paid) sales jobs to (the higher paid) managerial and commission jobs (see Scott 1988b). Like the rational actor assumption, the assumption of static and exogenous preferences rather than relational and endogenous preference formation, functions to simplify the task of explaining sex segregation in the workplace. However, both assumptions serve to mask inequalities created by the norms of gender. The partiality intrinsic to gender norms ensures a certain homogeneity in sex-linked preferences that has cumulative discriminatory effects. Such homogeneity, in turn, lends to discriminatory practices an appearance of neutrality and naturalness since the values which underpin sex-linked preferences may be widely shared, even by those who suffer from them.

The feminist question in this context is: Can our institutions be reshaped in such a way that they ensure the more equitable treatment of women? This question inevitably raises ethical issues: *ought* one seek to reshape human behaviour through intentional design? In the context of the institution of the family and the gender norms which govern it, this distinctively ethical question is brought into particularly sharp focus: ought one seek to alter not just the *behaviour* of individuals, but their very *identities*, their sexed '*selves*'? And, further, what is the appropriate means through which to collectively decide this?

'The man on the Clapham omnibus'

In a liberal democracy, the standard answer to the question above is that social change, or 'engineering', is a matter for the citizenry to decide. The values expressed by institutions should reflect the values of the citizens they serve. In a democratic society institutions should register what the citizens want and endeavour to achieve the outcomes that are desired by the population. There are a number of social institutions or mechanisms whereby this can be achieved, mechanisms which may be seen as vehicles of scrutiny: for example, the press, media generally, parliamentary scrutiny, the Senate, as well as the citizenry itself through special interest or pressure groups and social movements.

Now, here a feminist perspective runs up against a wellknown problem. Feminists believe, minimally, that women are unjustly discriminated against in a variety of social contexts merely on the basis of their sex. However, not all women are feminists and so feminists, often enough, find that their severest critics are women who deny that they themselves have ever been subjected to discriminatory practices (see Eveline, this volume). Obviously, this situation reveals a clear conflict of values. What one woman takes to be discrimination, another may see as appropriate treatment. These are not straightforward issues of fact but include value judgements concerning women's rights and entitlements. Once we acknowledge the moral and political dimensions of institutional reform alongside the purely instrumental dimension, the task of reshaping institutions begins to look rather daunting. It is at this juncture that Linder and Peters have argued against rational choice versions of institutional design. They argue that the

> rational choice approach becomes too thin . . . This is the view taken by the 'new institutionalism' literature. The argument there is that organisations can best be understood as governed by a logic of appropriateness that is in essence a moral statement about purpose and that provides a meaning for other actions of the institution. Without understanding that *embedded moral logic*, it is not possible to understand *the behaviour of institutions or their occupants*. (Linder and Peters 1995: 145, emphasis added)

A classic modern articulation of the problem may be found in Lord Devlin's influential essay, 'Morals and the Criminal Law' (Devlin 1965: Ch. 1). As Devlin observed, it is not possible in modern polities to gain the explicit assent of every person on each moral issue or on each proposal for social change. The standard which institutions such as law rely upon in order to gauge shifting social values is that of 'the reasonable man'. Devlin explains that this standard amounts to 'the viewpoint of the man in the street – or to use an archaism familiar to all lawyers – the man on the Clapham omnibus. He might also be called the right-minded man' (1965: 15).

If we were to pose to the 'right-minded man' the question: ought we endeavour to reshape norms of gender, the institution of the family and marriage? I doubt very much if we would get the green light. Why? Well consider those mechanisms through which policy and change are scrutinised: the press, media, parliament, Senate, and consider further the under-representation of women (feminist or not) in all these fields. There is little reason to assume that the 'right-minded man' would be willing to challenge the very norms which not only ensure him a privileged position, but which define his very sense of 'self'. Not only were women actively excluded from the historical process of constructing that which is deemed 'reasonable' or 'right-minded', they are not equally represented as participants in our present political context. This is perhaps the clearest case of the interpenetration of our social institutions and the diachronic as well as synchronic means through which their resilience is maintained. Men's advantage and women's disadvantage in one institution resonates throughout their participation in all the others. Social power operates across a dense network that needs to be acknowledged as a network, not in piece-meal fashion.

Let me provide just one example of the considerable effect of women's historical exclusion from, and present under-representation in, government. In 1983 government attempted to improve the situation of women through the introduction of a Sex Discrimination Bill. The debates that took place between the 'reasonable men' in the Senate do not strike me as particularly reasonable or 'right-minded'. Senator Brian Archer, for example, stated that:

> Not one Bill or even dozens of Bills are going to change the natural characteristics of men and women . . . most ordinary, natural women are homely and caring . . . they are not wildly ambitious . . . they are not naturally dominating . . . they are mostly inclined to avoid authority. They are, by nature, more cautious and more considerate. It strikes me that . . . [this] Bill makes it an offence for those characteristics to be taken into account. . . . Men by nature are more likely to be leaders, providers, protectors. (Quoted in Sullivan 1990: 176–177)

Senator Noel Crichton-Browne made his opinion of the bill clear in the following terms:

> The real intention and purpose of this legislation . . . is to redefine and to restructure the role of women, more particularly the family unit within the society. It is a not too subtle attempt to destroy the structure, the fabric, the values and the intrinsic role of the family unit which, for centuries, has been the foundation of our orderly and disciplined society.' (Quoted in Sullivan 1990: 176–177)

All the same, a version of the bill *was* passed and views such as those cited above do not always hold sway, even in contexts which are male-dominated. However, as Sullivan points out, the bill does little more than acknowledge that women have the 'right' to be treated no differently to men in public life. The bill does little, or nothing, to challenge those institutional structures which embody and perpetuate gender norms of partiality. It does nothing to redress the disproportionate burden that women carry in the so-called private sphere.

Concluding remarks

Dismantling fraternities which guard and promote men's privilege is a precondition for developing an equitable democratic community between men and women. Over the last few decades, the feminist movement has endeavoured to reshape the family and the domestic sphere. Yet, as recent feminist analyses of domestic work (see Baxter 1993 and in this volume) and child care have shown, the results are less than pleasing. The reluctance of men to share the burdens of child care and domestic work, as well as their reluctance to forgo unjustified advantages in the workplace (see Braithwaite, this volume) have been instrumental in recent feminist support for protectionist or paternalistic policies and laws specifically directed towards women as a class. If our institutions ceased to function to make women especially vulnerable then women would not require any 'extra' protection over and above that extended to any citizen in a democratic polity. In my view this does not imply any commitment to a notion of the 'sexually neutral' and disembodied citizen. Our future is not determined by an either/or dilemma of choosing between equality (understood as 'sexual neutrality') or an essential sexual difference. This dilemma is one created by the partiality of gender norms. Rather we need to consider a whole range of differences, including sexual, racial, ethnic, and class differences (see Bulbeck, this volume).

Recognizing that gender norms are norms of partiality may help us to see how and why this dilemma appears insurmountable. Understanding gender as a norm of partiality shows why the *content* of norms of gender may admit considerable change and variation – femininity and masculinity may carry very different meanings cross-culturally and transhistorically – provided that the *formal* opposition between the two categories remains constant. That is, gender norms *appear* to be quite flexible but this is mere appearance since what remains robust across time is the *hierarchical opposition* between masculine and feminine gender norms. It is this formal opposition between masculinity and femininity, as correlating with superordinate and subordinate social positions respectively, which constitutes the partiality of gender norms.

This is an important point that has far-reaching implications for feminist attempts to bring about institutional reshaping. For example, it suggests that legal, economic and political strategies that insist on a dichotomously conceived sexual difference do not challenge the partiality structure of gender norms. Strategies that involve agitating for, or bargaining over, *women's* rights, allowances, entitlements, and so on, do not challenge the *formal* structure of the norms of gender. One may by these means improve some women's future position relative to their past position but leave intact the basic structure of the norms which construct men's superordinate position.

Neither equality (conceived as sexual indifference) nor sexual difference (conceived dichotomously) are viable long-term strategies for reshaping society. Our institutions need to acknowledge differences that are irreducible to one standard and its deviations. Those who do not fit the abstract rational actor model should not be seen as failing to live up to a neutral ideal. Rather, that ideal should itself be exposed as partial and advantageous to white, middle-class, able-bodied men. This amounts to an argument for acknowledging multiple social actors. A more detailed criticism of the neutral rational actor would need to take into account not just sexual difference but other differences: for example, race and class.

This is not, however, to assume that all versions of institutional design theory are bankrupt. Institutional change *does* take place and the successes of the feminist movement are themselves proof that shared desires to reshape our institutions can improve women's situations. The larger task, it seems to me, is to challenge the linchpin of so many of our institutions: the normative power of gender difference itself. Linder and Peters have pointed out that

> institutions can become synonymous with cultural meanings and practices and thus *beyond the reach of designers* intent on reengineering an institution's organizational features. In these instances, the focus for design shifts to the broader canvas of *cultural change* as the medium of institutional reformation. (1995: 145, emphases added)

The institution of the family and the norms of gender which govern it *have* become synonymous with cultural meanings and practices. (Lloyd 1993; Nelson 1996: 3–19) Unlike the redesign or reshaping of other institutions, the reshaping of gender and the family assumes a preparedness to reshape not just our behaviour or actions, but a willingness to reshape our culture and our *selves*.

Notes

I would like to thank Robert E. Goodin and Geoffrey Brennan for helpful comments on an earlier draft of this chapter. I would also like to thank Alison Mackinnon and Deborah Mitchell for their comments on earlier versions of this chapter and for many helpful conversations.
1 For example, in Australia, the bombing of the Family Law Court in the early 1980s and the murder of a Family Law Court judge.

2 In liberal theory this failure to treat the family as an institution central to public life has the consequence that women and the family are subsumed under the category of 'the individual'. See, for example, Rawls 1971: 128, 146; and Friedman who, in 1962, wrote: 'as Liberals, we take the freedom of the individual, *or perhaps the family*, as our ultimate goal in judging social institutions' (p. 12).

3 For example, under coverture, marriage signalled the civil death of the wife and her legal 'death'. (See also Naffine 1995), from whom I borrow the notion that women lack a subject-position in law.)

4 One theorist who has argued persuasively for women's difference from *homo economicus* is Virginia Held. She argues that women's greater involvement in mothering suggests a quite different model than that of the rational actor (Held, 1990).

5 For a critique of 'enterprise bargaining' see Bennett, 1995: 112–143.

PART ONE

*Beyond the Male Breadwinner: Welfare,
housing and household labour*

CHAPTER 2

Life-course and Labour Market Transitions: Alternatives to the breadwinner welfare state

Deborah Mitchell

Introduction

The welfare state has been a central institution of the advanced industrial nations for most of this century. At the core of this institutional structure are policies, programs and practices which have developed over time around income security, community and personal social services, public housing and health. In the post-war period, the influence of Keynesian economics has seen other spheres of public policy – in particular employment, wages and taxation policy – either harnessed directly to the welfare state framework (as in the Scandinavian countries) or at the very least recognised as being critical to the effective functioning of the core areas of welfare state activity (as in the Anglo-American countries). The scope of the welfare state is such that it has the capacity to affect women's lives on many fronts. Apart from being a source of their economic and social well-being through the provision of transfer income, social services and public sector employment, it also has had a major impact on the life-course decisions which women make: for example, entry to the labour force, retirement decisions and even the timing of childbearing. More-over, the welfare state both reflects and entrenches gender roles and the division of women's lives into public and private spheres.

It is therefore not surprising that over the past two decades, one of the enduring features of Australian feminist strategies for achieving equality has been to target various aspects of welfare state provision for active campaigns which support and reinforce gains made in the areas of wages and employment.[1] These campaigns include increasing public child-care provision, gaining equal access to existing income security provisions and the creation of new entitlements which particularly meet the needs of women across the life course.

The changes initiated by feminist action have called into question many of the assumptions which underpin welfare state provision in Australia (Cass 1995) and have gradually shifted our institutional model of welfare state provision from being one which confers social citizenship on women through a male breadwinner towards a model which addresses social rights on an individual basis.[2] The resulting institutional structure is best described as being a hybrid, where policy assumptions based on the 'norm' of a male breadwinner family co-exist with policies which recognise gender equality and individual social rights. The incomplete nature of this structural change, coupled with a radical shift in Australia's wages system and the election in 1996 of a conservative government, raises the possibility that the position of Australian women may deteriorate under this hybrid structure.

Because the welfare state remains a strong element in feminist strategies, this change in the institutional structure of the welfare state raises a number of issues for Australian feminists. First, we need to consider the implications of adopting an individual rights model. For most of the 1980s, working towards this model – exemplified by reference to the Scandinavian countries – appeared to be an accepted ideal for Australian feminists, with very little discussion of either its content or appropriateness to the Australian context. Thus in the first section, an account is given of the male breadwinner and individual rights models of welfare state design. The contrast between these ideal-type models is then used as a backdrop for the discussions in later sections which highlight changing conditions in the Australian welfare state and the possibility of finding alternative pathways (institutional designs) outside of the breadwinner/individual dichotomy.

Although the shift towards an individual rights model in Australia is incomplete, there are several arguments to support the need for a re-evaluation of the implications of adopting the individual rights institutional design. The second section sets out some of these arguments and also discusses current trends in welfare, employment and wages policies which indicate that pursuing an individual rights model may be neither a realistic nor desirable alternative over the medium term.

Having considered the problems and issues arising from the breadwinner-individual hybrid transition, we need to consider what alternative patterns of welfare state provision may be practicable over the long term. This issue is taken up in last section of the chapter.

Models of welfare state institutional design

The comparative welfare state literature has a strong tradition of theorising and modelling different types or 'worlds', of welfare (see Titmuss

Table 2.1   Models of welfare state provision

Dimension	Breadwinner model	Individual model
Familial ideology	Strict division of labour	Shared roles
	⌠Husband = earner	⌠Husband = earner/carer
	⌡Wife = carer	⌡Wife = earner/carer
Entitlement	Differentiated between spouses	Uniform
Basis of entitlement	Breadwinner	Other
Recipient of benefits	Head of household	Individual
Unit of benefit	Household or family	Individual
Unit of contributions	Household	Individual
Taxation	Joint taxation	Separate taxation
	Deductions for dependants	Equal tax relief
Employment and wages policies	Priority to men	Aimed at both sexes
Sphere of care	Primarily private	Strong state involvement
Caring work	Unpaid	Paid component
Reference:	**Netherlands**	**Sweden**

Source: Sainsbury (1994: 153)

1974; Furniss and Tilton 1977; Esping-Andersen 1990, for example). Typically, these models take the nature or level of benefits (or both) conferred on men as the dependent (or classifying) variable, to be explained in terms of level of industrialisation, and class or interest group politics. In recent years, however, feminist scholarship has pointed out that models built around the benefits conferred on men provide an inaccurate – if not misleading – view of the nature of women's social citizenship rights in many countries (Lewis 1992). The theoretical and applied work undertaken to redress the gap between mainstream theory and the reality of women's entitlement has advanced the development of analytical models and generated new empirical evidence which can now be employed to re-examine the role and impact of the welfare state.[3] Diane Sainsbury, for example, has developed a framework which stresses the relationship between market, state and family as the starting point of a gendered analysis of the welfare state and arrives at two distinct models of welfare state design (1994: 150–169). These two models and the dimensions which characterise each are set out in Table 2.1 – the breadwinner model and the individual model.

In this chapter I follow the models developed by Sainsbury for several reasons. First, her work best captures the wider institutional setting of the welfare state, including not just social security entitlements but also the structure of the taxation system; the inclusion of women in wages and employment policies; the provision and financing of care work; and, most importantly, the familial ideology implied in the design of welfare state programs.

Second, in devising these models, Sainsbury takes as her starting point the characteristics of welfare states of the 1960s and delineates two formative institutional designs which have subsequently addressed women's social rights in quite different ways. She does this because during the 1970s and 80s these different institutional designs changed in response to social, economic, demographic and political pressures – including those of the women's movement – to arrive at the welfare states of today. The similarity of both the pressures on welfare states from the women's movement and the initial conditions of women's employment means that, when looked at from the perspective of women, most of the industrial welfare states are more similar than they were thirty years ago. For this reason, her framework provides useful markers for shifts between these two basic structures and thereby introduces a dynamic element into welfare state analysis, especially when compared with the mainstream models which are more 'fixed' in respect of men's entitlements. Nevertheless, as Sainsbury's schema indicates, these two basic designs have very different outcomes for women, perhaps not so much in crude terms, such as the levels of benefits or the services they provide, but more in terms of the life-course and labour-market decisions that each may influence. For example, the breadwinner model by virtue of its strict division of labour is generally associated with far lower labour force participation of women. This in turn affects women's entitlements to social insurance benefits and may further reduce pressure on the state to provide the types of services (for instance, child care) which improve women's labour force participation.

Third, Sainsbury's analysis makes a similar institutional design point to that raised by Robert Goodin (1996), which is that founding institutional characteristics have a strong influence on subsequent developments even if, in theory, the subsequent institutional overlays may appear similar. For example, the introduction of identical welfare policies into older institutional structures which have quite significant differences in their implementation, access and use will produce quite different outcomes.

To illustrate this point, let us consider a policy change which gives women full and equal access to unemployment benefits. In the individual model, where women gain these entitlements under a system similar to men, the criterion for access – like that for men – will rest on their prior attachment to the labour market. The benefit will be paid to them irrespective of their partner's labour force status and income. Under the breadwinner model, the institutional structure reinforces the supposition that a woman will be, at best, a secondary earner and so her entitlement may be conditional upon either her husband's labour force status or his income, or both. Although the change in theory is the same, the patterns of the older employment and social security structures will re-assert themselves and have a differential impact on the outcome. In the former case the woman picks up her entitlement in her own right, is recognised as a primary labour force participant, while in the latter her entitlement may be curtailed by virtue of her assumed economic dependency on her husband.

In what follows I employ the Sainsbury model at various points to track the shifting institutional structure of the Australian welfare state and, later, to propose an alternative design structure that incorporates some specifically Australian features into the individual rights model.

The Australian model (1969–1995)

The gendered nature of the Australian welfare state has been documented by many writers over the past fifteen years and the characterisation of Australia as developing from a male breadwinner model is an accepted part of the mainstream literature (see Baldock and Cass 1988; Castles 1985; Bryson 1992; Shaver 1995, for example). In some recent work Sheila Shaver (1995) has noted that since the 1970s the Australian social security system has gradually shifted the basis of entitlement from a 'logic of gender difference to one of gender equality'. In her analysis Shaver illustrates her argument by reference to numerous changes in the pension and benefits system in respect of sole parents, aged, widows and carers entitlements. While this provides us with evidence that change is occurring, it is far from clear that changes of this nature are sufficient to promote the types of institutional change which create greater equality, a point which Shaver makes herself (1995: 157). This is not to say that the efforts to make such changes are not worthwhile. They are in fact institutional adaptations which complement changes that have already occurred in the labour market, taxation and wages policies.

A fuller appreciation of the shifting design of the Australian welfare state can be gained by analysing the pattern of change across the wider dimensions identified by Sainsbury. Adapting Sainsbury's model to the current structure of Australia's welfare state provision, the first column of Table 2.2 suggests that Australia has moved strongly toward the individual rights model in many areas. It should be noted first that there are some elements of our institutional structure which have always been tied to the individual's social rights, such as separate taxation and equal tax relief.

The first major move toward an individual rights model was in the area of equal pay which was introduced following a ruling by the Conciliation and Arbitration Commission in 1969. This was not effectively phased in

Table 2.2 Australian models of welfare state provision

Dimension	Current Australian pattern	Proposed 'transitions' model
Familial ideology	Shifting roles	Flexible division of labour between:
	Husband = primary earner	(i) spouses
	Wife = secondary earner } primary carer	(ii) family and state
Entitlement	Minor gender distinctions remain	Uniform and/or by income
Basis of entitlement	Categorical unit	Life-course or labour force status
Recipient of benefits	Varies with category	Individual
Unit of benefit	Family (implicit in income test arrangements)	Individual/family
Unit of contributions	Not applicable, except for superannuation (individual)	'Smoothed' over the life course, according to care responsibilities and/or labour force status
Taxation	Separate taxation Equal tax relief	Separate taxation Equal tax relief
Employment and wages policies	Aimed at both sexes	Aimed at both sexes Enables smooth transitions between work and care
Sphere of care	Moderate state responsibility	Strong state responsibility
Caring work	In transition from unpaid to modest payment	Paid component

until 1975 and it has taken nearly 20 years for Australian women to reach parity (now around 90 per cent) on an hourly wage basis. In 1986 Equal Employment Opportunity/Affirmative Action legislation was passed by the federal government. In addition, as employers, the various state and federal governments have expanded women's employment in the health, education and welfare sectors and pursued equal access to labour market support programs. To complement the changes in the wages and employment areas, in the period between 1989 and 1995 public child care provision grew strongly and new financial support payments were introduced to meet the costs of child care whether children were cared for at home or outside the home.

Moving to the five dimensions in the top half of Table 2.2, those which characterise the income support system, change is also evident. The primary basis of income support entitlement in Australia is not determined by an income test, as is often perceived to be the case, but rather categorical eligibility. In other words, claimants are eligible for benefits only if they first meet the criteria of the category of payment (for example, entitlement to a retirement pension is on the basis of the age of the claimant). Income and assets test arrangements are secondary criteria which determine the level of benefit payable to the relevant unit. In the past, both the categorical and income test criteria have largely assumed the male breadwinner family as the norm and so categorical entitlements revolved around the extent to which a claimant matched this norm and this was reinforced by a family income test, which assumed the sharing of income within a household/family unit. As noted earlier, by 1990 entitlement to income support was open to both husband and wife, although family-based income tests may have had some perverse effects which to some extent have neutralised the uniformity (Mitchell and Dowrick 1994).

The recipient of the benefit will vary with the category of entitlement but it is the claimant who is usually paid. In some instances, such as child-related payments, the benefit is directed to the mother, even though the father can technically make the claim. In some areas the unit of benefit has theoretically moved toward a more individualised basis, notably in relation to retirement and unemployment payments. However, the reality is that family income and asset tests imply that the entire unit is held to benefit from the transfer. The unit of contribution, in the past, has been an irrelevant consideration in the Australian context, since all transfers are funded from general revenue. This has now changed in relation to retirement benefits with the introduction of mandatory employee superannuation contributions which are tied to the individual.

Taking these various dimensions of the Australian welfare state together, we can begin to assess the patterns of change which have brought about the hybrid character of the present institutional design. I begin with the labour force participation of women as a central motivation for change in the Australian welfare state. In the thirty years between 1966 and 1996, women's labour force participation rose from 36 per cent to just over 50 per cent. For married women the change was much greater, increasing from 29 per cent to just over 55 per cent. The adjustment to such rapid social change came not from within the private sphere (the family) but in the public sphere, as women's lobby groups pushed the state to support these changes through family-friendly employment policies, equal wages and the provision of child care. In Figures 2.1 to 2.3, I compare the changing patterns of women's labour force participation in Australia with The Netherlands (a breadwinner state) and Sweden (an individual rights state) in order to illustrate the extent to which women's labour force participation patterns are aligned with particular types of welfare state provision.

The characterisation of Australia as a breadwinner model can be seen from the pattern of participation of women in 1970 in Figure 2.3. The pattern is similar to that of the Netherlands (Figure 2.1), where women's participation peaks in their early twenties, followed by a major exodus from the labour force upon marriage or birth of children, leaving less than half their number by 30 years of age. While the base level of participation has increased substantially in the Netherlands, the pattern of exit remains similar to that of 1970. In both instances, the pattern of welfare state support policies was very similar with income support policies directed to the male breadwinner, whether directly through the social security system or indirectly, through the taxation system. Employment and wages policies favoured men and public provision of child care was non-existent.

The level and age profile of women's participation in Sweden (Figure 2.2) stands in strong contrast to both Australia and the Netherlands: while similar rates of participation are observed for women in their early twenties, labour force attachment for women is maintained across the major part of the life course, showing significant decline only after 55 years of age. While a slight dip in Swedish women's participation can be observed during the childbearing/rearing years in 1970, by 1990 this is no longer observed. The levelling out of this dip in Sweden is attributed to a combination of welfare state policies affecting child income support, generous maternity and parenting leave and extensive child care provision.

In Australia, a significant shift away from the male breadwinner pattern had occurred by 1980 and became more prominent by 1990 – women were

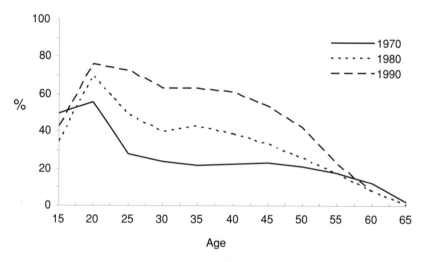

Figure 2.1 Women's age participation profile, Netherlands
Source: OECD (1993) *Labour Force Statistics, 1971–1991.* Paris: OECD.

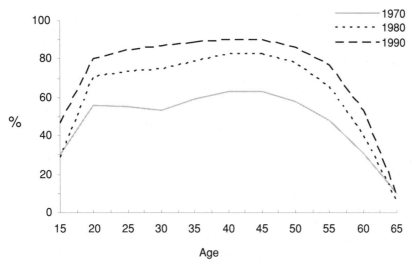

Figure 2.2   Women's age participation profile, Sweden
Source: OECD (1993) *Labour Force Statistics, 1971–1991.* Paris: OECD.

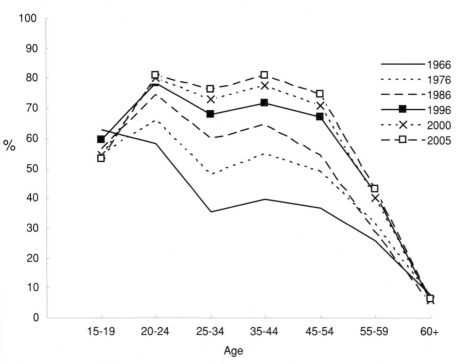

Figure 2.3   Women's age participation profile, Australia
Sources: ABS (1996) *Labour Force Survey, Australia.* (Cat No: 6203.0) Canberra.
            ABS (1996) *Labour Force Projections, Australia.* (Cat No: 6260.0) Canberra.

returning to the labour force after the birth of children resulting in a second peak of participation around 35 years – although this declined rapidly for women in their 40s and 50s. This seems to indicate that age cohort effects are quite strong in Australia and, as the ABS projections in Figure 2.3 show, the cohorts which returned to the labour force in 1990 are likely to remain longer than the previous cohorts. The shift of Australian women's participation patterns towards those of Swedish women, is also reflected in the increasing similarity of welfare state policies in both countries. Employment and wages policies in Australia moved toward greater equality; the social security system addresses women as individuals, rather than as dependants; and Australia is now closer to Sweden than to The Netherlands in terms of its child care policies.

Although the pattern of women's participation in Australia has moved away from a strict division of market versus care work between husbands and wives, it is clear that there is not the same shared breadwinner role as in the individual model proposed by Sainsbury, and represented here by Sweden. Rather, as indicated in Table 2.2, we have a shifting pattern of roles which varies with age[4] – so that older women are more likely than younger women to adhere to a strict division of labour – and within that division of labour, women have become secondary earners while remaining as primary carers.[5] This is reflected in other aspects of the welfare state structure: while wages and employment policies are strong, the lesser public provision of care and modest level of payments for care work remain as vestiges of the division of labour inherent in the breadwinner model.

While the framework of social citizenship in Australia seems to have shifted away from the breadwinner model and toward the individual model, the extent to which this transition has been effectively made is a matter for empirical investigation. In some areas it may be a matter of degree (for example, wages/employment; paid child care); in others apparent shifts may be masked or offset in practice by other institutional features (for example, uniformity of entitlement may be offset in practice by the effects of income tests); and in some instances changes may be reinforcing rather than weakening the breadwinner model (for example, the lag in labour force participation may mean that women have a lesser basis of entitlement, as is the case in the current arrangements for the Superannuation Guarantee Charge).

This apparent unevenness in the institutional structure of the Australian welfare state indicates that after a long period of commitment to a breadwinner model we are now entering a period of transition in our welfare state arrangements. It is therefore of interest to evaluate whether the individual model represents a feasible and/or desirable aim for feminist strategies. We also need to consider whether other changes in the economy and the Australian welfare state may require the scope of our search for an 'ideal type' of institutional design to be broadened beyond the breadwinner/individual dualism. These issues are considered in the following section.

Evaluating the individual model in the Australian context

Although Sainsbury (1994: 167) makes the point that her models are ideal types and that in the 1960s Sweden 'deviated from the breadwinner model but did not fit the individual model either', it is implicit in her argument that over time Sweden has evolved into the nearest approximation of the individual welfare state. Thus it seems reasonable to suggest that an assessment of the individual model should closely follow the developments and outcomes observed in the Swedish welfare state. In what follows, I raise challenges to the individual model – and what it implies in practical terms – by reference to Sweden.

Decommodification and the life course

One of the interesting debates which feminist critics of mainstream welfare state theory have generated – especially in relation to Esping-Andersen's work – concerns the apparent necessity that in order for women to become fully enfranchised as social citizens in the welfare state, their labour needs to move through the following stages: pre-commodification (care work), to commodification (in the labour market) and finally decommodification (entitlement to support by the welfare state, weakening dependence on the market). Despite Sainsbury's insistence that the Swedish welfare state derives its individualist character from an enfranchisement of women on the basis of motherhood and the valuation of caring work, it is difficult to separate the level of social citizenship enjoyed by Swedish women today from their initial, and continuing, high levels of labour force participation across the life course. In essence, achieving decommodification is strongest in the individual welfare state model and seems to be premised on high levels of labour force participation, for both men and women, across the life course. While a high level of participation is not, in itself, a necessarily undesirable aim, the extent to which welfare state development overall – and individual access in particular – should be contingent on participation is an issue which we should debate.

There is a number of objections which can, and have been, made to this progressive movement towards decommodification, especially as it affects women (Orloff 1993; Hobson 1994). For the purposes of this analysis, the major objection I raise concerns the apparent necessity to surrender a great deal of the shaping of the life course to the welfare state. The process of commodification followed by de-commodification deeply affects, and may even distort, the choices which women (and men) can make at different points in their lives. In their analysis of the relationship between the welfare state and the life course, Falkingham and Hills (1995) begin with the connections Rowntree observed in 1902 between the life course and material wellbeing. In particular, Rowntree noted the fluctuation in income observed during certain life course events, such as the birth of children, sickness, widowhood and old age. For a greater part of the twentieth century, the welfare state has sought to even out such fluctuations so that the dramatic loss in income and consequent fall in living standards has a minimal impact on families.

Over the past two decades, however, rather than reacting to such life-course events, the role of the modern welfare state has gradually shifted away from income smoothing to a more proactive role. According to Anne-Marie Guillemard (1991) and John Myles (1990), the welfare state now dictates the shape and timing of key events in the life course. The web of welfare state programs and policies governs entrance and exit to the labour force; determines what is and isn't included as 'work'; provides (or doesn't provide) services which allow women to move into the paid labour market; and through the provision of maternity, child benefits and child care may even determine the timing of women's decisions to raise children.

The welfare state, especially in its individual conception, appears as a two-edged sword. While it can – and does – smooth out life-course fluctuations in income, the cost of achieving this is an ever greater encroachment of the state on personal decisions in respect of market and care work. Moreover, a drive toward uniformity (as in the individual model) may limit the choices that can be made between market and care work, not only between the sexes but also between family units and the state.

A second concern I have with the individual model is that despite an underlying familial ideology of equal status between men and women as breadwinners, it is apparently not very successful in promoting changed gender roles in relation to care and household tasks. Empirical work by Michael Bittman (1991) and Janeen Baxter (1994), both employing time-use data, shows that it is just as hard in Sweden to get men involved in care and domestic work as it is in Australia. It would seem then that while the individual model does have definite advantages for advancing some aspects of equality in the public sphere, the same is not true for the private sphere.

Taking these points together, my view is that while the individual model, as exemplified by Sweden, may provide a relatively generous system of support for women, this support is strongly conditional on their collective commodification in the labour market. The individual model, however, does not seem necessarily to lead to equality in the private sphere – either in theory or in practice – and if we accept that decommodification may have some undesirable consequences in terms of encroachment on personal determination of the life course, then pursuit of an individual model as an ideal-cum-strategic aim for a feminist agenda may be questionable.

Changing employment patterns

For some time now, the increasing labour force participation rates of women in Australia have held centre stage in debates over social security and child care arrangements. These have tended to overshadow emerging debates over the trend toward transitory employment relations. The *standard employment relation* describes a pattern of employment which is full-year, full-time and carries the almost certain prospect of lifetime tenure in the same industry, if not the same job. By contrast, *transitory employment relations*, include work which is casual and non-permanent, part-time or part-year. In addition, during the individual's working life she or he may have to re-train and move into several different areas of employment, rather than along a single career track. The numbers currently affected by this pattern are probably around 15 per cent of the labour force, but some writers argue that this may rise rapidly after the turn of the century and that as much as 60 per cent of the working population will work outside the standard employment relation. This includes not just the people at the lower skill levels of the service sector where women currently predominate, but also professionals who will increasingly work on a contract basis.

One way of thinking about this is that, in the future, many more men will have employment patterns similar to those of most working women of today; but whereas women now have interrupted patterns due to child-bearing and rearing, men will have similar interruptions due to contract employment; the need to re-train; and to move in and out of the labour force in concert with the business cycle. A number of arguments have been put forward to explain the cause of these changes: for example, the sectoral shifts in the economy from the manufacturing to the service sector, giving rise to 'post-industrial' forms of work; heightened competitive pressures on the economy which require more flexible working arrangements; and the encouragement of the latter by government deregulation of the system of industrial relations. Whatever the cause, it is clear that the role of the welfare state will become increasingly important in providing some stability to these transitory employment relations.

To date, Australian responses to this trend have been rather backward-looking. John Langmore and John Quiggin (1994) for example, argue for a form of neo-Keynesian revision premised on a return to full-time employment. However, they and other analysts may be missing an opportunity in their critique of the loss of full-time male employment, to make a more radical revision of labour force participation along the lines of freeing up men to take greater child care responsibilities.

A resurgence of fiscal welfare?

It is interesting to note that while women are placing greater reliance on equality strategies via the welfare state, and remain comparatively optimistic about its emancipatory capacities (Meyer 1994), men are opting out of the public welfare state through various means and reconstituting a private system of welfare which Titmuss (1974) identified as occupational and fiscal welfare. Here I have in mind the changes to superannuation which benefit workers in a standard employment relation (mostly men), in the short term through tax savings; and in the long-term, through increased benefits in retirement. More recently, the newly elected conservative coalition in Australia has reconstituted tax rebates for male breadwinners with 'dependent' wives and children. These new paths of entitlement have been the subject of vigorous attention by feminist scholars who have identified substantial inequity in such changes (Cox 1992; Rosenman 1995; Sharp 1995; Mitchell 1997).

The viability of existing models in an era of retrenchment

The introduction to this chapter emphasised the expansionary tendencies of the welfare state over the greater part of this century. The historical evidence suggests that the expansion and diversification of the modern welfare state was relatively unconstrained in cost terms, supporting policies which led to increased coverage of the population and enrichment of programs, funded out of the dividends of growth. However, after almost 70 to 80 years of constant growth in welfare state programs and in public support for the welfare state, we have entered a period where we are witnessing declines in expenditure on some income transfer programs; restrictions, cutbacks and privatisation of health and personal social services; and falling public support for welfare programs in favour of tax cuts. These trends are evident both in Australia and elsewhere and raise questions about the constraints which may be placed on adopting alternative institutional designs. In particular, our evaluation of existing models and their outcomes may no longer be valid as we have no guide to the robustness of these models in a climate of considerable change.

Similarly, Pierson argues that retrenchment of the welfare state is in 'no sense a simple mirror image of welfare state expansion' (1994: 8). In other words, the constructs which we have developed to analyse and explain the welfare state in its era of expansion may give us very little purchase on the patterns of retrenchment. So, we shouldn't necessarily expect, for example, Esping-Andersen's "worlds of welfare" to provide us with a guide as to how retrenchment will proceed in different OECD nations.

Technical limitations on changing institutional designs

While cost constraints are an important issue, there are other insti-tutional design concerns which may prove more decisive. In his work on institutional design, Robert Goodin (1996) argues that incremental change in institutions is observed as a norm for several reasons:

(i) Co-ordination or coherence demands – that old and new policies be compatible; that there is a preference for smooth transitions.

(ii) Changes in political and social values move more slowly than environmental change – adherence to the original values which shaped the older policies (for example, moral, compassionate, social justice values) exerts a stronger effect than attempts to reshape policy according to current concerns.

(iii) There are technical limitations on change – the administrative complexities involved in implementing new policies, for instance, financing and distributional mechanisms.

These concerns are especially important in the context of the welfare state as it is an extensive institution in two senses. First, the sheer size and number of interdependent policies, programs and practices covered by the wider understanding of the welfare state implies that the co-ordination demands are extremely high. Second, the welfare state is extensive over time – it may affect people's behaviour (for example, saving for retirement) for periods of up to 40 years – and therefore it may be both difficult and undesirable to 'change the rules' too often.

In summary, moving towards a Swedish-style individual model as a basis for redesigning the Australian welfare state has a number of prob-lems: in practice, it seems to be linked to a pattern which requires citizens, whether male or female, to participate in the labour market as a preferred state. The incorporation of individual social rights does not necessarily promote gender equality in responsibility for care. The model is untested in a climate of economic restraint and problems may appear in maintaining its relatively strong outcomes over the long term. As changes in Australia to date indicate, it may also prove difficult to mesh with the existing institutional structure.

A life-course and labour force transitions model

What has been said above does not mean that the current pattern of provision represents a satisfactory set of arrangements, or that the trajectory of change is desirable. In my view, the current set of arrangements is best described as a hybrid institutional form or *partial individual model* where women are stranded between the breadwinner and individual models and may be subject to the worst features of both. On the one hand, married women have entered the labour market at a rapid pace over the 1980s and are now viewed as necessary, if secondary, earners in the family. On the other hand, patterns of care and the rules of welfare entitlement have remained relatively unchanged from the former legacy of the breadwinner model. In strategic terms, this pattern of change may require us to redirect our efforts in the welfare state arena away from the detail of social security administrative arrangements – and indeed much of the public welfare system – and engage in what Joan Eveline (1995c) has described as strategic reversals and the politics of advantage. For example, we should consider the many structural barriers that prevent men from participating fully in caring and housework.

Janeen Baxter (1994) asks 'Why don't men do more housework?' I think part of the answer to this question is tied up in two features of the design of our welfare state institutions. First, it is much more difficult for men to exit from the labour force to become full-time carers. Despite legislative changes to the social security system which theoretically make it possible for men to draw a limited range of benefits and become involved with child-rearing and domestic work, the reality is that the administration of benefits in relation to the *work test* presumes a primary breadwinner role. This may reinforce existing psychological and social barriers, for instance, being labelled as a dole bludger. Second, the economic reality is that most husbands earn around 15 to 20 per cent more than their wives (on an hourly basis) which, again, makes it difficult for couples to decide to share child care at home. Thus the removal of these sorts of penalties on care participation may provide one avenue for rethinking the institutional design of our welfare state.

The changes to our retirement income policy, which have prompted a withdrawal of men from the public welfare system, and its apparent reconstitution in the private sector – partially funded from the tax system it should be stressed – has elicited a strong response from sections of the women's movement (Cox 1992). Criticism of this change has quite rightly pointed to the relative disadvantage women face under this new policy, but perhaps stronger challenges need to be made in terms of re-integrating such occupational welfare back into the public sector, or at least expanding women's potential to participate: for example, government funding of both women's and men's contributions during periods out of the labour force.

A third consideration is formulating a feminist response to the emerging transitory employment relations trend. As I noted earlier, analysis of this change to date has been dominated by critics who seek ways in which to re-establish the standard employment relation that characterised the breadwinner welfare state. A feminist agenda might seek to use this change more constructively and highlight the opportunity presented to men to undertake care work during periods out of the labour force, rather than to get on the treadmill of re-training or work placement programs.

This is not, by any means, an exhaustive account of current changes – and possible adaptations to change – which could be the subject of feminist debate and analysis. Rather than proceeding to sketch out some policy prescriptions to address some of these issues, my purpose here is to shift debate away from specific policies and programs towards a more design-oriented consideration of the welfare state. In this section, I again employ Sainsbury's multiple dimension model to propose an alternative to the breadwinner/individual dichotomy which builds on some of the existing characteristics of our institutions while shifting some of the core assumptions about earning and caring roles within the family.

Adapting to change

In proposing the institutional design framework set out on the right hand side of Table 2.2, I have paid particular attention to several issues arising from the critique of the individual model as well as changes which are specific to the Australian model. These are:

- paying greater attention to the current trend towards de-commodification and what this implies for women without a similar re-evaluation of care work. This requires an explicit discussion and reformulation of the familial ideology which shapes the design of welfare policy, programs and practices.

- extending the theme of 'transition' from the life course to include transitions – especially for men – in labour force participation. This requires that equal status in welfare state support be given to individuals, whether they choose to take up life-course or labour force responsibilities, and involves the removal of a range of disincentives which currently limit the participation of men in care work.

- providing legitimate pathways of choice between work and welfare that do not disadvantage those who choose to move beyond the traditional breadwinner family model.[6] For example, adjusting contributions rules for retirement benefits to ensure continuity between care and market work.

Dimensions of a transition model

A central aspect of the framework I have proposed is the necessity to pay attention to the shifting character of familial roles. What I present here is only one way of thinking about this issue; there is clearly a great deal of room for debate. As noted earlier, the movement of women into the labour force in sizeable numbers has broken up the strict division of roles characteristic of the breadwinner welfare state, with the proviso that this shift may not obtain across all age cohorts. We appear to have moved to a situation where women are secondary earners in the household but maintain primary care/domestic responsibilities and this dual burden is reinforced by wage differentials and moderate, though changing, care provision and income support.

On the surface, the presumption of 'shared roles', which Sainsbury argues for as the hallmark of the individual rights model, has great appeal as a model for change. However, as I have indicated, in practice, this has not eventuated in the Swedish welfare state and I have reservations about what adopting this model would imply in terms of women's citizenship being conditional on an unequal labour market.

A more realistic conception of roles, and one which anticipates the loosening of the standard employment relation and the evolving pattern of transitory employment relations, is to premise welfare state structures on a flexible division of labour which will allow both partners to engage in alternating patterns of market work and care work across the life course. This model would imply a number of changes, for example:

- allowing men greater access to social security benefits during time spent out of the labour force. Rather than having to claim on the basis of being 'unemployed', men could opt for a care-based payment and not be required to submit to work tests.

- during those periods spent out of the labour market – for both men and women – the government should contribute to the super-annuation accounts of those who undertake care work.

- in other parts of the economy, current moves to make employment conditions more responsive to care participation should be encouraged.

- state responsibility for care should be guaranteed, especially where both partners are in the labour force.

The transitions framework described above represents one possible starting point for debate and re-consideration of feminist strategies for the Australian welfare state. This framework is a direct challenge to the long-held view that the Swedish model represents an ideal institutional design around which Australian feminists should build strategies for change. While current trends in the labour market seem to be leading us into a period of greater transience in employment patterns, I argue that rather than being a source of yet more gloom for the welfare state, there is now room for a feminist agenda which focusses on the increasing availability of men to undertake care work.

Notes

1 See Mitchell (1995) for a discussion of wage and employment outcomes for women.
2 A path of change which is also characteristic of most of the welfare states of the OECD in the post-war period (Lewis 1992).
3 The collection of papers edited by Diane Sainsbury, *Gendering Welfare States* (1994), provides a useful cross-section of feminist scholarship on this subject.
4 These age differential roles are acknowledged in certain social security payments, for example, Partner Allowances for the wives of unemployed men are restricted to women over 40 years of age without recent labour force experience.
5 See for example the evidence in Bittman (1991).
6 The notion of allowing greater choice to social security recipients, for example, was canvassed by the then Labor Minister for Social Security, Peter Baldwin, in his paper *Beyond the Safety Net* (1995). While Baldwin's notion of 'choice' is informed by a consumerist/client-based approach to income support recipients, there are some similarities in our arguments in respect of removing certain administrative controls over access, based on categories and moving toward self-election of the basis of income support.

CHAPTER 3

Reshaping Housing Policy and the Benefits of Urban/Regional Location: Why gender matters

Bettina Cass

Introduction: Gender and housing

In the project of the 'gender agenda' in 'Reshaping Australian Institutions', an institution of central importance which is often neglected in the mainstream of welfare state analysis is the social/economic/political institutional shaping of the distribution of housing – housing assets, amenities and services. Also neglected is the shaping of the social/environmental 'spaces' in which housing and community are located and where the opportunities for education, employment, sociability and community participation are differentially allocated. There is a flourishing Australian literature concerned with the distribution and redistribution of income through the market and the tax/benefit system (Castles and Mitchell 1992; Saunders 1994; Whiteford 1994); a flourishing feminist literature concerned with sex/gender difference and inequality in the shaping and the outcomes of work and welfare state institutions (Edwards and Magarey 1995); and a good beginning in feminist accounts of the gendered distribution of housing advantage and disadvantage (Watson 1988; Smith 1989). But there are few attempts to locate the institutions of housing distribution, as well as urban and regional planning, within the mainstream of welfare state analysis, and to do this in a way which identifies and explains the gendered outcomes of these institutional arrangements. To bring housing into the analysis is to recognise that welfare states are not only key players in the redistribution of income, but also in the distribution and redistribution of capital and assets, partly through housing policies (as well as through other forms of the regulation of property capital, not addressed in this paper).

This paper asks how women and their families have fared in the distribution of housing as shelter, asset and amenity; and in the distribution of locational resources. It raises major issues for the reshaping of housing policies and the distribution of urban/regional amenities and advantages.

Welfare regime analysis and the male breadwinner model

The European literature on 'welfare regimes' has focussed on the relationships between 'work' and 'welfare' in analysing the extent to which various welfare systems, in their economic, social and cultural interconnections, have enabled labour to be de-commodified: that is, enabled individuals to survive more or less adequately, outside the commodified relations of paid employment. These accounts have emphasised the concept of *de-commodification*, which is usually investigated through analyses of various forms of social security and the extent to which their rules and procedures of entitlement, coverage and generosity redistribute income to population groups who are excluded from market participation by unemployment, old age, disability or illness (Esping-Andersen 1990; Kolberg 1992).

Australian analysts, in contrast, have focussed on the principle of 'redistribution', on the extent to which tax/benefit systems redistribute income of a quantum which is sufficient to reduce the inequality of market incomes which would otherwise prevail, or which are insufficiently redistributive so that market inequalities are maintained or exacerbated (Castles and Mitchell 1992; Whiteford 1994). The concept of *redistribution* draws attention to the effectiveness of tax/benefit systems in reducing the inequalities which market-driven systems of income distribution would otherwise generate.

The feminist literature, however, notes that such analyses of the work/welfare relationship do not problematise 'work' in its market and non-market forms, and neither, paradoxically, do they problematise 'welfare'. Work is carried out not only within markets where it attracts remuneration, but also in the family/household/informal community where it attracts no remuneration but contributes substantially to the total of goods and services produced in national economies (Chadeau 1992) and to the welfare of those who benefit directly from this informal and unpaid provision of material goods and caring services (Ungerson 1990; Lewis 1992; Shaver 1992). As a consequence, the caring work largely carried out by women in family/household and local community and its treatment in social policy is either obscured by the privileging of the market/state relationship, or treated as no more than one other reason for being outside of labour market participation and its system of rewards. The masculinist and market-centred dichotomy of dependence/independence thus constructed enshrines market participation as the privileged source and site of all value, while other circumstances, including reliance on intra-family transfers or on social transfers, are seen as both stigmatising and less than adult: indeed outside the arena of social citizenship (Fraser and Gordon 1994). Omitted from these constructions is an appreciation of the interdependence of market workers and the work of care, and the interdependence of welfare systems and market participation, through an understanding of life course transitions, obligations and vulnerabilities which militate against full-time labour force participation or exclude people entirely from participation.

The mainstream welfare state literature also fails to problematise 'welfare'. Analyses of welfare are restricted largely to redistribution through the tax/benefit system, but seldom to the institutions determining the distribution of secure and affordable housing. If welfare is reconceptualised to cover all forms of 'social protection' (Polanyi 1944), to include the range of state interventions which aim to protect individuals from unimpeded market processes, then social policies in respect of housing and urban/regional planning, which redistribute the essential resource of shelter, public and private amenities, community services and the opportunity to participate in economic, social and political life are as important for welfare state analysis as are more traditionally understood social transfers.

One of the ways in which feminist analysis has explored the connections between social policy and women's market and caring work focusses on the strength and pervasiveness of the 'male breadwinner model' in labour market conditions, employment patterns and cultural expectations (Lewis 1992). The crux of the argument is that while all modern welfare regimes have subscribed to some degree to a 'male breadwinner' model, where men are expected to be either the only or the primary breadwinner in a couple family, and married women/mothers are expected to be either fully financially supported as home-based carers or partially supported as secondary earners, the extent to which such a model prevails in its pure form in actual social and economic arrangements (in all social classes and ethnic/cultural population sectors), and the extent to which such a model is institutionalised as one of the bases of social protection, vary. Jane Lewis identifies European countries where the male breadwinner model prevails (the UK), where a 'dual earner model' has been institutionalised in the post-war period (Sweden), and where the transformation of the male breadwinner model has manifested ambivalence and contradiction (France), a model which Lewis calls a 'modified male breadwinner model'.

All the planks of Australia's system of social protection in the post-Second World War period were predicated on a male breadwinner model, particularly in wage fixation (from 1907 until 1972–75), in the taxation system, the social security system and the paucity of provision of maternity/parental leave and child care (Baldock 1988; Cox 1988; Shaver 1988; Brennan 1994). However, the changes in women's labour force participation since the mid-1970s made significant inroads into the social validity of the model and have influenced social policy changes of a far-reaching kind. In an earlier analysis of whether Australian income support and employment/family policies since 1975 overturned the male breadwinner model and moved towards a dual earner model or merely modified the male breadwinner model, I concluded that the male breadwinner model has severe cracks in its edifice; these are as a result of women's increased labour force participation in the formal market economy and their struggle to combine the responsibilities and pleasures of employment and intimate life as mothers and partners. But at the level of social/cultural norms in sex/gender relations and in many public policies, Australian arrangements could best be described as a 'modified male breadwinner model', characterised by deep ambivalence (Cass 1995).

What is the purchase of this feminist analysis applied to the institutions of housing and the shaping of locational resources?

Housing, locational resources and the circumstances of women

Access to affordable housing for women in the industrial countries is based on three intersecting socio-economic and policy institutions: housing policy influencing the distribution of housing benefits according to each household's economic power; life-course transitions in gender relationships, marriage and family formation; and rates of labour force participation and access to earnings by women, who at the same time usually bear major responsibility for non-market, domestic work, the care of children and other vulnerable family members (Munro and Smith 1989; Cass 1991). Women's housing circumstances are an outcome not only of their access to economic power, as represented by paid employment and earnings from paid employment, but also of the variability of household and relationship formation and reformation. Access to secure and affordable housing is in turn a key determinant of the opportunities for women to enter and remain in employment, both in the geographical sense of access, through the location of their housing and its proximity to local labour markets; and in the socio-emotional sense, in providing (or not) a base of stability, on which movement into employment, education or training can be initiated and sustained (MacFarlane 1990; OECD 1990). When housing arrangements are insecure and housing costs unacceptably high as a proportion of individual or family income, not only is inequality, poverty and social exclusion exacerbated, but the fulfilment of the responsibilities of care for family members and the intimacy of domestic life are placed in jeopardy, as are a whole range of other activities crucial for women's economic participation. The ability to enter employment, seek a secure income and care for family members is gravely hampered when all energies are focussed on gaining and maintaining affordable and secure housing.

At the heart of the matter lies the realisation that housing is not merely shelter, cut off from the social and physical environment: rather, there is compelling evidence that women, in particular, conceive of housing within community settings, and emphasise that access to a range of community services, education facilities, employment, public transport, other social and cultural amenities and informal social networks is essential to their own and their families' economic welfare and their quality of life (Cass 1991). Housing is much more than merely 'a place to live'. There is an emotional symbolism around the meaning of 'home' which conceives of the dwelling not only as shelter, not only as a financial asset conferring benefits over the life course in the case of private home ownership, but also as the expected locus of security and autonomy, in which personal identities can be given full rein, and the emotional/caring responsibilities and pleasures of intimate life fulfilled (Stretton 1970; Watson 1988; Richards 1989).

A report of a consultation on housing carried out in Victoria in 1990, which covered more than 1,000 women from early adolescence to old age, living in a range of housing tenures, provides powerful evidence of women's understanding of housing (Barclay et al. 1991). Housing is viewed predominantly as a 'place to belong', a source of security and stability, which is intrinsically related to the high priority given to security of tenure. For women who have experienced housing-related poverty, frequent moves and disrupted personal lives associated with relationship breakdown, and sometimes associated with family violence, the importance of security of tenure providing control of one's dwelling and housing future are foremost considerations. For women whose lives and housing circumstances have been more stable and fortunate, there is a similar construction of the meaning of home. There is also evidence that men aspire to housing circumstances which provide a site of identity and a sense of control over the conditions of private life (Stretton 1970; Richards 1989). The powerful symbolism of the home, either already achieved or sought, involves the promise of security: financial, emotional, physical and security of occupancy.

Interviews of women with dependent children, held in Sydney and the central coast of New South wales in 1990, focussing on housing, employment and family circumstances, indicated the overwhelming importance of security of housing occupancy and housing stability, as well as housing affordability. But in conjunction with the emphasis on the home as a 'haven', the women interviewed were very aware of home in connection with its physical and social environment, and assessed the appropriateness of their housing in terms of location and access, as well as its affordability and security (Cass 1991). There was no perception of a dichotomy between the home as 'private sphere' and the surrounding locality as 'separate and public' in these understandings of the meaning of 'home', as evidenced by the sacrifices sometimes made by women, particularly those living in the inner city, who forgo housing quality and private housing space in order to enjoy the benefits of accessibility to public transport, child care, education, training and jobs, and the culturally diverse social networks of their community. The autonomy to construct a household which is secure and affordable was not seen as separable from the reciprocities of 'community' and the availability of supportive social networks, good public facilities, good neighbours, as well as access to child care and jobs.

But these aspirations may not represent actual experience for low income families and low income women, in particular those who are paying more than 25 per cent of their income on their housing costs and experiencing high levels of housing stress as a result (National Housing Strategy 1991). In addition, no form of housing tenure provides 'a safe haven' for women, children or young people in circumstances of family violence and abuse, indicating that assumptions cannot be made about the physical aspects of shelter without an appreciation of the social relationships encompassed within that shelter and the political/economic relationships which provide or withhold resources beyond the household.

Women's paid and unpaid work and labour market restructuring

Rates of home ownership in Australia over the last twenty years have been sustained by the increase in two-earner couples, where women's increased rates of labour force participation, deferral of the birth of the first child and smaller family size have contributed substantially to the savings and mortgage repayments necessary to achieve and sustain home ownership (Manning, King and Yates 1988). Women have been entering the labour force in increasing numbers in this period, as in all industrialised countries (Mitchell and Dowrick 1994). Over the last fifteen years, the most substantial increases have been for women with children: between 1980 and 1995 the labour force participation rate for married women with dependent children increased from 46 per cent to 64 per cent, while the rate for female sole parents increased from 43 per cent to 52 per cent (ABS 1980; 1995a).

Women's increased labour force participation has had a significant effect on the distribution of family incomes, reducing, to some extent, the increases in market income inequality which have occurred since the mid-1970s (EPAC 1995). When women with children in two-parent families are in full-time employment, their earnings contribute on average an additional 40 per cent to total family income; when they are in part-time work, the contribution is 24 per cent, and in lower income families the contribution made by women's earnings are considerably higher (ABS 1993a). In the case of sole mothers, the combination of family care and breadwinning is the major route out of poverty for the family; reducing the incidence of poverty considerably where the parent is in part-time work combined with partial receipt of social security benefit, and even more substantially where the parent is in full-time employment (Cass 1993). When women's earnings are added to their partner's earnings, the distribution of income across families is generally more equal (Mitchell and Dowrick 1994). In addition, women's increased labour force participation has sustained rates of home ownership for couples, keeping home purchase rates from falling as they might have done in the four periods of recession since 1975 and particularly in the latter part of the 1980s, when a long period of high interest rates reduced the affordability of home purchase for new entrants to the housing market (Yates 1994).

However, rates of labour force participation and full-time employment for women caring for dependent children or for frail elderly and disabled relatives are considerably lower than they are for men. A very significant proportion of women's employment is part-time when they have responsibility for dependent children: in 1994, 57 per cent of employed married women with children and 47 per cent of employed sole mothers worked part-time, compared with four per cent of employed married men and ten per cent of employed sole fathers (ABS 1994b). This gender-segmented pattern is attributable both to the increased proportion of all jobs which are part-time in the services sector of the Australian labour market and women's long hours of unpaid work in families and households, with women contributing more than three-quarters of all time spent in home-based child care (ABS 1993b). Involvement in long hours of unpaid work and the emotional commitments of family care reduce the time available to women to be fully attached to the labour force through the span of a (male-defined) 'working life', or to be employed full-time. These commitments reduce women's lifetime earnings capacity (Beggs and Chapman 1988), with significant implications for home purchase. Australia therefore may be characterised as a 'modified male breadwinner model', where contradictions abound.

In addition, increased rates of unemployment since the mid-1970s have resulted in a substantial proportion of families with no member in employment: in 1995, 21 per cent of all couple families, 28 per cent of male-headed sole parent families and 43 per cent of female-headed sole parent families had no family member in employment (ABS 1995a). These trends have profound implications for the distribution of housing benefits.

Market inequalities, the institutions of Australian housing and the unequal flow of housing benefits

The Australian housing system is composed of different types of housing and different housing tenures, which provide shelter, a 'merit good' essential for the welfare of individuals and households, and through private home ownership may provide the opportunity to acquire a major source of household wealth and increments to lifetime income (Stretton 1970; Yates 1991). The interaction of land and housing markets, financial systems, taxation and social security policies, and public housing policies at Commonwealth and State/Territory levels in the post-war period, and particularly over the last two decades, has resulted in a hierarchy of housing advantage/disadvantage, in terms of the long-term financial returns from housing and the long-term costs, and the conferral of rights over the disposition and use of one's housing, as well as security of occupancy. The greatest advantages flow in descending order to outright home owners, home purchasers, public tenants and private tenants (Kendig, Paris and Anderton 1987; Yates 1988; 1989a).

Additions to net wealth and income flow predominantly to home owners and are supported by taxation and social security arrangements which significantly advantage home ownership over other forms of tenure, for instance, the exemption of the owner-occupied residence from capital gains tax and the social security assets test, a privileged status not accorded to most other forms of asset accumulation (Kendig, Paris and Anderton 1987; Yates 1989b, 1991). In addition, while home purchasers are likely to have costly mortgage repayments and other outlays for equipping the household in the early years of purchase, these costs are more than offset in later years as equity in the home increases, and tax-free capital gains and imputed income benefits accrue. Further, owners and purchasers have a greater level of control over the use and modification of their home and greater security of occupancy.

Private home ownership, in which about 70–73 per cent of Australian households have lived since the early 1960s, is oriented towards the income circumstances of couples, and in particular to couples with at least a relatively well paid, securely employed male breadwinner, and increasingly oriented to the circumstances of couples with two income-earners (Watson 1988; Smith 1990). At the same time, non-couple households (single people and sole parent families) with the resources of only one adult income and households reliant on social security have considerable constraints placed on their financial capacity to achieve and sustain home ownership, which includes meeting the 'deposit gap' and maintaining loan repayments. In 1994, the 73 per cent of households in Australia who were home owners or purchasers were most likely to be comprised of couples, with and without children: approximately 83 per cent of all couple households were owner/purchasers, compared with 53 per cent of sole parent households and 63 per cent of single people (ABS 1995b). However, couples are not a homogeneous group and there are significant differences in home ownership rates depending on their position in the distribution of income. Low income couples, particularly those without earnings because of long-term unemployment, sickness or disability, are, like sole parent families and low income single people, at risk of being excluded from home purchase (Yates 1989a; ABS 1995b, 1995c). Couple families in the lowest 40 per cent of the family income distribution have lower rates of home purchase or ownership than higher income families: 64 per cent of low income families are home owners/purchasers, compared with 85 per cent of couple families in the highest 40 per cent of income groups. But for sole parent families in the lowest 40 per cent of the income distribution (accounting for more than three-quarters of all sole parent families), the rate of home ownership and purchase is much lower: only 28 per cent are private home owner/purchasers (ABS 1995c).

Public rental housing provided accommodation and housing services for only five per cent of all households in Australia in 1994, but that proportion varied considerably: only three per cent of couples and five per cent of single people were public tenants, compared with 19 per cent of sole parents and their children (ABS 1995b). In addition, almost nine per cent of single people aged 60 and over, but only two per cent of couples in this older age group were in public housing. Public housing provides resources to those most disadvantaged by low income and by very reduced access to employment, in particular women-headed households, and to others excluded from paid work which affects men as well as women; and, in the case of older people, provides secure and affordable accommodation to those least likely to have become private home owners through their 'working lives' because of low life-course income and, here again, women predominate (Cass 1986, 1991; Watson 1988; ABS 1995c).

The various methods of setting and subsidising rents in public housing which have been adopted in the post-war period, either to recover historical costs or reflect the application of market rents offset by income-tested rent rebates for low income tenants, have tended to keep the costs of public rental to an affordable level (Anderton and Lloyd 1991). Public tenants have much greater security of occupancy compared with private tenants, but they have very little freedom to modify their dwelling or to choose its location.

Private rental, on the other hand, may provide the advantages of housing flexibility for young people, households without children and higher income households; and provide cost advantages in the young adult years. It is the first form of tenure for most young people leaving the parental home, and may serve as a base for the accumulation of savings for entry into home purchase. But low-income private tenants, particularly families with children, who must remain in private rental for long periods, or even permanently, because they cannot afford home ownership and are not allocated to public housing, live in an insecure and expensive form of housing which attracts least advantages from the Australian taxation and benefits system. In 1994, private rental housed only twelve per cent of couples without dependent children, fifteen per cent of couples with children, 22 per cent of single people (not accounting for those who were boarding/paying rent to another person in their household), but 31 per cent of sole parent families (ABS 1994b).

The irony of this unequal distribution of housing benefits across the various housing tenures is that while women's significantly increased labour force participation rate over the last two decades has contributed substantially to the capacity of couples to achieve home ownership, this has not necessarily protected women and their children's access to home ownership or to an affordable and secure housing tenure when women are single, or when a marriage or relationship ends. Access to and retention of home ownership depends on relatively uninterrupted access to earnings from employment and to relatively high levels of income through the period of the working life, which is facilitated for women and men by being in a couple relationship. When a relationship is disrupted by separation or divorce there are limited safeguards for women with children that housing security will continue, unless they can call upon their own independent income and that income is adequate to sustain owner-occupation. In addition, for all people of working age, finding and retaining a job is crucial to housing security, since unemployment and joblessness reduce the chances of home ownership for all individuals and their families and significantly increase the risks of insecure and very expensive private rental housing, where housing costs drain unacceptably high proportions of income.

The unequal distribution of affordable housing

From the latter part of the 1980s, the affordability of housing for home purchasers in low and middle income ranges entering the market decreased considerably because of high interest rates and the property boom (Yates 1994). In addition, increased income inequality, as a result of high rates of unemployment, long-term unemployment and increased earnings inequality, interacted with increased housing costs to reduce the affordability of home purchase.

Turning to public and private rental housing, several public policies in Australia have made housing more affordable. The first, and the most effective and equitable, is the system of rent rebates for public rental housing, administered by the State and Territory governments with the objective of maintaining public housing rents at no more than 20–25 per cent of household income. The second policy is rent assistance, an additional payment in the social security system available to private renters who are in receipt of a social security payment because of old age, unemployment, sickness, disability, sole parenthood or because they are families with low employment earnings. Nevertheless, a large number of private renters bear significant housing stress associated with accommodation which is not affordable.

The National Housing Strategy, established by the Commonwealth Labor government in 1990, adopted a benchmark of 25 per cent or more of income spent on housing by households in the lowest 40 per cent of the income distribution as a reasonable indicator of 'housing stress', or 'crisis of housing affordability' (National Housing Strategy 1992a). In 1994, about 47 per cent of *private* renters paid more than 25 per cent of their income on rent, while 25 per cent of *public* renters were in this difficult and stressful circumstance. The groups most likely to be paying more than 25 per cent of their income on rent are predominantly people who are unemployed, employed part-time or not in the labour force, who comprised almost three-quarters of all renters paying more than 25 per cent of their income on rent, 79 per cent of those paying more than 30 per cent and 89 per cent of those paying more than 50 per cent of their income on rent. Couples without dependent children were least likely to spend more than 25 per cent of their income on rent (27 per cent); followed by couples with children (38 per cent); while single people were considerably more likely to be in this position (44 per cent). Sole parent families had the least affordable housing, with 62 per cent paying more than 25 per cent of their income on rent, 51 per cent more than 30 per cent of their income and 20 per cent more than 50 per cent of their income on rent (ABS 1995b).

A benchmark approach to 'affordability' was subsequently adopted in principle by the Labor government, which outlined in 1995 a policy objective to 'significantly reduce the number of people who have to pay high proportions of their income for suitable private rental housing', by improving the adequacy of rent assistance through the social security system (*Community and Nation* 1995). Such policies had not been implemented before the federal election in March 1996, when the Liberal–National Party Coalition was elected to government, and announced immediately, in a political climate steeped in promises of imposing severe reductions in social expenditure, that there would be no implementation of housing policy commitments made by the previous Labor government.

Public housing policy

In 1994 there were 375,600 households in public rental housing administered through State and Territory housing authorities. Single people (by far the majority over the age of 55) comprised 45 per cent of public tenants; and sole parent families comprised 22 per cent. Of the 33 per cent who were couples, by far the majority were not employed. More than three-quarters of public tenants derived their principal source of income from government income support; and the median amount of income paid in rent was 21 per cent (ABS 1995b). This profile indicates that public housing is a major resource of affordable and secure housing for low income individuals and families who have profound labour market disadvantages because of older age, sole parenthood, unemployment, disability and severe illness. It should also be noted that public housing is a very important resource for low income women, both the aged and sole parents. Almost one half (47 per cent) of households in public rental housing are either single women or women-headed families, compared with their representation of just sixteen per cent in other housing tenures (Australian Institute of Health and Welfare 1994).

The provision of low cost public housing has decreased the incidence of poverty after paying for housing. In 1990 the poverty rate after paying for housing costs (using the Henderson Poverty Line) for public tenants was *reduced* by 60 per cent, while the poverty rate after paying for housing costs of private renters *increased* by 50 per cent (Australian Institute of Health and Welfare 1994). In addition, public housing is effective in providing security of tenure: between 1986 and 1991, only eleven per cent of public housing tenants moved involuntarily, compared with 21 per cent of tenants in private rental; but households moving into or within public housing had less choice about the location of their dwelling than did those leaving public housing or moving within the private rental sector (Australian Institute of Health and Welfare 1994).

Long waiting lists for public housing indicate the dimensions of acute housing need. In 1994 there were 154,800 households who were registered on a public housing waiting list, showing that for every 100 households renting publicly, there were an additional 41 households waiting to rent a dwelling from a public housing authority (ABS 1995b).

The households most likely to be waiting for public housing were sole parent families (29 per cent) and couples with children (27 per cent); thus 56 per cent of those on a public housing waiting list were families with children, significantly higher than the 41 per cent of current public tenants who have children. Also, 35 per cent of those on the public housing waiting list were single people. People waiting for public housing were more likely to be younger than current public tenants, with 53 per cent aged between 15 and 34 years, compared with only 26 per cent of current public tenants. This reflects a shift in acute housing need to low income families with children, both sole parents and couples affected by unemployment and joblessness, and a shift to younger single people whose housing options are also profoundly affected by unemployment.

The gendered nature of regional advantage/disadvantage

Affordable, secure and appropriate housing is not just bricks and mortar: housing is located in a network of basic amenities, public transport, community services, education, training and job opportunities and other social and cultural facilities which may either support or undermine social and economic participation. Many low income households may be compelled, in seeking affordable and better quality private rental housing or home ownership, to forgo good access to services and amenities, while people allocated to public housing may have little choice about location, given the scarcity of public housing supply. On the other side of the 'affordability/accessibility dilemma', some low income households may be compelled to take less affordable and lower quality housing so as to have access to employment, public transport, services and amenities for themselves and their children (Yates and Vipond 1989).

There are stark differences in residents' access to services between regions where private tenants and households in higher priced, privately owned housing tend to live, and regions characterised by public housing and lower priced privately owned housing. Surveys carried out in Sydney, Melbourne, Adelaide and Canberra in 1991 show that residents in public rental housing were more likely to indicate difficulty in gaining access to services (51 per cent) than were those in private rental and private home ownership (40 per cent). Sole parent families and single people over the age of 65 reported greatest difficulty in accessing services – an indication of their low income, reduced access to public transport and reduced geographic mobility, as well as a reflection of the poorer distribution of services, jobs and amenities in regions where public housing and other low cost housing tend to be located (National Housing Strategy 1992b; Australian Institute of Health and Welfare 1994; Australian Urban and Regional Development Review 1995a; 1995b).

The relationship between housing location and employment opportunities is a central issue. Since the mid-1970s, economic downturns, industrial restructuring and high rates of unemployment have had clear locational manifestations. In some localities, in particular older industrial areas, there have been substantial falls in employment in manufacturing, which in smaller towns and cities can affect the supply of jobs in the whole community. Localities with high average rates of unemployment are also likely to have low average household incomes, housing disadvantage, lower-than-average labour force participation rates for women, higher rates of early labour force withdrawal for men, a relatively low proportion of young people attending higher education, high unemployment amongst young people and a relatively high proportion of children with no parent in employment (Australian Urban and Regional Development Review 1995b). In particular, it is women with child care and other family care responsibilities whose access to employment is most disadvantaged by housing location which limits local employment opportunities, particularly if public transport is also inadequate. The sacrifice of accessibility to housing affordability is too great a price to pay. Such a sacrifice may result in marginalisation from the labour force and from many other forms of social participation.

Deconstructing the male breadwinner model in housing policy

The implications for women and their children of the benefits derived from housing are very different from the generally expected lifetime housing profile. Private home ownership may not provide a lifetime flow of housing benefits to single women or to women when a marriage or relationship ends and with it the financial base for supporting mortgage payments and sustaining the costs of household maintenance, or if the distribution of property after separation or divorce results in their re-housing as tenants. Housing purchased for reasons of affordability on the outskirts of cities or in other low cost housing areas may severely constrain women's job opportunities. Home purchase may impose on a proportion of low income households, amongst whom women are considerably over-represented, an unsustainable debt repayment burden.

It is apparent that access to affordable housing is related closely to women's own access to secure labour market attachment and secure earnings through their life course. Where this pattern is never attained, or is disrupted by child care or other family care responsibilities, or by unemployment, illness or disability, the financial base for supporting mortgage payments and sustaining the costs of household maintenance is significantly eroded. Since women-headed households are over-represented in the lowest levels of the income distribution and under-represented among private home owner-purchasers, they are most likely to bear the high costs of private rental.

Public rental provides a major source of secure and affordable housing for low income households, redistributing to women and their children a major source of affordable shelter and relative security of occupancy. However, public housing provides these amenities for only five per cent of households in Australia overall, and the waiting lists for public housing indicate the substantial additional public investment which would be required to house the increasingly younger people, a majority with children, seeking public housing. The very parsimonious, residual involvement of Commonwealth, State and Territory governments in redistributing housing benefits to those households seriously dis-advantaged by their labour market location and their gendered life histories reflects the residual role of the state in decommodifying and redistributing housing. This places Australia, in terms of housing policy, among those liberal welfare states reluctant to intervene in the more equitable redistribution of benefits, whilst at the same time shoring up and reinforcing market-driven housing advantage.

Further, the historical development of large amounts of public housing on the outskirts of Australian cities and in once-thriving, now declining, industrial regions has often resulted in the sacrifice of accessibility to affordability for low income households. This observation applies also to private rental housing and home purchase on the urban fringe. Overall, housing policies which result in location in a declining local labour market can 'lock' low income women and men and their adult children out of job opportunities, exacerbating social and regional inequality and social exclusion. Location also matters to older women and men, if attaining affordable housing results in poor access to services, amenities and sociability.

These departures from what is considered to be a *normal* housing 'career', but what is clearly a *two-earner couple* housing career, where the full-time income earner is still expected to be the male throughout a working life-time, departures which occur when women are household heads and/ or when unemployment, illness or disability disrupt secure employment for couple households and for single people, indicate that while housing policy remains fossilised in a masculinist/market-driven set of assump-tions, it will not be able to accommodate emergent patterns of gender relations and labour market transformations. For housing policies to be effectively redistributive, to bring resources to those whose shelter would otherwise be determined by market relationships, requires a redesigning of the very assumptions on which the flow of housing benefits is based.

Institutional reshaping is indicated in a number of policy domains. A critical element of this project is supporting the chances for women as well as men to enter and remain in the workforce, to earn an adequate income while at the same time to fulfil their family responsibilities, according to the combinations of paid and unpaid work which they seek to make at different stages of life. The male breadwinner model in employment, wages and cultural norms is not only a model which subordinates women, it is also one which shapes a highly discriminatory set of housing outcomes, which advantages only those whose prior wealth and income circumstances equip them to conform to the maculinist and market-driven system of housing benefits. And it is clear that an honest appraisal of the contemporary housing system would recognise the overwhelming importance of two breadwinners in attaining secure and affordable housing – as this model fails to 'protect' women and their children when a relationship ends and when the responsibilities of caring work reduce the time available for paid employment.

The male breadwinner model also offers no protection to low income couple households – particularly those reliant on social security for more than short periods – because labour market participation is marginalised or denied, or for older people who have not been able to begin or complete home purchase through the course of their 'working' life. Clearly, a much greater sphere of the public and the social in housing policy is essential if state policy is to take seriously its role as equitable redistributor of housing as shelter, asset and amenity, in a period of profound transformations in employment and household composition. An expanded sector of public housing and community housing must be a corner-stone of an equitable housing policy which includes women-headed and other low income households within the ambit of affordability, security and social participation.

Setting and implementing an 'affordability benchmark' is also of particular importance for low income private renters, but is not a sufficient response to the other significant disadvantages which low income renters face: housing insecurity, limited financial capacity to find appropriate accommodation in locations which provide access to jobs, education, public transport and community services. Addressing these concerns requires the expansion of public housing and community housing options: that is, expanding very considerably the quality, choice and supply of social housing, and doing so in regions well served by locational resources and amenities. In addition, the close connections between locational disadvantage and employment disadvantage underscores the importance of expanding public and private sector investment in regional infrastructure and in employment growth (Australian Urban and Regional Development Review 1995c), as well as strengthening investment in education and training, as the major routes to employment security and to housing security through the life course.

Such forms of institutional reshaping would require greatly increased public investment in the sphere of social housing, urban and regional infrastructure, education, training and employment expansion, at a point in time when a neo-liberal political agenda is entrenched in housing and employment policies, and when social democratic agendas, never strong in Australian public policy, have been officially discredited. It is highly unlikely that political ideologies concerned with reinforcing the 'male breadwinner model' in employment and through the reduction of affordable child care will alter fundamentally the 25 years of change in gender relations, household formation and reformation, women's workforce participation and women's raised expectations about living a fully social life. At the same time, long-term unemployment is likely to be intensified in a period of severe reduction of social expenditure. If class and gender equity are to matter in the Australian welfare state, primacy must be given in institutional reshaping to the redistribution of the basic resources of a human and sociable life – secure, affordable and appropriate shelter – and to facilitating full social participation for people who would otherwise be excluded. These are critical issues in the project of feminist redesign towards more equal, inclusive and democratic social and economic institutions and practices.

CHAPTER 4

Moving Toward Equality?
Questions of change and equality
in household work patterns

Janeen Baxter

Introduction

The family-household is an institution that has been central to feminist
discussions of gender inequality. Women's continuing responsibility for
the bulk of unpaid caring and domestic work in the home is often viewed
as one of the most important factors restricting movement toward
gender equality in Western industrialised nations. While legislation
around issues such as voting rights, equal employment opportunity, sex
discrimination and wage inequality may have removed many of the
formal barriers to women's equal participation in the public sphere, the
constraints placed on women by their domestic responsibilities continue
to impede women's access to the public sphere.

The apparent intransigence of the domestic division of labour, then, is
a continuing political and intellectual problem for feminists. Men have
not substantially increased their involvement in domestic labour despite
married women's increased entry into paid employment. Although some
have argued that the gap between men's and women's time on domestic
labour is declining (Gershuny and Robinson 1988), the expected revolution in household work patterns has not taken place (Hochschild 1989).
On the contrary, women have shouldered a dual burden by developing
strategies to combine paid and unpaid work.

This chapter examines the institution of the family with particular
attention to the domestic division of labour. As Moira Gatens suggests in
Chapter One, the family is an institution which is often seen as timeless
and ahistorical. And yet, as the first section of my chapter demonstrates,
in many ways the family has been subject to as much social change as
other institutions. While the evidence suggests that the distribution of
labour between men and women has not changed radically in recent

years, it is possible to identify enormous changes in the organisation of, and time devoted to, household work since industrialisation. Additionally the family has undergone major demographic changes in relation to household formation and dissolution patterns which again have implications for changes in housework patterns.

The second section of the chapter turns to a discussion of recent theoretical and empirical developments in family research. It is possible to identify three main developments. First, there have been attempts to move away from the static notions associated with sex role theory to an examination of the construction and reconstruction of gender differences. Second, researchers have started to re-evaluate the meaning of housework in women's lives. Third, research has begun to look outside the household at the impact of differing institutional settings on domestic labour patterns.

The final section of the chapter considers the implications of this new research for understanding equality within the family. What do we mean by equality between men and women in terms of domestic labour? Is equality possible under the present institutional arrangements and how might we move toward a more equal division of domestic labour?

Changes in family work patterns

There are a number of different ways in which to think about change in domestic work patterns. First it is possible to identify historical changes in the definition of housework and the historical construction of housework as a job for women. Second demographic changes in the structure of the family (for example, age at marriage and number of children per marriage) may lead to changes in the amount of time women spend on housework over the course of their lives. And third, at a more micro level, we may observe changes in the day-to-day organisation of domestic responsibilities between husbands and wives, as well as changes in the amount of time men and women spend on domestic work.

The development of housework as a job for women

Housework as we know it today is a relatively recent phenomenon. Prior to industrialisation, most work was typically performed in small settings usually focussed around the family-household. Family members, including women and children, worked together to provide the labour and the resources needed to ensure the survival of family members. Women's activities were considered to be *real work* and were recognised as essential to the economic survival of the family.[1] With the emergence of industrialisation work patterns changed considerably. The development of factories and large-scale capitalist enterprises transformed the nature of work. Rather than working together in the household, most family members now went outside to work for factory employers. Many of the traditional trades and crafts that family members had practised within the home were now performed in factories using new skills based on new technologies and mechanisation. The small-scale domestic unit of production was thus gradually replaced by large-scale industrial production.

The changes brought about by industrialisation changed the definition of work. Work was now an activity performed outside the household, for an employer, in return for a wage. The household became a place where one returned after work to rest and recuperate. It became a private sphere as opposed to the public sphere of work and commerce (Cowan 1984). This had enormous implications for the development of a gendered division of household labour. Rather than working together in the family-household, men and women were now separated. Although working-class women and children initially followed their husbands and fathers into the factories, with whole families often working for one employer, various pieces of protective legislation aimed at reforming working conditions soon led to women and children being excluded from certain kinds of factory work (Barrett 1980; Barrett and McIntosh 1982; Brenner and Ramas 1984). Additionally, unionists worried about the threat of cheap labour advocated for the introduction of a family wage, payable to men – the idea being that a man should earn enough to support his wife and family. Hence women were actively excluded from paid labour outside the household.

This legislation was buttressed by the development of new ideologies of gender. The modern notion of masculinity emphasised the father/husband as sole breadwinner and economic provider. The modern notion of femininity emphasised the wife/mother as central to the domestic arena – caring for the home, servicing the needs of husband and children. The family-household was no longer seen as a place of work, but as a sanctuary away from the world of work. Women were increasingly economically and socially dependent upon men.

As most traditional home crafts were taken over by factory production and many household necessities could be easily purchased, it now seemed as if women might be left with very little to do. But rather than having increasing leisure time on their hands, women found that housework took on a new significance (Ehrenreich and English 1979). It was promoted as a new profession with new standards of cleanliness and hygiene, combining a range of managerial, scientific and creative skills. The domestic economy movement played an important role in the professionalisation of housework. Not only did it help to entrench beliefs that women should do domestic work, but it also changed the nature of domestic work. New tasks were created, ostensibly to make housework more efficient, but actually resulting in an increase in the amount of time spent on housework. For example, women were instructed to draw up schedules of tasks to be completed during the week, and then more precise timetables for daily activities, as well as records and files of the weekly household budget, recipes, medical histories of family members and so on (Strassser 1978; Ehrenreich and English 1979).

As new technologies were introduced into the household, housework changed again. With the introduction of gas and later electricity to many Australian urban homes in the 1920s and 1930s, the washing machine, vacuum cleaner and refrigerator rapidly became essential household appliances (Reiger 1985). But these mechanical devices did little to reduce the amount of time spent on housework (Vanek 1980; Cowan 1984). Far more important in terms of lightening women's load was the provision of public utilities such as piped water, gas and electricity. The introduction of domestic machines such as the vacuum cleaner and washing machine led to higher standards of domestic cleanliness and may have actually *increased* women's domestic work. The idea of the spring-clean disappeared and was replaced by the necessity of daily or weekly dusting and vacuuming. Similarly, clothes were washed much more frequently with the advent of washing machines, and this of course increased the amount of ironing and folding and sorting of clothes. The introduction of technology into the home went hand-in-hand with new standards of cleanliness and hygiene set by the domestic economy experts and both resulted in an increase in the amount of time women spent on housework.

Historically, then, it is possible to document the emergence of housework as a distinct activity, as well as its development as a job for women. Just as getting out of the house and going to a paid job emerged as an integral component of masculinity, or what it means to be a *real* man, doing housework and taking care of children developed as an integral part of femininity. Moreover housework and childcare are activities that have taken up increasing amounts of women's time. The introduction of new domestic technologies has done little to lighten women's load (Robinson 1980), while at the same time, the 'emotionalisation' of housework (the equation of housework with love for one's family) has helped to justify the large amount of time and energy that women in the late twentieth century are expected to devote to housework (Pringle 1983).

Demographic changes in the structure of families and households

Demographic changes in the structure and formation of family-households have also led to changes in housework patterns. Declining levels of fertility, an increase in age at first marriage, rising divorce rates and increasing diversity in living arrangements, in combination with greater participation by women in the paid workforce, have resulted in greater levels of independence and autonomy for women (Hartmann 1987; ABS 1995d). While there is clearly debate about how much *real* autonomy women have achieved in contrast to their grandmothers (Hartmann 1987), it seems clear that over the course of their lives women are spending less time in purely traditional family-centred activities than was the case up until the early 1970s. The implication is that women will also spend less time on domestic work over their lifetime.

A brief look at some demographic data illustrates the changes taking place in household formation patterns. As shown in Table 4.1, in 1971 there were 9.1 marriages per 1,000 mean population compared with a rate of 6.6 in 1991 (ABS 1994a: 9). At the same time, following the introduction of new divorce laws, the divorce rate climbed from one per 1,000 in 1971 to 2.6 in 1991 with a peak of 4.5 in 1976 (ABS 1994a: 11). Over the same period, the median age at first marriage increased by approximately three years for both men and women (ABS 1994a: 9) and fertility levels declined markedly (ABS 1995d: 29). In addition, it seems that women are delaying starting families, perhaps until after their careers are well established. For example, nine per cent of all births in 1971 were to women having their first child, compared to 24 per cent of all births in 1991. Table 4.2 shows changes in living arrangements over the ten years 1982–92. The biggest change has been the growth in de facto families and one-parent families. The former have more than doubled since 1982 while the latter has grown by 42 per cent.

These trends suggest that women are spending less time in conventional nuclear family living arrangements than in the past. Even though most women will marry and have children at some stage in their lives, women are spending significantly greater periods of time living outside marriage and significantly longer periods living without children than previously. From a life-course perspective this implies less time spent in traditional domestic pursuits. On the other hand, these patterns should not be taken to imply that women living alone, or as heads of households, have access to the same kinds of financial and material resources as their married counterparts. Single mothers in particular are usually at the lower end of the socio-economic scale in terms of income and material goods (Mitchell, Harding and Gruen 1994). Nevertheless it might be argued that these women have managed to escape from some family-centred patriarchal control in their daily lives and may spend less time on domestic labour than their married counterparts.[2]

The demographic changes noted above have been accompanied by an enormous increase in the numbers of married women participating in paid labour outside the home. In 1973 the labour force participation rate

Table 4.1 Selected demographics on family formation and dissolution: Australia 1971–1991.

	Registered marriages		Median age at first registered marriage		Fertility rate[a] (females 15–49 years)	Divorce	
	Number	Crude rate[b]	Males	Females		Number	Crude rate[c]
1971	117,637	9.1	23.4	21.1	2,945	12,947	1.0
1976	109,973	7.8	23.6	21.2	2,061	63,230	4.5
1981	113,905	7.6	24.4	22.1	1,938	41,412	2.8
1986	114,913	7.2	25.6	23.5	1,870	39,417	2.5
1991	113,869	6.6	26.7	24.5	1,855	45,630	2.6

Source: ABS 1994a Catalogue No. 4420.0: 9–12

[a] Total fertility rate is the number of children 1,000 women would expect to bear in their childbearing lifetime if they experienced the rates of the year shown.

[b] Crude marriage rate is the number of marriages per 1,000 mean estimated resident population.

[c] Crude divorce rate is the number of divorces per 1,000 mean estimated resident population.

Table 4.2 Families: growth in selected family types: 1982–1992.

Family type	1982 '000	1992 '000	Change 1982–1992 percentage
Couple only			
De facto	102.4	204.6	99.8
Registered married	1,176.5	1,415.3	20.3
Total	1,278.9	1,619.9	26.7
Couple, others			
De facto	66.2	140.6	112.4
Registered married	2,226.6	2,337.1	5.0
Total	2,292.8	2,477.7	8.1
One-parent, others	436.6	619.4	41.9
Other family	62.1	58.1	−6.4
All families	4,070.5	4,775.1	17.3

Source: ABS 1994a Catalogue No. 4420.0: 6.

of women was 42 per cent, in 1983 it was 45 per cent and in 1993 it was 52 per cent. Over the same period the labour force participation rate of men declined from 82 per cent to 77 per cent and then to 74 per cent (ABS 1994d: 5). This suggests that women may have greater access to financial resources than in the past. Of course, increased access to paid labour does not automatically imply increased access to financial rewards; women tend to be concentrated in low-paid, part-time work in specific sectors of the labour market, particularly in clerical and service occupations. Moreover, women's work is often defined as additional 'pin' money for the family and may be paid into joint accounts over which women have little control (Sharpe 1984; Yeandle 1984). Nevertheless, research has shown that time spent in paid labour outside the home and an increase in women's wages relative to their husbands does lead to a reduction in women's time on domestic labour (Ross 1987; Baxter 1993).

These data suggest then that women are spending less time on domestic labour over the lifecourse and also that women's time as wives and mothers may be concentrated into shorter periods of their lives. Marrying later and having fewer children, for example, suggests that women will have more time, at both ends of the lifecycle, free of full-time domestic responsibilities. These demographic changes, combined with some measure of economic independence, may have given women greater autonomy from men than at any time in the past.

Individual variations in men's participation in domestic labour

The third area of change is the reorganisation of the day-to-day allocation of tasks between husbands and wives and variations in the time spent on tasks within households. This is the area where most sociological research attention on domestic labour has been focussed in recent years (Berk 1985; Pleck 1985; Ross 1987; Goldscheider and Waite 1991; Baxter 1993). Women's increased labour force participation rates and changing values about men's and women's position in society led many researchers and commentators on this subject to predict that men would increase their involvement in household work and that couples would negotiate more egalitarian divisions of labour. But the evidence for such change is variable and contradictory at best (Goodnow and Bowes 1994; Bittman 1995).

As early as the 1970s Michael Young and Peter Willmott coined the term 'symmetrical family' to describe the emergence of a new family type in the UK in which husbands and wives contributed equally, although in different areas, to the running of the household. This theme continues to appear in later studies. Joseph Pleck (1985) for example in the US concluded that men and women are moving toward convergence in family time, but he admits that this is largely due to a reduction in women's time on domestic labour rather than an increase in men's time on domestic labour. Johnathan Gershuny and John P. Robinson (1988), in a re-analysis of time budget studies from the US and the UK, argued that domestic work time for women had been declining since the early 1960s while men's domestic work time has been increasing, albeit rather slowly. Michael Bittman (1995), on the basis of Australian time-budget data, finds no evidence of an increase in men's time on housework, but does suggest a decline in women's time spent on housework. In particular he finds significant reductions in the amount of time women spend on cooking. He also suggests that both men's and women's time on child care has increased by between one and two hours per week over the last five years.

Other studies have found little evidence of a significant increase in men's involvement in domestic labour (Sharpe 1984; Hochschild 1989). A national survey conducted in Australia in 1996–1997 found that men report spending about eight to nine hours per week on housework compared to women's 24 hours per week (see Table 4.3).[3] In addition to the large gap in men's and women's time spent on domestic labour, there is also evidence of a clear gender division of labour with women doing a large proportion of indoor tasks (cooking, cleaning and laundry, for example) and men more heavily involved in outdoor activities, such as mowing and home maintenance and improvements. There is little evidence here of the convergence in men's and women's levels of involvement in domestic work which was so confidently predicted by earlier studies.

The question that remains, then, is why don't men do more housework? Most research has focussed on three factors as the key determinants of the domestic division of labour – sex role attitudes, women's time spent in paid employment and economic power in the household (Pleck 1985; Spitze 1986; Ross 1987; Hardesty and Bokemeier 1989; Coltrane and Ishi-Kuntz 1992). Basically the expectation is that men do not do housework because both men and women have been socialised into traditional gender roles, because men spend more time than women in paid employment and because women are economically dependent on men. The results from studies testing these models, however, tend to be quite contradictory. For example, some studies find no relationship between housework involvement and sex role attitudes (Geerken and Gove 1983; Coverman 1985); others suggest that sex role attitudes are one of the most important predictors of household labour patterns (Perucci et al. 1978; Baxter 1993), while others report that sex role attitudes have only marginal effects (Huber and Spitze 1983; Pleck 1985; Ross 1987).

Table 4.3 Average hours per week spent on child care and housework for cohabiting men and women, 1996–1997.

Tasks	Men		Women	
	Self	Partner	Self	Partner
Child-care[a] (N = 918)	23.5	50.2	57.9	22.3
Housework (N = 1405)	8.8	21.9	24.2	6.7

[a] The child care scale is calculated on a sample restricted to couples with at least one child under 15 years living in the household.
Source: See footnote 3.

In terms of paid work time, the available research tends to suggest that the domestic division of labour is more closely tied to women's time in paid labour than men's time in paid labour with relatively few studies finding a significant relationship between men's paid work time and domestic labour arrangements (Walker and Woods 1976; Coverman 1985; Baxter 1993). If paid work time was a key variable, however, we would expect that in households where men are retired or unemployed we would see more egalitarian divisions between husbands and wives, but this is not usually the case (Healy 1988).

The third issue concerns men's economic power over women. The argument here is that the spouse with the most economic power, usually measured in terms of relative earnings, will have the least involvement in domestic labour. The assumption is that housework is unpleasant and monotonous work and that men by virtue of their economic power will have control over women's labour within the household (Hartmann 1981). Again, however, empirical studies of this relationship produce quite varied findings. Some studies find a strong relationship between women's relative earnings and husbands' participation in domestic labour (Stafford, Backman and Dibona 1977; Ross 1987; Baxter 1993), while others find no relationship (Huber and Spitze 1983).

While there is clearly much more work to be done in sorting out these relationships, it is also apparent that the domestic division of labour is a more complex and enduring pattern of arrangements than originally thought. The number of households in Australia, for example, in which men and women participate equally in domestic labour is extremely small and this pattern persists despite women's increased labour force participation and the widespread acceptance of egalitarian gender role attitudes (Baxter 1993; Bittman and Lovejoy 1993). More recent research has begun to move in several new directions in an attempt to move beyond these earlier attempts to equate the domestic division of labour with variations in power, attitudes and time. The next section examines these new directions, all of which are broadly concerned with explaining why men do not do more housework.

New directions in housework research

Beyond sex roles

One of the most important developments has been the critique of sex role theory. Although this critique is not new (see, for example, Edwards 1983; Connell 1987), the implications for housework analyses have not been examined in any detail and much research on housework still relies on notions of male and female roles to explain the domestic division of labour. But as many have argued, role theory suffers from a number of critical problems.

First, sex roles are assumed to be unitary, internally consistent and ahistorical (Connell 1987; Ferree 1990). In other words, individuals are presumed to be socialised into appropriate sex roles early in life and, once socialised, their ensuing behaviour and attitudes are clear, consistent and uniform (Ferree 1990). As Bob Connell and others have noted though, this ignores evidence of struggle, contradiction and resistance (Stacey and Thorne 1985; Connell 1987; Ferree 1990). It also assumes the dominance of the normative standard case. Exceptions to the normative are usually theorised in terms of deviance, further implying that the conventional sex role is typical of the majority (Edwards 1983; Connell, 1987).

Second, role theory is often assumed to be an explanation of social behaviour rather than a description of expected or observed behaviour. As Edwards (1983) states: 'In this way, a concept of role which is only an analytical construct, useful for describing expected or actual patterns of human behaviour, becomes reified and thereby assumes the power of an independent and empirically existent causal variable' (1983: 391).

Third, sex roles are typically presented as free-floating, unconnected to social structure and ahistorical. According to Connell, the missing element of social structure is supplied by the biological category of sex (1987: 50). While appearing at first to offer a clear solution to the problem of connecting individual behaviour to social structure in the form of socially learned categories of behaviour, role theory slides inexorably into a biologically based theory of sex differences.

Fourth, role theory is unable to theorise power and differing social interests. In terms of sex roles this means that the female and male role are implicitly treated as different but equal. This kind of conceptualisation ignores the obvious power differences between men and women. Furthermore women's roles are primarily defined in terms of marriage, family and housework, areas that are socially subordinate to those which constitute the main identifiers of men's roles, primarily their occupational position.

In place of sex role theory, feminists are increasingly focussing on what Ferree (1990) calls the gender perspective. One of the key elements of this new perspective is the proposition that gender is not an individual characteristic, but an emergent property of social situations; it is continually constructed and reconstructed in interactional settings. In other words, gender is not a role, but is something one 'does' in relation to others (West and Zimmerman 1987).

> While it is individuals who do gender, the enterprise is fundamentally interactional and institutional in character, for accountability is a feature of social relationships and its idiom is drawn from the institutional arena in which those relationships are enacted. If this be the case, can we ever *not* do gender? Insofar as a society is partitioned by 'essential' differences between women and men and placement in a sex category is both relevant and enforced, doing gender is unavoidable (West and Zimmerman 1987: 137).

This new understanding of gender has important consequences for understanding the domestic division of labour. Rather than examining housework arrangements in terms of sex role attitudes and men's and women's roles within the family, feminists are beginning to look at the way in which housework produces gender. Sarah Berk has argued that the domestic division of labour is much more than an allocation of tasks between men and women. It is a set of institutionalised practices that supports two production processes – household goods and services on the one hand, and gender on the other (1985: 201).

> Simultaneously, household members 'do' gender, as they 'do' housework and child care, and what I have been calling the division of household labor provides for the joint production of household labor and gender; it is the mechanism by which both the material and the symbolic products of the household are realized. (Berk 1985: 201)

Doing housework, then, is a means of producing gender. This perhaps goes some way toward explaining the enduring nature of women's responsibility for housework. The domestic division of labour is not a rational allocation of labour based on attitudinal variations, time availability or economic power. It is a much more fundamental system of producing and reproducing differences between men and women. Doing housework means doing gender and doing difference (Berk 1985; West and Zimmerman 1987; West and Fenstermaker 1995). Establishing new patterns of domestic labour therefore requires a fundamental reorganisation of gender itself, not just of the allocation of tasks. Perhaps more fundamentally, this understanding of gender undermines the causal relationships inherent in many studies of the domestic division of labour. Rather than gender being causally prior to the domestic division of labour, the relationship is dialectical; gender produces the domestic division of labour, but at the same time, the domestic division of labour produces gender.

The meaning of housework

Understanding housework as a significant factor in the production of gender also raises questions about the meaning of housework in men's and women's lives. This is an area that has come under closer scrutiny in recent years. In the 1970s Ann Oakley documented women's feelings about housework and argued that most women disliked housework, describing it in very negative terms, such as monotonous, low status, long hours and low rewards (Oakley 1974). Other studies have reported similar findings showing that women often view paid work in much more favourable terms than unpaid domestic work (Ferree 1976). But some recent research has noted that women, and not so surprisingly men, report high levels of satisfaction with household arrangements, even though women are doing the bulk of the work (Thompson 1991; Blair and Johnson 1992; Sanchez 1994; Baxter and Western 1998). The data presented in Table 4.4 support this view. In households where women are spending most time on housework, 41 per cent are very satisfied with the division of labour.[4] Not so surprisingly, seventy-five per cent of men in these households are also satisfied with the division of domestic labour. Overall, very few men (0.5 per cent) and women (3.8 per cent) report low levels of satisfaction with housework arrangements. Similar patterns emerged in relation to satisfaction with child care.

How can we explain these apparently contradictory findings? Recent feminist work has suggested three issues to be considered here – the meaning of equity in the household; the comparison referents; and justifications for existing arrangements. First we need to reconsider the meaning of equity and fairness in the household division of labour (Thompson 1991). In other words, equity may not be judged in terms of time and tasks, but in relation to other desired outcomes, such as avoiding tasks that one dislikes, having tasks done to a certain standard, having a responsive, caring partner, who values your input into domestic work, peace in the household, and having 'down time' or 'time out' (Thompson 1991). For many women, then, the immediate goal may not be to increase the number of tasks that men perform in the household, or the amount of time that they spend on domestic labour, but to achieve some other desired outcome. In particular, analyses of the determinants of women's levels of satisfaction with housework show that if husbands participate in some conventional female chores, such as preparing meals,

Table 4.4 Relationship between satisfaction with housework and the division of time on housework, 1993.[a]

	Husbands spend most time on housework		Husbands and wives spend equal time on housework		Wives spend most time on housework	
	Men	Women	Men	Women	Men	Women
Very satisfied	39 (15)	61 (14)	84 (117)	78 (118)	75 (557)	41 (324)
Somewhat satisfied	42 (16)	35 (8)	13 (19)	21 (32)	24 (176)	42 (337)
Not very satisfied	16 (6)	4 (1)	2 (3)	1 (2)	1 (10)	13 (105)
Not at all satisifed	3 (1)	–	–	–	0.5 (4)	4 (30)
N	38	23	139	152	747	796

[a] Figures are column percentages with N in brackets.
Source: Class Structure of Australia Project 1993, machine-readable data set, M. Western, J. Baxter and J. Western, St Lucia, University of Queensland.

cleaning up after meals, cleaning the house or doing the laundry, women's levels of satisfaction are higher than if their husbands do not participate in these activities (Baxter and Western 1998). The relative amount of time husbands spend on housework also matters, but time spent overall by husbands is less important than which tasks men actually do. For most women, it seems that the benchmark against which their own household arrangements are judged is not some ideal in which men and women contribute equally to domestic labour (and against which almost all households fall short), but a pragmatic assessment of reality, in which men do much less and in which there is a pronounced gender division of labour. Against the yardstick of a highly traditional gendered division of labour, any consistent participation by husbands in non-traditional male activities is better than the alternative.

Second, if women compare their domestic loads to those of other women, such as their mothers or grandmothers, rather than to their husbands, then they are less likely to be dissatisfied with the division of labour. In other words, we should not assume that women will always compare their workloads to their husbands'. If they typically make within-gender comparisons, that is comparing themselves to other women, and comparing their husbands to other men, they are likely to judge their own circumstances as more favourable. Similarly men may compare themselves to other men, such as their fathers, thereby justifying their own contributions. The comparison referent, then, is an important determinant of women's level of satisfaction with household arrangements.

Third, the assumptions underlying these kinds of justifications, of course, is that women should be the primary care-givers and men the primary breadwinners. Even though many married women do contribute to the household income, research has shown that both men and women regard this income as secondary to men's income (Haas 1987; Hood 1986). For example, women's work is often defined as an outlet for personal needs rather than a necessary source of income (Weiss 1987). The corollary is that for both men and women domestic work is women's primary responsibility and while husbands may be expected to help out, they are not expected to take full or even equal responsibility for household work. Other justifications may include the belief that women have a greater personal need for clean houses and well-prepared meals than men, that women have more natural talent for domestic work than men, or that women have more time than men.

As Linda Thompson (1991) has noted, consideration of these issues points to the importance of understanding justice as a social process, defined in interaction with others, as well as the gendered nature of justice. What is considered fair and just may be different for men and women and may differ depending on the sphere of social life under consideration. Justice in the home, for example, may be something different to justice in the labour market. This also raises questions about equality. The main goal for women may not be to achieve a 50–50 split on tasks; rather equality in these terms may take second place to other goals, such as devising strategies that commit men to at least some level of involvement in housework chores. A contribution to housework, rather than equivalence in housework responsibility, may be the main goal because the only conceivable alternative that most women can imagine is not an equal division of labour, but a situation in which men do even less.

Institutional variation

The third area that has emerged in housework research is investigation of the impact of institutional and political variations on domestic labour patterns (Blau and Ferber 1990; Kalleberg and Rosenfeld 1990; Calasanti and Bailey 1991; Wright et al. 1992). The question underlying these studies is to what extent variations in institutional arrangements, such as variations in welfare state arrangements, women's levels of participation in paid labour, the gender gap in wages, demographic patterns and political processes influence the division of labour within households.

The implicit theoretical schema underlying much of this work derives from mainstream comparative welfare researchers. Gosta Esping-

Anderson (1990), for example, has developed a typology of countries – liberal, conservative-corporatist and social democratic – which are characterised by various levels and kinds of social provisions. Although this schema explicitly excludes consideration of social provision in the private sphere, elements of the schema have informed studies of cross-national variations in housework patterns.[5] In particular, the assumption is that social democratic regimes, such as the Nordic countries, will exhibit more egalitarian gender relations compared to liberal regimes, such as Australia and the United States, and conservative-corporatist regimes, such as France, and the Netherlands. As Mitchell's chapter in this volume shows, it may be argued that Sweden has made the most progress in moving away from a male breadwinner welfare state model to an individual welfare state model. As a result, Sweden is usually identified as the key example of a country which has done the most to assist women in combining paid and unpaid work (Ruggie 1988; Moen 1989). A combination of parental leave policies, flex-time, a progressive taxation system, fewer penalties for part-time work, and extensive child care facilities, all of which may be understood as elements of institutional design, have raised expectations about moves toward equality in the private sphere.[6] In contrast it is assumed that in countries such as the United States and Australia, where comparatively little effort has been directed at redesigning institutions to accommodate work and family demands, there will be little evidence of change in gender relations within the home.

The data presented in Table 4.5, however, indicate that, at least in relation to the five countries considered here – the United States, Sweden, Norway, Canada and Australia – there is little evidence of significant variations in men's participation in housework.[7] In all countries men report doing about 25 per cent of total housework activities, with the exception of Sweden, where they report a slightly higher level of involvement – 27.9 per cent. These results are remarkably consistent across all five countries and tend to undermine the view that institutional variations in political, cultural and economic settings will lead to variations in men's involvement in domestic labour.

More broadly, these results suggest that policies aimed at integrating work and family demands, such as the provision of extensive child care facilities, parental leave rights and a progressive taxation system, have little impact on the gender division of labour in the home. One possibility, of course, is that these five countries do not really vary in terms of social and political regimes – even in Sweden, women earn less than men, tend to be concentrated in part-time employment, have a high level of occupational segregation and tend to take up the option of parental leave. A greater variety of countries may exhibit greater variations at the

Table 4.5   Husband's percentage contribution to domestic labour for dual-earner couples in the United States, Sweden, Norway, Canada and Australia as reported by men.[a]

	United States 1980 (N=267)	Sweden 1980 (N=350)	Norway 1982 (N=497)	Canada 1982 (N=384)	Australia 1986 (N=228)
Cooking meals	21.9	27.6	23.2	23.7	25.3
Cleaning up after meals	28.5	25.7	32.1	30.5	38.1
Laundry	20.1	19.1	12.8	16.3	16.1
General house-cleaning	25.9	30.5	22.3	24.7	20.8
Grocery shopping	30.3	37.4	36.5	34.4	29.3
Total housework	25.1	27.9	25.1	25.8	25.9

[a] Percentages are constrained to equal 100%. This controls for the fact that in some households, someone other than husband or wife may do some domestic labour.
Source: Baxter 1997.

household level. Nevertheless it seems clear that the domestic division of labour is not greatly affected by variations in welfare state design.

Conclusion

The problem of explaining men's lack of involvement in domestic labour is clearly central to the feminist agenda and I believe will remain on our agenda. The fact that men have not significantly increased their domestic involvement in recent years, despite married women's increased participation in paid work, presents both a political and an intellectual problem for feminist research. Intellectually we must identify the social forces that maintain the gender division of labour in the home. Politically we must develop and implement institutional mechanisms that will reshape the gender division of labour in the home.

But it is clear that we must look beyond the kind of social democratic welfare policies that have characterised attempts to institutionalise equality in Scandinavia. Clearly, women's responsibility for domestic labour is not just based on structural impediments such as wage inequality, the lack of child care facilities and the availability of suitable parental leave options. If this were the case then we would expect to see much greater participation by Swedish men in domestic labour than in other countries. Social democratic policies may have made it easier for women to combine paid and unpaid work, but they have done little to reshape gender relations in the home. It may well be easier to develop strategies that enable women to carry out both kinds of work, rather than strategies which will encourage men to do more domestic labour.

Part of developing these strategies involves understanding the domestic division of labour as not just a means of allocating tasks between men and women but as a set of institutionalised practices that operate to produce gender and to produce difference. Reshaping the domestic division of labour, then, requires reshaping not just the division of tasks, but more fundamentally gender itself. Moreover the domestic division of labour does not operate in a vacuum. It is part of a broader gender division of labour that equates the private sphere of the family with women and the public sphere of paid work with men. Reshaping the domestic division of labour is dependent, therefore, on reshaping these broader divisions as well.

Notes

1 It is interesting to note that in the nineteenth century domestic labour was classified in official statistics as economic activity (Bryson, 1994c). At the beginning of the twentieth century domestic labour was redefined as non-economic and taken out of the national account figures. So it was officially defined as non-work and made invisible. Recently the Australian Bureau of Statistics (ABS) has started collecting data on domestic labour and housework. So while it is not included in national accounts, there is some recognition that domestic work is real work. According to the ABS, in 1992 the total value of unpaid work was $227.8 billion and the ratio to Gross Domestic Product was 58 per cent (ABS 1994c: 88).

2 Data that I collected in 1993 (as part of the Class Structure of Australia Project) show, for example that married women spend almost twice as much time on domestic labour each week as unmarried women.

3 The survey was carried out as part of the project entitled 'Negotiating the Lifecourse: Gender, Mobility and Career Trajectories' at the Research School of Social Sciences, Australian National University. The data were collected by telephone interviews using the CATI system.

4 These data come from a national survey in Australia in 1993 conducted as part of the Class Structure of Australia Project (see Western, Baxter and Western 1993). The question asked: 'How satisfied are you with the way you and your partner divide housework tasks?' Response categories were very satisfied; somewhat satisfied; not very satisfied; and not at all satisfied.

5 Ann Orloff (1993) has extensively criticised mainstream comparative welfare research for ignoring gender relations.

6 Although some feminists have raised doubts about the extent to which Sweden does exemplify gender egalitarian ideals (Ruggie 1988).

7 These data come from the Comparative Project on Class Structure and Class Consciousness. The data, collected in the early-to-mid-1980s, are based on questions asking respondents to indicate what percentage of each task was

done by them and what percentage was done by their spouse. Note that the percentages are a measure of the proportion of domestic labour done by husbands in comparison to wives, rather than a measure of husbands' share of the total housework performed in the household: for example, in some households men may do 30 per cent of the housework and wives may do 30 per cent and the remainder may be carried out by some other member of the household or paid help. In this case husbands would be scored as doing 50 per cent since they are actually doing half of the work compared to their wives. The total housework measure is the average of each of the five housework tasks combined (see Baxter 1997 for more detail).

PART TWO

Triumphs and Failures of Feminist Design: Reshaping the workplace

CHAPTER 5

Changing the Sexual Harassment Agenda

Carol Bacchi

Introduction

Over a relatively brief period historically speaking, sexual harassment has been identified as an institutional 'problem'.[1] It came onto the political agenda in the mid-1970s, largely in the first instance due to the campaigns of feminists in the United States. The term had sufficient currency in 1975 for the *New York Times* to assume that its readers would be familiar with it (see Nemy 1975: 8). The first book-length study was by Lin Farley (1978). Not long after another was published by Catharine MacKinnon (1979). In Australia in 1978 the Australian Union of Students (predecessor of the National Union of Students) conducted a media campaign against a phenomenon which it termed 'academic rape', describing the pressure some academics exerted for sexual 'favours' in return for grades (Nicholls 1995: 1). In 1980 the Melbourne Working Women's Centre initiated a campaign to incorporate the issue of sexual harassment into the ACTU Working Women's Charter, a campaign which was successful the following year (Bryson 1994b: 10).

Government regulations currently stipulate that organisations have a responsibility to create work environments free from sexual harassment. Sections 28 and 29 of the Commonwealth Sex Discrimination Act (1984) make sexual harassment in employment and education unlawful. As Chris Ronalds describes, under this legislation, '... it is usual that both individual employees and management generally are held liable for specific instances of unlawful discrimination' (1987: 120). It follows that '... only an employer who can demonstrate that a policy statement against sexual harassment has been issued, that staff training about legal responsibility and management disapproval of such behaviour have been conducted may be able to avoid the liability provisions'.

Institutional responses are generally in line with government directives. Typically the response has been to set up forms of grievance procedures. These vary but generally involve the creation of a committee to investigate sexual harassment complaints. The purpose of this chapter is to suggest the limitations of this approach and to show that these limitations stem from a particular way of viewing the relationship between sexual harassment and institutions. To this end I consider the 'problem' of sexual harassment in universities, though the analysis is relevant to other organisations.

In brief, the argument is that the grievance procedures approach to sexual harassment sees sexual harassment as a problem for institutions, as something exogenous to them in a sense, and hence something 'they' must manage. The focus of analysis becomes, in this vision, a question of which procedures will best curtail or limit this dysfunctional behaviour. All the limitations of grievance procedures – the fact that they are difficult to access given imbalances in institutional power, the way in which they constitute the recipient of the behaviour as the attacker and the sexual harasser as the attacked – flow from this particular under-standing which places the institution outside the process of harassment. An alternative vision and the one I advance here, by contrast, sees the institution as the problem and sexual harassment as a symptom of the problem. That is, sexual harassment is seen as an institutional by-product of a setting unwelcoming or even hostile to women. This understanding of sexual harassment produces a very different reform agenda, one detailed later in this chapter.

Here I wish to note that illustrating the limitations of a grievance procedures approach does not suggest the wish to eliminate such pro-cedures; nor does it in any way imply criticism of women who have fought hard to obtain and sustain them. Rather the point is to draw attention to how women's best efforts at change are being 'managed'.

Feminism and institutional design

As was explained in the Introduction, this volume is the product of feminist scholars working in the 'institutions of gender' strand of the Reshaping Australian Institutions project (RAI), undertaken by the Research School of Social Sciences, Australian National University. The 1994 Progress Report for the project (1994: 14) defined institutions as 'sets of regulatory norms that give rise to patterns of action, concrete social structures or organisations'.[2] As an example, the report explains: 'we can speak of the institutions of gender as gendered sets of regulatory norms'. This description is useful, as many feminists would agree that many of society's rules and principles are shaped by expectations about appropriate behaviour for women and men, and that these rules and principles are operative in many important organisations.

However, in much institutional design theory, including that produced by members of RAI, institutions become more than simply 'regulatory norms'. In Robert Goodin's work, for example, social institutions become 'stable, valued, recurring patterns of behavior' (1996: 21).[3] If we are talking about 'gendered regulatory norms', an obvious question, unasked here, is valued by whom? Many feminists would suggest that the norms regulating male-female behaviours benefit men and oppress women. Theory which equates recurring behaviour with valued behaviour involves a problematic investment in stability, which I see as part and parcel of much institutional design theory.

This investment in stability reveals itself again in Goodin's middle-level principles of institutional design. While he insists that 'disharmony is far from disadvantageous' and that optimal institutional design ought actually to prescribe 'institutional irritants' (1996: 38–39), the emphasis remains on robustness of institutions, 'resistant to sheer buffeting by changes in the social circumstances that have no bearing upon the assumptions upon which those institutions were predicated' (1996: 40).

One wonders what this means for 'gendered regulatory norms', deemed by most feminists to be oppressive of women. To put it bluntly, few feminists find much in the gendered regulatory norms or in the organisations or social structures to which they give rise which they would wish to remain robust. Their emphasis rather is on disruption and change. Of course, feminists, no less than any other group of change agents, may disagree about the best channels for change, as is apparant in this book. Still there is a privileging of stasis in institutional design theory which many feminists find worrisome.

The vision of 'collective norms' institutionalized in organisations which then either constrain or liberate 'individuals' has a number of additional problems. As the Introduction points out, this model assumes self-interested individual actors set within and against institutional structures. Although Goodin sees the goal of institutional design theory as breaking down the structure/agency dichotomy, as striking a 'rapprochement' between the 'warring camps' of Enlightenment liberals and communitarians (1996: 18), he still lists as the first proposition of a consolidated new institutionalism that 'Individual agents and groups pursue their own particular projects in a context that is collectively constrained', and as the second proposition that '(T)hose constraints take the form of institutions' (1996: 19). In a word, we still have 'individuals' pursuing self-interest within but against 'institutions'. It is this model which produces as one of the key questions of institutional design theory: whether institutions (and here institutions are treated as synonymous with organisations) ought to be 'designed' for knaves or saints, whether 'institutions' ought to encourage desired behaviours through penalties for undesirable behaviour which is the outcome of pursuit of self-interest, or through mechanisms which produce desired behaviour by rewarding self-interest, for example by drawing upon an individual's desire for a 'good name' (Goodin 1996: 41).

Many feminists and some in this book (see Gatens, Cass) challenge the assumption of the self-interested individual which underlies this model. They offer counter-models of motivational behaviour, models which privilege caring and altruism, and models which do not set the 'individual' against 'the group'. In addition, many feminists have trouble with the parallel impression that 'institutions' are regulatory norms that are almost self-generating, that how they operate has little to do with the characteristics of those who contributed to their evolution. Feminists have sought a number of ways to draw attention to the non-innocent nature of institutions, to show them as operative in the subordination of women.

In the next chapter Joan Eveline elaborates one such attempt, the notion of organisational culture and the focus on culture as practices. As a way of identifying dominant norms and rules, and showing how some discourses dominate over others, Eveline focusses on the stories which justify institutional practices. In a sense I am doing something similar. I am retelling the 'story' of sexual harassment, suggesting that the dominant story leaves in place organisational values and structures which actually spawn sexual harassment. The counter-story I offer is one of institutions as peopled.

Identifying institutions as peopled means that who people are, their background, their race, their gender, within organisations makes a difference to the values associated with those organisations. Institutional cultures do not spring ready-made from above; people make culture. Clearly, people are complex and have a number of affiliations and factors influencing their values and assumptions (Bacchi 1996: 12). This explains in part the existence of institutional sub-cultures (Harman 1989; Mayer and Bacchi 1997). Feminists, however, have emphasised the differences made to institutions by the predominance of white, middle-class men in positions of influence within organisations (Ramsay 1995a).

The difficulty and the need for complexity of theory comes in recognising that indeed men of influence 'do' culture while recognising as inadequate a model of explanation for sexual harassment which attributes the 'problem' to individual aberrant men. While not wishing to exonerate individual harassers,[4] such a model of explanation posits sexual harassment as a problem of 'deviant individuals', leaving in place the culture which makes such behaviour possible and even likely. My goal is to explore the deeper problem, the male-dominated character of universities and other institutions, and to show how the 'deviant individual' explanation of sexual harassment leaves that deeper problem untouched.

Sexual harassment and institutions

To re-open understandings of sexual harassment, I borrow here an idea from Murray Edelman (1988: ch. 2): that social problems do not exist 'out there' waiting to be discovered and solved, but that in a sense they are 'created' by the policy community. By this, Edelman means that a 'problem' will assume a particular shape, depending upon how it is thought about and represented. It follows that the specific policies recommended to 'solve' the problem will reflect and follow from the particular way in which a problem is construed. The approach developed by Edelman draws attention to those doing the construing, the policy analysts, who in many accounts are portrayed as functionaries or experts simply putting forward possible policy options, possible 'solutions' to 'problems'. Similarly, the approach developed in this chapter draws attention to those inhabiting positions of influence in organisations and highlights their non-innocent status, their stake, institutional and gendered, in organisational cultures and norms, including decisions about how best to 'deal with' sexual harassment.

Most commonly, as mentioned earlier, sexual harassment is considered a 'problem' for or within institutions/organisations.[5] The task then becomes finding ways to 'deal with' sexual harassment while managing to continue to preserve institutions from 'sheer buffeting by changes in social circumstances that have no bearing upon the assumptions upon which those institutions were predicated' (Goodin 1996: 40). A second and contrasting understanding begins with the assumption that universities are gendered at their core and that, hence, universities are the problem, with sexual harassment a symptom of that problem. Clearly in this understanding the 'problem' of sexual harassment cannot be addressed without addressing the gendered character of institutions.

This position builds upon the insight of Joan Scott (1988: 2) that '(G)ender . . . means knowledge about sexual difference' where knowledge means '. . . the understanding produced by cultures and societies of human relationships, in this case of those between men and women'. Knowledge, as Scott explains, extends beyond ideas to '. . . institutions and structures, everyday practices as well as specialized rituals, all of which constitute social relationships'. In this understanding, institutions are profoundly implicated in the '. . . social organization of sexual difference'.

It is clear, for example, that deep historical assumptions about gender characteristics and gender roles are constitutive of universities. In fact, it could be argued that universities are archetypal patriarchies. Historically they were created to educate men, and women were excluded. Today a significant number of students are women, but positions of authority and influence are still largely in men's hands. Robyn Kemmis (1995: 2) notes that '(W)hile women now make up more than 50 percent nationally of undergraduate university students and about one third of academic staff, they hold less than 15 percent of senior decision-making roles' (see also Gale and Lindemann 1988; Bacchi 1994a; Castleman et al. 1995).

Gender is also constitutive of other institutions, of course (see Eveline, this volume), but the nature of this constitution can and often is very different. Universities privilege an individualistic ethic captured in the notion of academic freedom which seems on the surface to make them open to individual women. Jane Nicholls (1995: 3) describes the university as '. . . an idealised entity, (which) has traditionally been a place in which academics were supposed to have enjoyed significant autonomy tempered by little formal accountability'. However, the image of the isolated scholar in search of 'truth' continues to sit uncomfortably with the characteristics associated with womanliness – emotionality, particularity, attachment to others – and with the fact that women in the main assume responsibility for society's caring labours. For most women 'isolation' is hardly an option, even to pursue 'truth'.

A contrast here could be made with an institution like the armed forces which insists on internal cohesion and group effort. Women's exclusion from the armed forces, only recently challenged, was based on an understanding of defence of home and country as men's duty and was associated with the presumed masculine characteristics of aggressiveness and physical strength. In both universities and the armed forces it could be argued that there is such resistance because the presence of women upsets some of these assumed configurations, and in the process upsets their raison d'etre (see Ruddick 1989; Bryson 1994b).

Typically universities have responded to legislative requirements in the area of sexual harassment by setting up forms of grievance procedures. These vary, both in their terms of reference and in the penalties they can inflict. Generally committees are established to investigate sexual harassment complaints. Some universities have not even gone that far.[6] Experiences with students' reluctance to use grievance procedures have produced on some campuses networks of contact officers to allow students easier access to the complaint mechanism (Bacchi 1992).[7]

These responses can be seen to fit the kind of institutional design theory which locates 'individuals' within and against 'institutions' and which describes institutions as constraints upon the 'particular projects' of individuals and groups (Goodin 1996: 19). Here, it is interesting to note the alacrity with which businesses and other institutions, including universities, have set up grievance procedures for sexual and other forms of harassment. There was a readiness here to concede that harassing behaviours were hardly conducive to effective institutional functioning and that something needed to be done to constrain such antisocial behaviour. It is this readiness to intervene which has made sexual harassment the apparant 'success story of twentieth-century feminism' (Gallop 1997: 27). Here, however, I highlight the need to pay attention to the shape of this intervention.

For institutional design theorists, the problem becomes one of punishment and deterrence, or of mediation and education through publicity. Models of deterrence see sexual harassers as knaves; models of mediation and education see sexual harassers as misguided or as 'victims' of socialisation, and hence in need of re-socialisation. A recent article in the *Independent Monthly* (O'Neill 1995) showed that universities perceive their role chiefly as mediation, not punishment.[8] In all these cases, the problem is construed to be the individual harasser. Granted, in both government regulations and in more recent university guidelines, there has been an insistence that institutions create environments free of sexual harassment, but this is given little content and generally it is considered adequate for institutions to institute grievance procedures and to distribute leaflets describing the illegal nature of sexual harassment.

The rationale for these forms of 'intervention' also fits comfortably with other institutional imperatives, efficiency, effectiveness, and so on. In fact, one could argue that the response of universities and other institutions to the 'problem' of sexual harassment has been facilitated by its easy placement within this managerialist discourse. Unfortunately, however, locating sexual harassment within such a discourse positions the managers as the ones who decide the shape and limits of the intervention (compare Braithwaite, Chapter 7, this volume). While it might seem useful to describe sexual harassment as a waste of human resources, one must remember, as Suzanne Gibson reminds us, that the 'proximate calculation' here is '. . . of the economic consequences of failure to protect employees: the cost of any claim made by an aggrieved party, the costs of impaired performance in the workplace, the costs of poor labour relations, for example' (1994: 45). When inserted in a cost-benefit analysis, therefore, the outlay on response will be determined by the presumed costs and benefits. If, as currently, these are minimal, we can expect little in the way of serious organisational change. We should remember that in universities the vast majority of the members of sexual harassment committees and contact officers are women who serve in a voluntary capacity and who receive no recognition or monetary compensation for the service.[9] The response, therefore, is a cheap one and, as Clare Brant and Yun Lee Too contend, policies like grievance procedures usually 'represent the end of individual (meaning here institutional) responsibilities rather than the start' (1994: 12).

Moreover, once a grievance procedure policy is in place, it becomes the responsibility of the one who is harassed to use it: 'it becomes their failure, rather than the institutions'' if they do not' (Brant and Too 1994: 12). As with any complaint-based procedure, sexual harassment grievance procedures are reactive and wait upon the complainant. As Margaret Thornton explains, complaint-based mechanisms are notoriously poor responses to hierarchically ordered relations of domination: '(C)omplainants are always vulnerable in the face of corporate power' (1994: 219). This observation is particularly appropriate when considering the possibility of students charging lecturers with sexual harassment. In some cases, the lecturer concerned could hold some power of assessment over the student; in every case, the student is being asked to challenge the integrity of a member of a prestigious profession.[10]

Elsewhere I have written specifically about the way conflicts of interest, and potential conflicts of interest, between staff and students make it difficult for students to press sexual harassment charges (1994). Diane Purkiss (1994: 25) confirms my conclusion that in the academy '. . . the professor's authority, a complex construction of gender, intellect and historical credential, places students at an institutional disadvantage'. Ignoring this locates power in personalities rather than in a profession: '. . . it skims over how power accrues to them [professors and lecturers] from their authority within their institution, and from the status of that institution in wider society' (Brant and Too 1994: 10). Institutions, then, are not abstracted 'regulatory norms'; in this case they are coterminous with the ones doing the harassing!

A related limitation of the grievance procedure approach is that such mechanisms suggest implicitly that the problem we are dealing with is one of individual aberration. Diane Purkiss shows how this tone was established in one of the first texts to draw attention to the problem of male staff – female student sexual harassment, *The Lecherous Professor* (Dziech and Weiner 1984). As Purkiss explains, this title suggests '. . . the separability and opposition between the professor and his lechery'. The 'lecherous' professor becomes the 'odd man out'. Such a construction also opens up the possibility of a defence along the lines that the professor (generally) is 'a pillar of the profession' and hence cannot 'be equated with that which is deviant from it'. Purkiss concludes: '[S]eparating the professor from his lechery by coding it as deviant from professionalism can be unhelpful juridically, and it is also unhelpful to the victim' (1994: 189).

Writing about the problem of sexual exploitation in the caring professions, William White (1993) identifies a number of what he calls 'reductionist models of explanation . . . which tend to define the problem of sexual exploitation in ways that narrow our view of etiology, and restrict our vision of prevention and intervention strategies'.[11] Two of these, the Perpetrator Morality Model and the Clinical Model, have clear similarities with the tendency to see sexual harassment as deviant behaviour. The first sees the problem as '. . . emerging from the evil of the perpetrating professional helper'. Such an approach '. . . allows the organisations to believe that they have addressed the problem of harassment or exploitation solely by extruding an identified sexual predator'. The Clinical Model sees the problem as psychopathology, either chronic or transient emotional disturbance. In this case the organisation is again seen to be doing all that is required by taking steps to deal with the emotional disorder of the perpetrator, through counselling for example.

Jenna Mead talks about the way in which some explanations of sexual harassment are similarly reductionist (1995: 169). She is particularly concerned, as is Jenny Morgan (1995; see also Bacchi and Jose 1994), with the tendency to see the problem as sexual deviance. Here the problem is pathologised in a way which reduces the possibility that the deeper problems of sexual inequality, of sexism, of gender will be identified and dealt with. Seeing sexual harassment as sexual deviance also tends to focus attention on egregious sexual harassment, bypassing wider forms of sexual harassment such as persistent sexual comments and innuendo, which highlight the issues of institutional culture particularly clearly (see Eveline, Chapter 6, this volume).[12]

We also need to consider how sexual harassment grievance procedures constitute those who use them.[13] The sexualising of sexual harassment just described means that women who use the procedures or who encourage their use become, in one interpretation, 'puritans', '. . . trembling creatures innocent of desire' (Garner 1995: 210). In this interpretation such rules and guidelines contribute to a disempowering paternalist construction of women as needing protection from men predators. This perspective can be seen as part of the recent characterisation of some feminist approaches as encouraging a sense of victimhood in women (see, for example, Garner 1995: 168; Gallop 1997).

There is no doubt, however, that it takes great courage to press a sexual harassment charge, especially in cases where the harasser holds institutional power over the one harassed. Hence, there is no clear logic linking sexual harassment procedures to a protectionist interpretation. The problem is that, due to power differentials and other disincentives, few charges will be pressed, leaving the paternalist understanding of sexual harassment dominant and suggesting simultaneously that the 'problem' has been exaggerated – that is, that little harassment is taking place.

One way to undermine the charge of paternalism would, counter-intuitively, involve creating the conditions to facilitate the making of charges – hence showing women actively contesting men's presumed sexual prerogative (in contrast to being passively protected). But we are caught in a circularity here since in a sense complaint-based procedures constitute the accuser as aggressor and the accused as victim, innocent until proved guilty, a point made earlier.[14] The appearance of larger numbers of women accusers could serve, then, to cement the view that it is men who are under attack. The discourse of the mendacious woman creates an opening here to suggest that men are under attack 'without cause'.[15] Instead of images of strong women challenging men's beha-viour, use of sexual harassment procedures becomes trivialised as part of a 'culture of complaint' (Mitchell 1995).

Women are caught in a situation of damned if you do, damned if you don't. If grievance procedures go under-utilised, they are considered protectionist or unnecessary, or both; if they are used, they become part of a 'culture of complaint'. It is important to consider what it is in the nature of these procedures that produces these effects. I am highlighting how grievance procedures locate the 'problem' in individual aberration, leaving the impression that the 'problem' is containable, and that 'institutions' have indeed taken care of the problem. Here, 'institutions' project themselves as 'protectors' of women, and 'objective' arbiters of 'interpersonal' disputes. In this scenario 'institutions' are innocent, located outside of and overseeing the sexual harassment 'problem'.

William White adds the Anomie Model to his discussion of reduc-tionist explanations of harassment and exploitation. In this case the problem is considered '. . . the absence of a clear body of ethical standards defining appropriate and inappropriate conduct in worker-client relationships'. The result is often the proliferation of codes[16] and 'awareness' training sessions. In all these examples, as White sums up, we have a response in which '(A)n appendage is added – a policy, a person, a training seminar – none of which is intended, or likely by itself, to alter the nature of the organisational culture' (1993: 82).

A recognition of universities as gendered at their core would produce a very different agenda. It would start from White's (1993: 81) premise that sexual harassment or sexual exploitation can best be viewed as a process rather than an event, a process '. . . ecologically nested within professional, organisational, community and cultural environments'. Here the problem becomes the institution itself and not simply aberrant individuals within it. By this, I mean that the 'institution' does not stand over and above 'individual agents' who either conform or deviate from desired behaviour. Rather, the institution has a character and this character is gendered. Moreover, part of that gendered character comes from the gender of those holding positions of influence within it. This is what I mean by seeing institutions as peopled – the need to recognise that those designing institutional responses to diagnosed 'problems' shape responses which fit their understanding of the nature of the problem, and this in turn is shaped by their gender and by their willingness or lack of willingness to re-think seriously the nature of the institution. To see the problem of sexual and other harassment as a problem of deviant behaviour keeps the problem within narrow and inexpensive boundaries and makes it unnecessary to probe further into the causes of the problem.

In the next chapter, Joan Eveline provides evidence that women are more likely to be sexually harassed in occupations where there are fewer of them. A study in the Netherlands similarly makes a connection between the position and numbers of women in organisations and the existence of sexual harassment. This study revealed a link between low risk of sexual harassment and workplaces characterised by 'relatively small inequality between the sexes with respect to numbers and hierarchical position' (in Bryson 1994b: 23). Here we are provided with a starting place for re-thinking the relationship between institutional climate and sexual harassment, suggesting that sexual harassment is a product of a particular climate – one in which women hold little institutional influence – not the deviant behaviour of deviant individuals.

The feminist community has over the last ten years at least drawn attention to what has been called the 'chilly climate' for women in universities (Sandler and Hall 1986). In April 1995 the University of Technology Sydney's Women's Forum hosted a national conference entitled 'Women, Culture and Universities: A Chilly Climate?' (UTS 1995). The brochure advertising the conference described it as 'on the effect of organisational culture on women in universities'.

Just what is this 'chilly climate' and what is its relationship to sexual harassment? Here we need to be aware of feminism's characterization of sexual harassment as a way of telling women they do not belong, a way of making them feel as if they do not fit. The 'chilly climate' is the agglomeration of factors in universities which mark women as 'ill-fitting'. Here I note the lack of responsiveness to child caring responsibilities and children, the style of learning and debate which is competitive and gladiatorial, the content of the curriculum which in general privileges men's activities and marks women as non-contributors to something called 'knowledge'. The list goes on. What I wish to suggest here is that sexual harassment is a product of the kind of anti-woman climate which dominates in universities; it is not a problem of individual aberration. As a result, grievance procedures are unlikely either to curtail harassment or to alter that environment.

The way in which current institutional approaches to sexual harassment isolate causal factors and so reduce the chances of meaningful change is illustrated in a survey I conducted of staff and student attitudes at the University of Adelaide in 1990 (see Bacchi 1991a, 1991b, 1991c).[17] Staff were asked to record their attitudes to a number of university services and programs, including affirmative action, sexual harassment, and curriculum content. Attitudes to affirmative action differed sharply by gender and by faculty, with the strongest opposition coming from men and from members of the science, engineering and economics faculties.[18] In contrast there was overwhelming support for sexual harassment policies.[19] Opposition and indifference, again mainly from men, characterised the response to increasing the curriculum content on women.[20]

While on the one hand the enthusiastic endorsement of sexual harassment policies is encouraging, the sharp contrast with the responses to affirmative action and curriculum content on women suggests the need to think about the reasons for that endorsement. Sexual harassment policies, I would argue, owe their popularity in part to the fact that they fit more comfortably into conventional discursive constructions of 'fairness'. Harassment is deemed contrary to the 'fair go' mentality. At the same time such policies require no real commitment to doing anything; staff and students are being asked only not to harass.

By contrast, affirmative action policies and the suggestion that course content ought to reflect the experiences of women and other out-groups[21] and their interests imply that something actively needs to be done (see Braithwaite, Chapter 7, this volume). The rationale behind affirmative action is that little meaningful change for women at the university will occur until women are given voice through increasing their presence and their access to positions of authority and influence. Drawing attention to the gendered character of much course content exposes the shallowness of the claim that universities pursue 'truth' and 'excellence'. The extent of opposition to changes in these areas, set in sharp contrast to the wide endorsement of sexual harassment grievance procedures, illustrates a successful narrowing of understandings of the problem. As White perceptively notes, '(O)rganisations tend to respond to crises with responses that minimize real change' (1993: 82).

Diane Purkiss similarly insists upon the need to place the events of sexual harassment in their academic context (1994: 194). Her particular target is pedagogy. She draws attention to the evidence that in mixed seminars women students tend to talk less than men and tend to be taken less seriously. On these grounds, she calls it a scandal that single-sex classes have not even been considered in universities (1994: 215 fn 13).

There is also a clear need to examine the sexual culture of universities (see Hearn and Parkin 1987; White 1993: 82). As I have argued elsewhere (Bacchi 1992, 1994a), sexual harassment grievance procedures will achieve little until the ambiguities surrounding staff-student personal and sexual relations generally are addressed. The fact that this issue is successfully avoided indicates only, as White says, that '(I)t is easier to focus on one sexual exploitation incident than to focus on widespread boundary problems (1993: 82)'.[22]

All these proposals confront the presumed sanctity of academic freedom and the 'idea' of the university as a place to seek 'knowledge'. In effect, they lead to the conclusion that these notions, as presently constructed, are themselves gendered protections for ways of working and thinking which have little to do with women (see Allen 1996).

Conclusion

Recognising that gender is constitutive of universities means recognising that the effects of this constitution, of which sexual harassment is one, can be dealt with effectively only through challenging the culture of the university. This is not a matter of managerialist tampering. It is a matter of re-thinking the university. The argument here, in summary, is that to address sexual harassment we need to address the culture of universities. We need to see what it is about universities which encourages an atmosphere of maleness, an atmosphere where women are only just tolerated. The problem is complex and includes institutional history, elitist traditionalism and male-dominated hierarchies. To do something meaningful about sexual harassment means confronting these issues. From this perspective, firm commitments to increase women's representation throughout university structures, a willingness to review curriculum for content on women, better child care, an examination of the effects of pedagogic practices on women, a reviewing of the nature of staff-student relationships are better indications of a desire to do something about sexual harassment than instituting grievance procedures, however necessary these may be.

The point here is to emphasise that anything less than the kinds of changes detailed in the paragraph above will leave the problem of sexual harassment as it is, all the while suggesting that it is being addressed. We need this kind of analysis, therefore, in order to set a new agenda for change. This agenda identifies institutions as peopled, rather than seeing them as something operating outside of and on people. It also suggests the limited usefulness of middle-level principles of institutional design which attempt to bypass hard political discussions about institutional goals and institutional culture, discussions which by their nature must consider whose interests are served by existing institutions.

Notes

1 I use quotation marks here to signal that we need to start thinking about how something becomes characterized as a social 'problem' and the variety of possible ways of so characterizing a particular social condition. This point is elaborated below.

2 While there is a distinction in this definition between 'norms' and the organisations to which they give rise, the two are often treated as coterminous in institutional design literature. Clearly, this literature is concerned with elucidating principles conducive to the production of smoothly functioning organisations. This aspect of the literature is the primary focus of this chapter.

3 Here Goodin is quoting Huntington 1968: 12.

4 Recognising the ways in which organisational culture produces sexual harassment does not render harassers 'guiltless'. As the National Committee on Violence Against Women makes clear, we cannot punish individuals for the 'context in which violence . . . [and sexual harassment] . . . flourishes'. But we can hold individuals responsible for 'violent behaviour', including sexual harassment, which reproduces those conditions. This argument is developed and defended in Bacchi and Jose 1994.

5 Sue Wise and Liz Stanley (1985) usefully discuss limitations in the 'social meanings' given to sexual harassment, focussing on the kind of problem sexual harassment is often seen to be.

6 Jenna Mead (1995: 173) describes how, at Ormond College, Melbourne, the site of a much publicised sexual harassment case (see Garner 1995), a committee was set up to formalise the students' complaints but it never undertook an investigation. The inadequacy of this response led the students to complain to the Equal Opportunity Commission. This resulted in an apology to the students by the Ormond College council.

7 In some settings contact officers perform a number of roles, of which facilitating access to complaint procedures is only one. At the University of Adelaide, for example, contact officers provide a known first point of contact, assist in clarifying the nature of the concern and explore possible strategies (1995: 5). Their most important function is to provide '. . . support to the complainant throughout any stage of the complaint resolution'.

8 On this subject, see Bacchi and Jose 1994.

9 This may be a little harsh as some policies (for example, University of Adelaide 1995: 6) specify that '(B)eing a Contact Officer is not a formal part of the duties of University staff, but is evidence of service to the University'. Still, no specific compensation or recognition is offered.

10 It should be noted that power at a University takes many forms and does not necessitate direct control over assessment or appointment. There is a kind of social power exercised by the nature of staff-staff relationships where individuals may be reluctant to press a sexual harassment charge as they may

have to work closely with the alleged harasser for years to come. I'd like to thank Carol Johnson for this point.

11 Although White is concerned specifically with sexual exploitation of clients by professional helpers, his categories of analysis are useful for understanding the ways in which organisations deal with sexual harassment.

12 I'd like to thank Carol Johnson for this point.

13 Here I am adopting insights from Fairclough (1992) into interdiscursivity.

14 Note, for example, how Garner (1995: 96, 100, 197) describes the taking of action on the part of the young women in the Ormond College affair in terms of retribution and punishment, as 'punitive', as revengeful.

15 For a discussion of the strength of this discourse in legal writing see Naffine 1992: 746–747.

16 See, for example, the discussion of a draft code of ethics for academics in the recent newsletter of the National Tertiary Education Union (NTEU 1997: 15–22).

17 Because I am interested here in the attitudes of those having authority in universities, I will contain my comments to staff responses. The survey elicited 320 responses from academic staff, a response rate of 40%.

18 The survey posed several questions about affirmative action in an attempt to find out just what people understood by the term. For my purposes here it is adequate to note that 46.6% of men staff felt that affirmative action programs were little needed (compared to 24.5% of women staff), while 46.6% of men staff thought they ought to be maintained (compared to 75.5% of women staff). For breakdown by faculty, see Mayer and Bacchi 1997 (unpublished).

19 Some 88.1% of staff saw a need to maintain policies against sexual harassment; only 11.2% thought that they were little needed. Neither gender nor faculty were statistically significant in this response (Bacchi 1991b).

20 The questionnaire asked if more content on women should be introduced into the curriculum. Among men staff 42.2% disagreed, 30.7% were neutral, and only 27.1% agreed. Among women staff 21.3% disagreed, 24.5% were neutral, and 54.3% agreed (Bacchi 1991b).

21 I use 'outgroups' to refer to those inhabiting the borderlands of positions of power and influence in Western democracies.

22 On the subject of appropriate boundaries in staff-student relationships, see Hunt 1994; for a different view see Gallop 1997.

CHAPTER 6

Heavy, Dirty and Limp Stories: Male advantage at work

Joan Eveline

Introduction

When United States economist Donald McCloskey changed his gender to become Deirdre in 1996, peers predicted his professional demise. Some believed Deirdre's work would be more difficult to publish, others claimed that her research topics would become 'softer', less important. Feminist economists were particularly dismayed. Their cause had lost, they said, the most supportive male voice the field had produced – Donald McCloskey's (Wilson 1996: 24).

McCloskey's colleagues evoke and entrench a deficit model of the feminine. They displace 'the problem' of gender onto McCloskey's new gender identity. Revealingly, none of them mention the advantage that their story of female deficiency generates for men. Male advantage is normalised through such discursive forms.

Drawing on research in labouring work, skilled technology and management, this chapter examines the politics of advantage in the institutions of paid employment. Despite two decades of equal employment opportunity (EEO) programs, Australian occupations are among the world's most sex-segregated. Many Australian feminists have looked hopefully to EEO as a means of changing the sex-marking of jobs as either 'men's work' or 'women's work', a major factor in the higher incomes of men over women. My question concerns how people identify 'the problem' when they argue for and against the re-gendering of work through equal opportunity.

A key term in arguments for EEO is the concept of disadvantage. It is fair to say that equal opportunity, particularly in Australia, has institutionalised talk of disadvantage. 'The problem' is identified as 'women's disadvantage', or 'Aboriginal disadvantage' or 'disadvantaged groups'. In fact, the 'disadvantaged' are often 'commatised', as Mary O'Brien (1984:

43) reminds us: where the lists of disadvantaged sweep across 'blacks (comma) women (comma) unemployed (comma) gays (comma)' and so on. This form of argument 'otherises' the problem and normalises the standards by which those terms are measured – whites, men, employed and employers, heterosexuals and so on. In Australia more recently, we see the discourse of disadvantage turning to encompass groups who were previously the unnamed advantaged, with the news media trumpeting about 'boys' disadvantage' in schools (Foster 1996), 'men's disadvantage' in university admissions (Maslen 1995), or 'men's disadvantage' in unemployment.

Throughout these justifying tales, the absence of any talk of 'advantage' – 'men's' or otherwise – is notable. When we ask why this relation is rarely spelt out we are groping for an insight into the normative characteristics of 'advantage'. In the case before us here (gender), we are dealing with 'male advantage'.

Interestingly, feminist research also suffers from a lack of talk about advantage. If you scan the indices of recent feminist books on almost any topic you will seldom find a listing for 'male advantage'. A comprehensive recent collection on the institutions of work and welfare (Edwards and Magarey 1995), for example, pursues the track of 'women's disadvantage' carefully throughout. Yet, apart from Lois Bryson's contribution in that book, it fails to raise a whisper about the topic of 'men's advantage'.

There are a couple of good reasons why feminists find it difficult to use the term 'male advantage', one theoretical and one pragmatic. For those concerned about universalising, it is obvious that the term can be used to imply that *all* men have a similar set of advantages, which denies in particular questions of class and ethnicity. Then, too, for those not so much intimidated by theory but engaged in the everyday business of promoting and pursuing equity strategies, it is politically expedient to avoid upsetting men around them who need persuading on reforms (Eveline 1994b). Given these good reasons for avoiding the term, then, why bother with it?

My response is that there is still a story to be told, retold, and heard about how women's lack of advantage, in the institutions of gender and of work, is portrayed as a lack in women themselves.

To illustrate the case, I describe three narratives, calling them the *heavy work* story, the *dirty culture* tale and the *women go limp* fable. These stories share a central theme: that women lack whatever is needed to do the job. In heavy industry, for example, we are told that women lack the 'physical capacity to do the work'; in technological and trades occupations they are said to lack the ability to tolerate 'the male culture'; and in the managerial story about 'limp women' they simply lack motivation.

Significantly, these tales also share a particular outcome – they explain why men are over-represented in their occupation by identifying women as 'the problem'. This approach leaves women *with* 'the problem' and men with the advantage.

Questions about pan-institutional and inter-institutional inequalities built on gender are rarely addressed by institutional theorists. While Giddens (1990), Goodin (1996) and Dryzek (1995) all provide useful starting points for analysing the outcomes of instituting practices, only Goodin mentions gender – and then only briefly. Moreover, none of those writers attend to the point about dominant interests that feminist Jan Pettman (1992) makes about what institutions *do*. 'Institutions', argues Pettman, 'validate rules, roles and certain understandings about entitlements which are often seen as fair or universal, but which actually reflect and protect dominant social interests' (1992: 57–58). By focussing on what institutions do, she claims, we can examine how patterns of social inequality are reproduced, not simply as a matter of individual pathology or ignorance, but through the distribution of social resources.

Yet from a feminist perspective, focussing generally on what *institutions* do can deflect our attention from the ways in which individuals discriminate against women (Waring 1985: 18–19). As Carol Bacchi reminds us in the previous chapter, institutions are always 'peopled'. In similar vein, Eleanor Ramsay (1995a: 7) suggests that the use of 'apparently benign, neutral and abstract terms', such as 'institution', can obscure men's behaviour, and ensure that 'women's reactions remain the problem to be explained and solved'.

The issue of agency and structure is a particularly thorny one for those theorising institutions. Pettman's question of what institutions do, I suggest, should include the repetitive stories, or discourses, that shape and reflect their regulatory norms. Through stories, subjects are discursively constructed, and in turn have access to a range of discursive strategies (Foucault 1980; Hollway 1989). By examining the stories through which individuals define and justify their institutions we can gain a sense of how an institutional culture is being reproduced, what the norms and rules are and how some discourses dominate over others.

In the following sections I outline the fables about 'heavy work', 'dirty culture' and 'limp women'. I show how, in embracing a deficit model of women, they normalise male advantage. While feminist research counters these deficit tales, we find writers rarely emphasise advantage in so doing.

Heavy work

In its simplest form, the story about heavy work situates women as physically incapable of doing the job. While 'heavy' is the principal term used, it is often followed by descriptors such as 'dirty', 'dangerous' and 'noisy'. In a study of employer attitudes in the Australian building industry, for example, they (employers) most commonly perceived the key problem as women's incapacity for heavy work. Another concern was 'a dirty or unhealthy environment', while many respondents also said that 'noise levels are very high' (Pyke 1993: 33). Case studies of butchering (Pringle and Collings 1993), baking (Steiger and Reskin 1990), engineering (Sampson 1991), metal trades (Kyle and Wright 1993) and printing (Roos 1990: 285) repeat these findings.

The stress is on women's physical unsuitability for the work, while working conditions are often cited as detrimental to female health. In the words of an Australian female miner: 'They said if I became a dozer driver I was sure to damage my womb' (Eveline 1989).

Feminist researchers are quick to reject the logic of this narrative. Across all cultures, they show, women do *heavy* work (nursing, child care, farming, labouring), *messy* work (housework, factories, subsistence) and *noisy* work (child care, factories, marketplaces, schoolyards). In many historical and contemporary situations it could be argued that women are given the heaviest and messiest work to do.[1] Women's capacity to manage heavy, dirty or noisy *work* is not the problem, the feminist argument goes; rather, the issue is the gender hierarchy in which jobs are defined as 'men's' and 'women's' in the first place (Bradley 1989; Cockburn 1983; 1985; 1991; Game and Pringle 1983). Portraying the jobs men do as inherently more demanding than the jobs women do 'is part of the very ideological framework that stigmatises women as marginal workers' (Schultz 1992: 333). Moreover, as many point out, if work practices and environments endanger the health of women, they will also be detrimental to the health of men. Displacing the danger onto the bodies of women, this feminist counter-story suggests, is no adequate substitute for changing the work practices and environment in the interests of better health, fewer compensation claims and lower worker insurance premiums. Yet even when safer weights and work practices become a lawful requirement, research shows that men still vie with each other to lift more than they need (Cockburn 1985; Eveline 1989: 35–6; Roos 1990; Steiger and Reskin 1990).

An embellishment on the heavy work fable is the notion that the work is abhorrent to feminine taste. Managers often use this story about women's 'lack of interest' to explain why only men operate heavy-duty machinery, such as cranes, dozers and forklifts – 'it is hot, heavy, dirty work and women don't want to do that' (Beechey and Perkins 1987: 105; Eveline et al., 1989: 20; Cockburn and Ormrod 1993: 63).

Feminist challenges to the lack-of-desire narrative take a similar line to their critique of the heavy work story. First, they argue that it is erroneous to suppose that women per se avoid doing heavy, dirty, noisy jobs in all contexts (Bradley 1989; Dahlerup 1990; Reskin and Roos 1990; Sampson 1991; Schultz 1992). Second, they show that women's preferences are not static and fixed, created through early socialisation, nor that they are simply shaped by gender norms or practical responsibilities beyond the workplace. Quite the contrary, they show that the language and practices produced by those workplaces themselves are major factors in stimulating or constraining women's preferences.

For example, when a mining company in Australia's north-west advertised that under an equal employment opportunity scheme *women* were encouraged to apply for training on all tasks in the mine operation, over a thousand women applied for the four hundred jobs offered (Eveline 1995b). A few weeks earlier, when an advertisement stressed that 'trainee miners' were wanted for small, co-operative work teams, there were no applications from women. The term 'miner' in the first advertisement, was read as coterminous with 'men'. The lesson here is that when job advertisements are couched in masculine-favoured language women see them as 'more of a warning than an invitation' (Cockburn 1985: 18). By contrast, when given signals that they are *expected* to apply for 'men's work' there is evidence that women respond in considerable numbers, particularly when employers intimate in their advertising that they are interacting with a government-sponsored scheme (Bem and Bem 1973; Dahlerup 1990; Reskin and Roos 1990; Sampson 1991; Schultz 1992; Kyle and Wright 1993).

Yet the story that, *as a gender*, women lack desire for the heavily mechanised and better-paid jobs done by men is still prevalent amongst employers in industry. In this context Pettman's advice to focus on what institutions *do* becomes highly pertinent, in particular if we relate it to the stories spun by people within them. Through a series of ongoing narratives about the 'men's work' of heavy industry, the institutions of the labour market intersect with those of gender and law to protect most closely the advantages of men.

Dirty culture

Originating in the technical and trades areas, the dirty culture story holds that such work is conducted within a rough, dirty, aggressive, noisy and alien *culture*. Rather than 'the problem' being women's physical inadequacy, it is now that they are deemed *psychologically* unfit. The rationale for this story relies heavily on cultural practices called 'dirty jokes', 'dirty pictures', 'dirty language', 'dirty environment' and 'dirty tricks'. Yet when we unpick this story about 'culture' we find proponents contending that women cannot tolerate the *behaviour of men* in certain workplaces. Therefore, the argument goes, they should be protected from it.

Feminist critics encounter a particular complication when they challenge this story: they usually agree that women need protection from men's harassing behaviour. They cannot, therefore, straightforwardly claim the account is incorrect. Kyle and Wright, for instance, suggest that 'the greatest barriers to female advancement are male workers and male work culture and work practices' (1993: x), while Lois Bryson writes (in her study of the Australian Defence Forces), that 'acts and language are used by men to exclude women from full acceptance and to limit their participation' (1994b: 10). This is precisely the argument that employers use to explain why women are not in industries such as building, butchering and metal trades. An Australian study on employer attitudes in the building industry, for example, shows some revealing results. A majority of employers (57%) cited 'men's behaviour' as the biggest problem women in the trade would face. They forecast that women would receive a 'lack of acceptance by co-workers, sexual harassment and intimidation, lack of power in the workplace and bad language' (Pyke 1993: 12).

It is too simple to say that, in refusing to consider women for jobs, these employers show an attitudinal bias. The 'lack of acceptance' by men to which they refer includes practices that studies refer to time and again as outright hostility. The spectrum of men's 'lack of acceptance' of female co-workers ranges widely. It includes men refusing to work on the same tasks as women (Cockburn 1983; Kanter 1984; Cockburn and Ormrod 1993; Eveline 1995b), it traverses 'dirty jokes', 'unpleasant atmosphere', 'swearing', 'pornographic pictures', 'rough' and 'loud' behaviour of men (Cockburn 1983; Eveline et al. 1989; Pyke 1993) and it covers women being endangered by harassing behaviour and by 'practical jokes' or 'stunts' (Schultz 1992: 321 ff; Eveline 1995b: 97–99). Feminists agree, therefore, with the justificatory story that women find this 'culture' hard to take. They differ from employers, however, in their analysis of what should be done.

Broadly speaking there are two outcomes when women enter the jobs that men have claimed as their own. First, there are the practical stories that invent enclaves of 'women's work' so that all else is recast as 'men's work'. There are two mechanisms involved here: (i) fables that gender certain tasks as 'women's'; and (ii) stories that normalise what we might call demands for 'extra service' by women, so that men are positioned as advantaged beings, the ones to be served. Second, there are the practices generating what Cockburn calls a 'hostile environment' (1985: 176–185). Again there are two components to this: (i) various forms of harassment which mark 'women' as highly visible through exploitative and objectifying practices; (ii) a male norm which effaces the lived experiences of female bodies, and casts women as non-workers.

Reinventing men's jobs by creating women's work

Marking women's work. Studies of non-traditional workplaces show repeatedly that when women move into 'men's work', demarcations that belittle women's contributions are invented. Sometimes women are complicit in forming these divisions, pleased enough to have a more woman-friendly space: 'Now I don't try too hard, I just drive a truck in place of a dozer'; 'So I thought, why not hold the hose instead of the drill? we all get paid the same' (Eveline et al. 1989). At other times they contest the designation of 'women's machines' with varying degrees of success (Eveline 1995b). By the invention of these divisions, those who are most like 'men' understand that whatever jobs are deemed the most desirable, the most skilled and the most lucrative are manifest as their prerogative (Cockburn 1985; Eveline 1989; Bradley 1990).

In all cases, the tales marking the 'women's work' code it as inferior. Even the story, told by mine supervisors, that women were 'better' at truck-driving because they tended to drive more carefully and took better care of the equipment, did nothing to make truckdriving itself as valued as working on the explosives team, although the amount of training and responsibility was directly comparable. Revealingly, the rationale that women were 'better' at certain tasks was applied also to menial jobs like cleaning, hosing down and acting as assistants, all jobs that men usually felt should be left to women and trainees (Eveline 1994c). In similar studies, Cockburn and Ormrod (1993) and Game and Pringle (1983) show how work institutions gender tasks across technologies, from welding to computing.

Extra service. A similar generating of masculine superiority operates through the story that women's presence will automatically accomplish 'extra services', ones that will benefit men, employers or both. The term that managers of Argyle Diamond Mine, in Australia's north-west, use to describe their employment of women miners is 'normalisation'. Bringing women into mining, for the mine's designers, tempers the established ways of mine workers: having women miners 'has improved the behaviour of males'; 'they dress better, stay cleaner, behave more appropriately, when there are females around than when there are not' (Eveline 1995b: 97).[2] Here, women are discursively located as servicers of the men, a strategy of which they are well aware ('we're not only miners but minders'). For the mine's managers, women's mining takes second place to their minding. Women certainly become miners, yet the work retains its masculine focus, and men – the assigned beneficiaries of women's domesticating presence – retain their normative advantage (Eveline 1995b).

Hostile environment

Singling out. Research in the United States tells us that women in male-dominated occupations are more likely to be subjected to harassment than are women in other occupations (Gutek and Morasch 1982: 67–68; Martin 1989). Anecdotal evidence in Australia shows similar findings. It is now well understood that sexual overtures are only a small part of this harassing behaviour, and that by far the greatest difficulties for women come from a systemic form of workplace harassment engendered by sex segregation itself: 'it's a form of harassment every time I pick up a sledgehammer and that prick laughs at me'; 'the foreman puts me in a dangerous situation, gives me the wrong instructions, and jokes along with the rest when I try to cope'; 'he calls me love and I've asked him over and over not to'; 'they all stop and leer when it's my turn to unsnag the moving conveyor' (Pollack 1990: 221–222; also Eveline et al. 1989).

As Rosemary Pringle argues, 'For a woman to enter one of these trades is to put her gender on the line' (1994: 206). Many women describe being 'on the line' as continual sexual surveillance. In such environments harassment is what I call atmospheric. Other terms feminists use for this constitutive antagonism towards women and the feminine are 'gender harassment', 'sex-based harassment' and 'hostile work environment' (Cockburn 1985; Eveline et al. 1989; Schultz 1992; Blackmore 1993; Still 1993; Bryson 1994a).

Atmospheric harassment occurs when employers condone men's resistance to women. Take, for example, the mechanical fitters who papered walls and ceiling of their workspace with hard core pornography. One of the men described this action as a way of reminding women that they are 'intruders': 'You don't try to make it better for women', he said, 'if anything you make it worse. If women want to come into our workforce they can put up with it, and if they don't like it they can bloody leave' (Eveline 1995b: 98). By driving women away and hindering their performance abilities harassment *produces*, rather than simply reinforces, the idea that women are inferior workers who cannot cope with a 'man's job'. Women 'understand that behind the symbolism of masculinised job descriptions lies a very real force: the power of men to harass, belittle, ostracise, dismiss, marginalise, discard and just plain hurt them as workers' (Schultz 1992: 321).

Since the 'normal' atmosphere of non-traditional jobs begins with a training system which is dependent upon devaluing and excluding the feminine, the demerit women are accorded appears intangible and impersonal, and therefore non-discriminatory. The intangible, the forgettable and the unnameable efface the female body and generate male advantage. Yet, as Bacchi argues in the previous chapter, the institutions and organisations in which these actions occur, providing they have grievance procedures in place, are deemed 'innocent' of this atmospheric harassment 'problem'.

Masculine norms and men's advantage. Women in male-dominated fields often describe the ways in which the specificity of their bodies is denied (Pringle and Collings 1993; Eveline 1995b). Everyday examples of this are described in a case study of a mining enterprise, in that safety gloves for handling dangerous chemicals came in one size only – large – and supervisors invariably addressed workers as 'men', 'blokes' and 'guys' (Higginson 1994: 4–5). Moreover, until women's complaints were acted upon, they had to walk 400 metres to the toilets and neither toilets nor the mine's supermarket carried sanitary towels and tampons. Pringle and Watson describe a similar process of negating women's experience, in the relation between women and the state: the problem, they say, is a recurring pattern of 'discursive marginality' (1992: 57). This marginality necessitates no explicit opposing of 'men's interests' to women's; rather, it operates as 'government conducted as if men's interests were the only ones that exist'.

The normalising of men's interests and bodies is enabled by the story that the working body per se is gender-neutral or a 'merely human' body. A neat example of this again comes from mining. When women miners made a group protest to deal with the continual erasure of their interests, the first thing they asked the company to do was provide them with 'women's working clothes'. In the mine's tropical climate all workers and managers wore regulation blue shorts, shirts and sleeveless overalls. Many women experienced discomfort with the proportions of these garments, across chests, waists and hips. Yet their request annoyed many of their male co-workers: 'These aren't men's clothes', said the men, 'they're *work* clothes'. The normalising of men's interests, an unremarkable form of privilege, locates women outside the designated norm of 'worker' and obscures the advantaged status of men (Eveline 1994c).

The dirty culture story centres on men's behaviour and 'male culture', rather than the physical 'nature' of women. Yet the theme – of women being treated as the problem – remains the same as in the heavy work tale. So does the answer.

Nonetheless, some women will not abide their exclusion, nor will they accept the culture of 'men's work' as it stands. Instead they demand 'a strategy of organisational change which aims to change the culture' (Bryson 1994b: 6).

In blue collar work, women have occasional allies in their concern for change. Spurred by the need to comply with the legal requirements of affirmative action and the escalating costs of workers' compensation and lost productivity stemming from the 'macho' culture of men, companies and supervisors can have an incentive to change the narratives, and to some degree the practices, of both 'heavy work' and 'dirty culture'. For still other organisational designers the desire to change the culture is an attempt to make a potentially unruly workforce more industrially malleable. However, when we examine the jobs of those managers and leaders themselves, as in the next section, we find few pressures for change.

A limp story of women

The third tale 'flashes its gender rather obviously'.[3] Told to justify the over-representation of men in the senior ranks of professions and management, it suggests that women lack the necessary drive, motivation and testosterone to get to the top. Complicating the gender dimension with questions of class, this narrative prompts the question of how women oppress each other.

In August, 1995, Dame Leonie Kramer, the chancellor of Sydney University, was rebuked by her university's senate for views she had expressed about senior women. Some weeks earlier, Kramer had stated that her institution's previously poor performance on the indicator of women in senior positions could be put down to the fact that women 'go a bit limp when the going gets tough'. Applications for vice-chancellor of the university were being invited at the time, a decision over which Kramer as chancellor had the final say (*Australian* 8.8.95: 1).[4]

Dame Leonie was unswayed by her senate's rebuke. In a subsequent radio interview she argued her case, adding that she herself 'can go limp at times'. Denying that her remarks would 'disadvantage' women in any way, Kramer charged her female critics with a 'victim mentality'. Women 'overused', she claimed, the notion of disadvantage in pursuit of 'their own ends' (ABC, Radio National 8.8.95). Carrying her own swag of financial and educational advantage, not only does Kramer take her privileges as an unmentionable right, she allows no place for relative disadvantage in her view of aspiring managerial women.

Given her opinion that women and men in Western democracies start from equally unencumbered positions, Kramer can only describe women's lack of success as 'a mystery'; it should be attributed to nothing other than women's individual choice. Time and again, she said, she has 'observed women who, when faced with the challenge to go to the top, decide not to, for various reasons'.

In sum, Kramer rehearses the lack-of-desire story that is also invoked in the heavy work and dirty culture narratives. Told by an employer – and a woman who marks other women as outsiders – this fable reiterates the theme of women as a group against which men are pitted as the desired and desiring standard. Like others of its kind, emanating from its class, it helps to ensure that while a limited number of women may trespass on the paths of upper management, the job will still retain the status and symbols of 'men's work'.

In such stories, the practices that generate women's exclusion are seen as the normal way to achieve successful managers and competitive institutions. Those practices are viewed as gender-neutral and non-discriminatory. Importantly, as I indicate below, they share common ground with the stories encountered by women in blue-collar and technical occupations: they project a deficit model of women, via a pervasive normalising of gender discrimination.

Women inadequate to the task

At the beginning of the eighties, the management literature on women was dominated by the narrative that female under-representation could be explained and remedied by attention to women's own behaviour, characteristics and motivations. In the nineties, the literature usually recognises that women's past exclusion has been fostered by discriminatory practices within organisations and institutions. Among policy-makers, however, there often remains the comfortable view that such discrimination has now been addressed by equal opportunity and affirmative action and it is only a matter of time before women 'catch up' (for example, as in DEET, 1993). This view is echoed amongst employers who believe that 'discrimination is past and time will fix all' (Eveline et al. 1989; Burton 1991; Cockburn 1991; Poiner and Wills 1991; Castleman et al. 1995).

Like Kramer, other employers imbue professional and managerial jobs with characteristics which women are then normalised as lacking. In a recent study, managers believed that senior personnel must be 'highly committed', 'single-minded' and prepared to contribute 'more than a forty-hour week'. General agreement that 'it's a *hard* job', often used in selection panels, was tantamount to saying that 'we want a man for this job' (Castleman et al. 1995: 106). Cockburn shows similar stories being used, along with what she calls the 'chill factor', against women in the upper echelons of the British civil service and in retail chains (1991: 64–68). Similar narratives are exposed by Marshall (1984) in her study of women managers, by Pringle (1994) in her account of senior women in law and by Burton (1991: 100–101) in her analysis of the 'halo effect' and 'expectancy bias' in job evaluation.

The converse of the story that women lack the necessary 'hardness' is condemnation when they demonstrate it. Both Cockburn (1991: 69) and Schultz (1992: 320) show that even when women do emulate these stereotypical managerial requirements they are excluded on the grounds that they lack feminine virtues.

Despite considerable research revealing that women are more likely than men to apply for jobs at a level well within their capabilities and qualifications, men are advantaged by the idea that female applicants have generally lower qualifications and less experience than their male counterparts (Marshall 1984; Schultz 1992; Castleman et al. 1995). The focus on women as lacking in certain characteristics sets the standard for what the job is said to entail. According to one study, the primary requirement of university employers is '(c)ontinuity and concentration of effort', which women are deemed not to have, since 'a number of people suggested that the problem of women's status lies with women's choices and attitudes' (Castleman et al. 1995: 114).

Not all women are excluded by stories of demerit and lack of determination. Research shows, however, that successful women are those who emulate the requirements associated with stereotyped (male) career paths (Holton 1988). As a senior lawyer said: 'You have to be one of the chaps to succeed. This means not that you dress like a man but that you act like one' (Pringle 1994: 213).

'Acting like a man' can mean that maleness triumphs over merit, since studies show that successful men have lower qualifications than women who apply for the same positions (Castleman et al. 1995: 88–90) and that successful men have lower qualifications than successful female peers (Marshall 1984; Cockburn 1991; Schultz 1992). Moreover, women in middle management, at least, perceive that male colleagues produce less and work fewer hours than they do (Marshall 1984; Eveline 1994a). Heather Carmody (of the Business Council of Australia) claims that the required output, for executive level women, is 150 per cent (*Four Corners* 12.10.92).

Normalising gender discrimination

Whether the work is in heavy industry, in technical and trades occupations or in executive levels of organisations, it is normal to describe the work as '*hard*', and to embody incumbents as 'highly committed', 'single-minded', as well as 'selfish and arrogant'. By definition, male-dominated occupations position 'women' as lacking in these characteristics and 'men' as 'one of us' (Castleman et al. 1995). Another study shows how the under-representation of women in management is fixed as a women's problem, since the behaviour and processes which exclude them are 'taken as acceptable, expected and thoroughly normal' (Still 1993).[5] The normality of stories and exclusions ensures a lack of counter-stories and effective challenges to men's behaviour. Thus 'the absence of adequate terms in which to identify what is occurring continues to normalise both the behaviour and its effects' (Ramsay 1995: 5).

Women competing on institutional ladders face the added disadvantage that the culture of professional and managerial work is seen as the *most* normal of arrangements, a perception indicating, and enhanced by, institutional hierarchies. Compared to blue-collar work, decision-making duties are light, clean and relatively quiet and it is considered rather unprofessional to display overt forms of sexual discrimination and harassment. Whereas in industry, and occasionally in bureaucracy, managerial attempts to extract greater cost benefits from workers may sometimes prompt employers to intervene in the 'dirty culture' of more junior employees, the upper echelons of management are not about to generate a self-critique, particularly one which would prescribe a sex change. In an unremarkable way, the ordinary business of institutional leadership simply institutes gender as usual.

The problems that women face in senior white-collar jobs are linked to their being implicated in normalisation procedures. Since their work has to be done regardless of interaction with colleagues, women (like men) will usually try and follow as 'normal' a life as possible. Amongst everyday pressures, systemic discrimination will often go unchallenged: 'they thought I would have to consult my husband before booking an interstate trip'; 'the CEO always has an eye out for contacts for Simon, but if I don't remind him he doesn't worry about me' (Eveline 1994a). Such assumptions and exclusions, which cash out as advantages for men, are likely to remain invisible *as* discrimination against women, precisely because they are seen as normal.

Organisationally generated obstacles

As in trades and blue-collar work, recent feminist research on professions and on seniority finds that women are excluded and marginalised by practices emanating from organisations themselves, rather than from factors extraneous to the workplace (such as their early socialisation). Metaphors of 'glass ceilings' and 'brick walls' are attempts to describe organisational discrimination, as invisible 'things' which have to be removed in order for women to succeed (Bacchi 1993; Bryson 1993; Pratt 1993; Still 1993). Talk of cultural discrimination has become more prevalent in recent literature and is an attempt to deal with norms, myths and images that shape and reflect discrimination (Blackmore 1993; Sofoulis 1993). The concern for culture attempts to address the intangibility of institutionalised inequality, which for Posner is 'the new problem that has no name' (Still 1993: 146).

Giving the problem a name, for some writers, means concentrating on direct discrimination, although often placing it against a background of systemic bias. On this point Kaplan (1985) argues that men treat women

with non-verbal hostility, ostracism and exclusion from informal networks, while Sheppard (1989: 153–155), Kenway (1991: 30) and Schultz
(1992: 317–321) outline a range of practices by which men belittle,
undermine and ignore female colleagues. In an effort to have such
behaviour addressed, the Women's Alliance of Sweden's Social
Democratic Party produced a booklet itemising how male politicians
attempt to minimise and dominate female colleagues: (i) robbing them
of the right to be heard, by talking over the top of them, shuffling papers,
walking out of the room; (ii) generalising about 'women's behaviour'
in a derogatory fashion; (iii) withholding vital information; (iv) con-
demning women (but not men) for supposedly neglecting family
responsibilities; and (v) attempting to make women feel responsible for
men's sexism and abuse (Swedish Social Democratic Party 1993: 11–16).
On the question of men's motivation, Davies concludes that the very
presence of women is experienced by many male decision-makers 'as a
threat to their male values, practices, and conceptual frameworks,
perhaps especially where they are seen to have an equal chance (of
success)' (1982: 19).

By contrast with the heavy work and dirty culture stories, those
encountered by women near the top of organisational hierarchies are
particularly difficult to designate as illegitimate. There is room for more
investigation into just what it is that men in senior positions *do* to exclude
and alienate women, since the very pervasiveness and normality of
stories that advantage men 'shroud in vague generalities the actual
occurrences to which they allude' (Ramsay 1995: 2).

Kramer's 'women go limp' story expresses the ordinariness by which
women are marginalised and belittled in organisations. For Kramer the
institutional advantaging of men, in which she shares as a token female,
is so pervasive as to be invisible. In the university setting from which she
comes, the link between the regulatory norms and the being male is
hidden by the concept of the liberal individual (see Carol Bacchi on this
point, Chapter 5 in this volume).

It is this 'hidden text'[6] of women's challenge to leadership – the
institutional favouring of men – that poses 'a mystery' for Kramer. Rather
than the over-supply of men being a source of insight, she accepts it
without question: there is no advantage for 'men' or those who act like
them, it is just how things should be. Any mystery involved can be
explained by displacing the problem back onto women: after all, a
woman who is *being* one 'goes limp'. Amongst the ordinariness of male
privilege, then, Kramer's limp story is hardly extraordinary. Rather, it is
one of the more colourful, and less discrete, expressions of how tilts at
the men's work of upper management, by women *qua* women, are constituted as ill-fitting.

Gender: a relation

Recognising the relation between the institutions of 'men's work' and 'women's work' is crucial to assessing how each is reshaped and reinvented. To say that these institutions are inventions is not to deny that they have real effects in the world.

For a start, statistical and qualitative studies show that while the content of each is subject to historical change, the division between the two is continually reinstated (Game and Pringle 1983; Cockburn 1985; Cockburn and Ormrod 1993). Secondly, research shows a consistent undervaluing of women's skills and work (McNeil 1987; Pocock 1988; Cockburn 1991), that this is built into the development of technology (Wajcman 1991; Cockburn and Ormrod 1993), and how in turn the gendering of skill reflects and shapes the worth put on women's work (Phillips and Taylor 1980; Burton et al. 1987; Acker 1989). A point often downplayed in these latter analyses, however, as Cockburn and Ormrod point out (1993: 1–3), is that the undervaluing of women's skills, occupations and work is relational; it can also be described as the overvaluing of men's skills, jobs and productivity.

We can apply this relational analysis to the 'limp', 'dirty' and 'heavy' stories, to show how they protect their sectors by devaluing the efforts of women who enter them. When we analyse the stories that protect men's work we find that their common outcome is to displace the explanation for women's under-representation onto women themselves. In the heavy story women lack a capacity to do the *work*, in the dirty story they lack a capacity to tolerate the *culture* and in the limp story they lack a capacity to remain *erect, hard and determined*. Their common theme, that women lack the necessary, has long-running historical forbears. Feminist counter-stories, by contrast, drawn from studies across each of those fields of work, indicate how women's exclusion and minimisation is generated by practices and behaviours within organisations and institutions themselves, which displace the explanation, and 'the problem', back onto women.

For those who are most like 'men' there are considerable advantages flowing from those acts of legitimation by displacement. They derive advantage both from the norms being as they are, and from discussion of advantage remaining muted.

In the institutions of work, some women are trying to gain some of that cultural advantage, others are working to persuade men to do some of the work that currently gets cashed out as cultural disadvantage (generally, for women). Those at the top, who make most of the decisions, who have most effect on which organisational practices become normative, are still invariably white men. They rarely do heavy, dirty or dangerous work, but what they do fits closely with the preference given to hard, acquisitive and aggressive action. The understanding that a stable, competitive and renewable society must value such practices above all others, and indeed cannot survive without them, is exactly their advantage. Until those who reap the most advantage from that understanding no longer fit the currently predominant model of 'men' a case for emphasising not only a story of 'women's disadvantage', but of 'men's advantage' will be difficult to deny.

One way of retelling that story is to incorporate it into affirmative action and sex discrimination guidelines. If the major source of obstacles to women's careers come from organisations themselves, and if, as studies show us time and again, work institutions continually discriminate against women, there is a good case for doing what Valerie Braithwaite suggests in the next chapter: exerting more pressure through affirmative action and sex discrimination legislation.

A precedent for highlighting and delegitimating unfair advantage is to be found in a proposal by the Labor government in 1995. The proposal called for a toughening of the Trade Practices Act so that powerful business interests cannot take advantage of smaller enterprises. The amendment proposed that the act would 'prohibit harsh or oppressive conduct' where 'the nature of the relationship' between two parties 'gives one party a significant advantage in its bargaining power' and 'where the stronger party knowingly exploits their advantage' (Lewis and Clout 1995). This radical shift of focus was aimed at explicating unfair business advantage. The question is whether, and how, a similar concern for advantage can be transported into other policy areas. Could it be applied to gender equality legislation? Does the proposal set a logical precedent for how to address gender advantage at work? Can we envisage such policies on present-day agendas, under a federal government bent on diminishing, if not indeed disbanding, our already minimalist strategies of affirmative action and sex discrimination?

Policy that uses the criteria of unfair advantage in affirmative action and sex discrimination law looks increasingly remote, but it is still conceivable. Criteria for work practices and behaviour can be imagined whereby affirmative action could delegitimate 'men's' advantage' in a forthright and systematic way, and where sex discrimination cases could be judged on the basis of systemic advantage. If the criteria for reporting on affirmative action, and the criteria for judging sex discrimination, were to include proof that work practices and behaviours of personnel enabled no unfair advantages to men, a clear message that unfair advantage is socially unacceptable may yet be sent, and the source of the problem directed away from 'women'.

Notes

1 In nineteenth-century British mines, it took two men to lift a basket of coals, weighing 170 lbs, on to the back of a woman (Bradley, 1989: 107), and in many unmechanised societies women still do the heavy labour of road work and building (Bradley, 1989:42). As for messy work the amount of cleaning that women do far outstrips that done by men, in both paid and household labour (Cockburn, 1985; Beechey and Perkins, 1987; Baxter et al. 1990).

2 For reasons of costs and industrial relations stability the company decided against a mining town complete with families, and instead bases miners in the city and flies them to the remote mine for two-week stints. With no families at the mine, women miners are expected to stabilise and civilise the men.

3 Barbara Brook (Victoria University of Technology, 1995: 7) coined this phrase in response to an early version of this chapter.

4 Somewhat predictably, the job was won by a male applicant.

5 Cited in Ramsay (1995a: 3).

6 Microsoft Word word processing program has a facility called 'hidden text' which allows material compiled in a file to remain hidden when the file is printed. While a lot of this material may be essential to the final structure of the printout, it remains unexposed to public view.

CHAPTER 7

Designing the Process of Workplace Change through the Affirmative Action Act

Valerie Braithwaite

Introduction[1]

The blindness of labour institutions to the interests of women has led to the creation of a body of legislation to mandate equal wages between the sexes, equality of opportunity and family friendly workplace policies. In spite of almost a decade of legal apparatus at the international, national and State levels, movement toward gender equity has seriously lagged behind women's rapid entrance into the Australian workforce (Mitchell 1998). As Baxter, Eveline and Bacchi point out in this volume, culture remains remarkably resistant to change in spite of legislation and political rhetoric promoting gender equality.

The imperviousness of masculine work culture to change through law in Australia has been attributed to reliance on legislation that does not demand enough of employers, that gives too much latitude for compliance and that does not impose heavy penalties on those who fail to take gender equity seriously. These facets will be referred to in this paper as the law's gentleness, looseness and weakness respectively, and will be examined in relation to the legislative centrepiece for cultural change in Australia, the Affirmative Action (Equal Employment Opportunity for Women) Act 1986.

The objective of the Affirmative Action Act (AAA) is for each employer to rid the workplace of sexual discrimination so that women have as many employment opportunities as men. The AAA does not prescribe outcomes but rather processes that align closely with standard business practices. In this sense, the legislation is gentle. Its looseness stems from the fact that the mechanisms for correcting discrimination are left entirely to the discretion of employers and employees. The weakness of the AAA lies in the absence of an array of institutional artillery that theorists of regulation claim are necessary to bring about cooperation between regulators and regulatees (Ayres and Braithwaite 1992). The AAA does not provide a range of sanctions, escalating in severity, to encourage persistent non-compliers to reconsider their options and see advantage in finding co-operative, law-abiding solutions.

This paper argues that while the penalties associated with failure to implement affirmative action legislation in Australia are low, the psychological stakes associated with interpreting the legislation and implementing it in the spirit in which it is intended are high. Under such circumstances, strengthening legislation may fail to produce the psychological surrender that is a necessary part of changing culture. In the long term, 'loose' and 'gentle' legislation may be the more productive option, providing that implementation is properly planned, resourced and monitored. This paper proposes four principles of implementation: (a) value consensus, (b) empowerment, (c) institutional redundancy, and (d) interlocking social chains. All four strategies were used to achieve bipartisan support for the AAA in parliament, but they were not carried over into the stage of implementation.

The paper is divided into six parts. The first delineates the central features of the AAA. The second section examines the way in which psychological stakes can be high even while recognising the legislation as loose, gentle and weak. The third section uses parliamentary debates to illustrate that the loose, gentle and weak nature of the legislation was fully recognised by politicians, but was also feared. The fourth section shows how these qualities enabled the building of consensus among politicians from opposing parties, a left-right alliance that was crucial to getting the legislation passed by both houses of parliament. The process of designing and building support for the legislation also involved the operation of the principles of empowerment, institutional redundancy and interlocking social chains. The fifth section argues that the strategies are generalisable beyond the parliamentary setting and can be developed as institutions (as norms or accepted practices) that facilitate social adaptation and the constructive resolution of conflict in organisational contexts. Evidence is presented to show the patchwork way in which value consensus, empowerment of employees, institutional redundancy, and interlocking social chains were at work at the implementation stage. Where they were employed, changes in workplace culture were evident. The final section reviews the recent changes in implementation that offer hope for the evolution of workplace cultures that meet the needs of both women and men and directions for the future.

Central features of the AAA

Australia's Affirmative Action (Equal Employment Opportunity for Women) Act 1986 mandates change in the workplace to remove gender-based discrimination. When first introduced, it affected all private sector employers with 100 or more employees and institutions of higher education. In 1992, it was amended to also include community organisations, non-government schools, unions and group training schemes.

The legislation requires employers to set up an affirmative action program that incorporates eight steps:

- issuing an equal employment opportunity policy statement to all employees;
- appointing a senior officer responsible for the affirmative action program;
- consulting with trade unions;
- consulting with employees;
- collating and analysing the employment profile of the workplace by gender and job classification;
- reviewing employment policies and practices to identify sources of discrimination;
- setting objectives and forward estimates for the affirmative action program; and
- putting in place self-regulatory procedures to monitor and evaluate progress.

Companies are required to report on an annual basis, in writing, to the Director of the Affirmative Action Agency detailing their progress in implementing their programs. If a report is not submitted without good reason, or if the report does not indicate sufficient progress in implementing an affirmative action program, the employer is sanctioned by being named in parliament. A further sanction added after the five-year effectiveness review of the AAA was that government contracts would be denied to companies not in compliance with the legislation.

Since 1995, changes have been made to the reporting form used by companies and the feedback provided by the Affirmative Action Agency (Affirmative Action Agency 1995). The eight steps specified in the act have been incorporated into a best practice model so that affirmative action activities can be fully integrated into the strategic business plan. These reports are given an assessment on a five-point scale by the agency staff to provide feedback to individual organisations and benchmarks for different industries.

Loose, gentle and weak – yet threatening

From a traditional legal perspective, law that is not backed by punitive sanctions and that is vague and non-specific is bound to be cast aside as unimportant law, as a nice display of social etiquette, or a cynical display of political rhetoric. The AAA has always suffered from such characterisations. Where the objective is workplace reform, the law's looseness, gentleness and weakness have been widely regarded as serious liabilities (Sawer 1990; Thornton 1990; Poiner and Wills 1991; Bacchi 1994b).

Pessimism is understandable in view of the social changes envisaged, changes to (a) how work can be done, (b) what constitutes effective performance, (c) organisational goals, (d) interpretations of workplace behaviour and (e) workplace behaviour itself. The social change required to reform workplaces is not cosmetic, but deeply cultural (Burton 1991; Eveline 1994c: 1995a).

Change of this kind impinges on the psychology of individuals. If it does not, one is left with no more than lip service to a new social order. Substantive change to work practices means that basic beliefs, social truths, habits and lifestyles of individuals must be challenged and re-evaluated at the micro level of social interaction. This process is threatening to all individuals, whether they be AAA sympathisers or antagonists. Under these circumstances, the law does not have to demand or threaten much. The threat is the change. Fear of change in this context is rational. The gender-friendly workplace is an ideal rather than a tried and proven organisational structure, and getting there involves taking chances, making mistakes and frustration enough to dampen the enthusiasm of the most ardent supporters.

Having outlined the reasons for insecurity and resistance at the individual level, how can individuals be accommodated in programs to transform workplace culture? Why not use law to impose a new order from above? The answer is that change imposed from above within a democracy does not probe deeply enough into the culture to affect what really matters, the way men and women view each other in day-to-day interactions. A realistic objective in changing the culture of a workplace is to win over a critical mass to the idea of change, communicate clearly the desired end point and achieve the co-operation of key players to get there. Obviously, legislation that is highly prescriptive and punitive will have an effect, but change of this kind is likely to be too narrow, too circumscribed, and easily overturned.

Examples of the way in which specific directives to a workforce can yield effective, but narrow, change abound. In academia, the adoption of rules to remove sexist language from the print media has had a clear impact on the written word. These days, within universities, senior academic staff invariably display exemplary compliance with such rules, but sophistication in linguistic practices has not been accompanied by equally sophisticated insights into the barriers facing women in academic environments.

Furthermore, specific prescriptive rules tend to be owned by their makers rather than by those who are expected to obey them. When the Australian government banned smoking on airlines, airline staff regrettably explained to passengers that smoking was prohibited due to government regulations. It took a considerable period of time for the regret to fade, for tones of blame to be set aside and for airlines to accept responsibility for safeguarding their passengers' health. Where change in culture is the goal, ownership for regulations needs to be more quickly transferred to the regulated, along with the responsibility for identifying the breadth and depth of the change that is required. Psychological research has provided a body of evidence that warns of the way in which external controls on behaviour can reduce feelings of self-determination and subsequent motivation to take the initiative in achieving related goals (Festinger 1957; Festinger and Carlsmith 1959; Lepper 1973; Boggiano et al. 1987).

A third argument against prescriptive, punitive regulation is that of a psychological backlash. Brehm and Brehm (1981) use the term 'reactance' to describe the counterproductive effects of trying to force individuals to take actions that impinge upon highly valued freedoms. Under such circumstances, sanctions designed to have a deterrent effect can increase the likelihood of undesirable behaviour. A similar effect has been observed among those who have a highly emotional disposition (Makkai and Braithwaite 1994). They became less compliant when faced with deterrence.

These findings can be drawn together to postulate that prescriptive, punitive law incurs significant psychological costs that may work against the objectives of the legislation. The notion of affirmative action threatens core aspects of individuals' beliefs systems, their identities. In such cases, the 'sticks and stones' thrown by others are less of a threat to the individual than the 'names' one is forced to call oneself if one complies.

The central propositions of the argument as to why prescriptive, punitive legislation may not work more effectively than loose, gentle and weak legislation are as follows. Threats to a person's sense of self can override threats from external sanctions. Culture plays a pivotal role in the definition of self. Attempting to change culture through legislation threatens individual identity. The threat will be greatest among those most attuned to that culture. The AAA is a piece of legislation that explicitly seeks to change culture through changing individuals' work-related identities. The legislation targets employers and senior managers, most often men who are well socialised into a culture that perpetuates discrimination against women. These senior executives are required, by law, to listen to women as well as men, and to identify their own discriminatory practices in appointing staff, allocating tasks and recommending promotions. Having faced their shortcomings in their work performance, they are required to find solutions. For these reasons, senior business executives might be expected to shirk their responsibilities under AAA, but they can also be expected to show high levels of psychological reactance when force is applied to elicit compliance.

Individuals who perceive assaults on their identities are not without means to protect themselves (Braithwaite et al. 1994b; Braithwaite 1995). Indeed they are particularly powerful in launching a defence at the psychological level. One posture is resistance, in which individuals engage in active defiance, forcefully opposing the government and its rules and regulations. Resistance is likely to result in campaigns to oppose, overturn or undermine legislation. The fate of affirmative action in America demonstrates the power of resistance to undo social justice initiatives. The second posture is disengagement. This response involves passive withdrawal and the placement of an impenetrable psychological barrier between oneself and government. Under such circumstances, regulators have limited capacity to have any effect at all on compliance, even with powerful sanctions at their disposal. Those who disengage don't trust government, don't feel socially connected to the regulatory community, and don't care about the consequences of non-compliance.

Both these postures are consistent with theoretical accounts of how individuals choose groups that define, maintain and enhance their social identities (Tajfel 1978; Turner 1987). As part of this process, differences from out-groups are as important to self-definition as similarities with in-groups. For employers faced with change through affirmative action legislation, work identities are protected by defining government and its agents as the out-group which is forcing destructive regulations on the workplace and the community at large. Once an in-group and out-group construction is in place, group processes work to keep the identities of these groups as different from each other as possible. Thus, employer groups are likely to become entrenched in present culture, closing themselves off from that group that most wants to influence them and change their practices. This process is the antithesis of what is required to achieve the legislative objectives of the AAA. The process should be one of opening the doors to new ideas and sharing identities. Gentle, loose and weak legislation can allow such a process to occur providing implementation builds a consensual framework, provides for institutional redundancy, empowers workers at the grass roots and promotes networking across diverse groups.

Before discussing the use of these strategies in winning support for the legislation, parliamentary debates and newspaper reports will be used in the next section to substantiate the proposition that loose, gentle and weak legislation carries threat. The Affirmative Action Bill was publicly acknowledged by all sides of politics as being loose, gentle and weak, much to the ire of those wanting social change. Yet there was genuine fear, even among sympathetic politicians, at what it might do.

Reviewing political reactions to the bill in 1986

Parliamentary debates

The frustration aroused by the looseness of the legislation was articulated by the then leader of the Opposition, John Howard, who referred to the legislation as 'symbolic' and doing less for women's work opportunities than the Coalition parties' policies on 'freedom of choice in industrial relations, permanent part-time work, retraining schemes, income splitting and child care tax relief'.[2] Others, such as Andrew Theophanous, who were more supportive, also had reservations about how much could be accomplished with such open-textured legislation: 'It is a waste of time establishing any such [affirmative action] program if the matter of child care is not taken into consideration . . . and given due prominence in rearrangement of the working conditions which women face.'[3]

The second characterisation of the AAA was identified by Senator Coates when he described the bill as 'a very gentle piece of legislation',[4] that was neither demanding nor threatening to Australian business. The first director of the Affirmative Action Agency, Valerie Pratt, confirmed that the requirements of the act were not intended to be particularly taxing for business, being no more than 'a blueprint for good management of human resources' (Affirmative Action Agency 1990: vii).

The fact that the only punishment for non-compliance — being named in parliament — was a social rather than financial sanction led to a widespread view of the bill as weak. While the business sector and some politicians[5] echoed the position of the social scientists (Anderson et al. 1977; Tittle 1980; Braithwaite 1989; Grasmick and Bursik 1990) that loss of reputation can be as punitive – if not more so – than economic sanctions, others, particularly trade unionists and feminists, were sceptical (Ronalds 1990). Their scepticism was understandable in the light of some observations made during the parliamentary debates. Senator Crowley, after defending the bill's sanctions, added: 'I might say that the naming of a firm or an organization will happen only after that firm or organization has had the opportunity to advance good reasons for its inability to produce a report on time or actually to implement a program. The other penalty that ought to be noted is that there is a fine and/or jail term if any of the confidential information in the private report is released improperly'.[6] The message given was not one of legal invincibility on the part of law enforcement agencies, but vulnerability.

The looseness, gentleness and weakness of the legislation were regarded widely as symptoms of backdown and compromise. Senator Hill argued that 'the major problems facing women are really beyond the competence of this bill to remedy'[7] and that the beneficiaries will be a small elite group: 'Basically, this Bill provides a tool for women whom I might describe as being in the know, women who are already in the bureaucracy, femocrats with their networks, women in middle management, women in tertiary and financial institutions, women who already have access to the system, generally with education and reasonably available prospects of opportunity.'[8] Senator Hamer concluded that if there was nothing more behind the bill than 'creating non-binding programs which employers may or may not carry out . . . the Government [had] indeed laboured mightily and brought forth a mouse'.[9] More deeply held regrets were expressed by feminists who believed that the government had compromised its commitment to the principle of equality for women (Sawer 1990). Peter Baldwin spoke on the 'cogent criticism of the legislation coming from such women's groups as the National Women's Consultative Council, and also from the Australian Council of Trade Unions, which feels that the Bill has not gone far enough'.[10] Janine Haines, the leader of the Australian Democrats at the time, criticised the legislation as 'desperately weak'[11] and 'essentially defective,'[12] not going as far as many people wanted and, in effect, being an affirmative action bill without a great deal of action.[13]

In spite of this convergence of opinion that the bill was innocuous, if not useless, conservatives were far from complacent. While part of their rhetoric was undoubtedly intended to impress their constituency and play to the gallery, part also reflected deep-seated fear, even insightfulness. The conservative forces in the parliament couldn't believe that the government had put up legislation which was 'to be a toothless tiger'.[14] It had to be, according to Senator Knowles, 'the thin end of a wedge'.[15] Senator Crichton-Browne described the bill as 'diabolical and draconian' – 'a frank, factual and fair description',[16] he added, because 'there is far more to this legislation than meets the eye'.[17] Those who were suspicious of the bill searched hard to discover the hidden powers that were going to be used to unravel the social fabric of society. The debate against the bill raised the themes of family values, women's self-esteem, the merit principle and the rise of mediocrity. Senator Crichton-Browne attacked the bill as a threat to family tradition and as a deep offence to those women who spend their time as wives and mothers: '[The Bill] is an attempt to undermine the confidence of these women, to leave them feeling inadequate and feeling that they have not fulfilled a complete and absolute role in the community'.[18] The senator extended his objections to the domain of paid work, expressing the view that the bill would 'Demean the achievements of women who have already succeeded', 'but will be of great assistance to all those incapable women applying for jobs'.[19] This was a reference to what Senator Powell referred to in a later debate (on the 1992 amendment to the AAA) as 'The old bogey of quotas'.[20] The reference to the setting of objectives and targets in the legislation was regarded as softened language for quotas which would overturn the merit principle and, according to Senator Short, take Australian society down a path of 'mediocrity and the demise of excellence' with a resulting 'dreadful greying effect of bringing people to a common denominator'.[21] The debate was colourful and passionate.

Looking beyond the speeches at the amendments proposed and particularly at the divisions that were called in the Senate, a more credible picture emerges of the major concerns of the Opposition and of the business community. Senator Baume, who was on the Working Party that was set up to look into the need for legislation and to plan the legislation, proposed some 40 amendments in the Senate, four of which are particularly revealing. The Opposition wanted the affirmative action program to be voluntary.[22] They did not want to see an increase in government bureaucracy and regulation.[23] The Opposition wanted clarification on the title of the bill, specifically they wanted Affirmative Action taken out entirely, leaving just Equal Employment Opportunity.[24] Third, the Opposition wanted a sunset clause in the legislation so that it would no longer be operational after five years[25] and, finally, the Opposition wanted to curb the powers given to some of the actors under the legislation, specifically the director of the Affirmative Action Agency and the trade union movement.[26] In short, the Opposition did not want the creation of a new institutional base to counter entrenched practices.

The loose, gentle and weak nature of the legislation did not sit comfortably on the shoulders of the Opposition and there is little evidence that they considered it to be necessarily ineffectual. Instead of triumphing over the weakness of the legislation, the Opposition invested a high level of energy in limiting its influence. As Senator Crichton-Browne noted: 'Owing to the imprecise words used in the Bill it is impossible to foretell exactly the effect that this Bill will have. In large part it will depend on the mood of the person occupying the position of Director of Affirmative Action.'[27] It was also going to depend on the mood of ordinary Australians.

Robert Goodin (1982) uses the term 'loose laws' to describe legislation that specifies goals without specifying any particular mechanisms for achieving them. The Affirmative Action (Equal Employment Opportunity for Women) Act 1986 fits this characterisation well. Goodin has argued that the kind of uncertainty recognised in the above quote from Crichton-Browne is a by-product of loose law, but not a by-product that is necessarily undesirable. Loose laws 'offer opportunities for realizing efficiencies impossible with rigid rules' (Goodin 1982: 66). Those whose explicit goal is to avoid the implementation of the legislation are seriously disadvantaged by 'not knowing how far they can safely go before incurring legal liability' (Goodin 1982: 67).

The media

The controversy over the bill was widely reported in the media and the community was given the message that life would never be the same again. The *Australian Financial Review* (24.7.84) reported the composition of the Working Party under the heading, 'Women's program watchdogs named'. The *Bulletin* (22.4.86) announced the new legislation with a story entitled 'New law, new threats to get women more "male" jobs'. As the legislation reached implementation stage, the *National Times* (15.3.87) proclaimed that the 'Government faces tough public relations job on affirmative action', while the *Age* (11.4.87) ran a story headlined 'Companies prepare for female invasion'. Newspapers focussed on quotas, threats to male breadwinners, feminist unrest and changing family traditions.[28]

Furthermore, newspaper reports on the consultation process among interest groups exposed friction and tension. The *Australian* (11.7.84) headlined their story as 'Affirmative action plan unleashes angry debate', and the *Age* (6.6.84) anticipated differences on the working party with the business sector pushing for non-interventionist legislation. The *Australian Financial Review* (4.9.85) announced the Business Council of Australia's opposition to prescriptive legislation, fearing it to be counter-productive because it conveyed a message of positive discrimination rather than support for the merit principle. The opposition of State branches of the Chamber of Commerce was also given coverage (*Australian* 7.6.84). The rift between the government and the business sector at the time of the second last meeting of the working party made news in the *Australian Financial Review* (4.9.85), with the government expressing a willingness to negotiate. The angered response from feminists about government being too accommodating to business was subsequently reported in the *Sydney Morning Herald* (19.9.85). The concern from women's organisations – that the legislation did not go far enough – was aired in the *Australian Financial Review* (7.6.84) with the legislation described as a 'sop to business and unions' by the Women's Electoral Lobby. While all these accounts were a fair representation of the divisions that existed, the positive side of the affirmative action story, that of successful negotiation and bipartisan support, was not given an equal hearing. Later it will be argued that public ignorance of the positive aspects was one of the major impediments to the affirmative action legislation being implemented as intended.

Designing principles for cultural change

How can loose, gentle and weak legislation be an effective means of achieving broad social change? The story of the passage of the legislation through both houses reveals four useful principles.

At the centre of the success of legislating for affirmative action in Australia was the widely recognised negotiation style of the Prime Minister, Hawke-style consensus. The strategy was familiar to the Opposition. William Coleman opened his speech in the House of Representatives as follows: 'I fear that the Affirmative Action (Equal Employment Opportunity for Women) Bill is a characteristic Hawke Government measure. It is put forward to advance a cause we all support – the removal of barriers to equality of opportunity for women. However, . . .'[29]

The openly acknowledged point of consensus was the value, equal opportunity for all, a value that was at the heart of Liberal Party ideology, Labor Party ideology and at the heart of Australian society. Academic lawyers have been dismissive of such values as 'motherhood statements' that have no imperative for action (Krygier and Glass 1995; Ziegert 1995). Elsewhere it has been argued that values, like mothers, are greatly underestimated (Braithwaite 1994a; Braithwaite and Blamey 1996). Values that enjoy social consensus, like equal opportunity for all, provide the impetus for engagement by civil society and are the umbrellas under which dissension can be aired with confidence and conflict dealt with constructively (Fisher and Ury 1981).

The government initially secured agreement, 'at the level of principle', from the Opposition, other government members, business, trade unions and women's groups, that equality of opportunity was something for Australian society to honour. The government then pursued the next step of amassing data, undertaking consultations and running affirmative action pilot programs to gain support for the proposition that women were not getting a fair go in Australian workplaces. Staff were seconded from the private sector to the Affirmative Action Resource Unit, set up by the government to provide advice to pilot programs and government, and to undertake public speaking engagements with business representatives, trade union organisers, women's organisations and other individuals and groups in the community. It was a select group that held consensus together, but it was an influential group, crossing party lines and incorporating representatives of the major players in the workplace. Furthermore, the foundations were laid for future implementation of the legislation through strengthening linkages between the private and public sectors. The consensus surrounding legislation for equal opportunity for women was nurtured painstakingly from the time the Discussion Paper was introduced in 1984 until the Affirmative Action Bill was passed in 1986.

The parliamentary records demonstrate clearly that consensus surrounding equal opportunity framed the debates. At the second reading, speakers for the Opposition repeatedly placed their commitment to equal opportunity on the record: 'The Opposition does not object to this legislation because we accept wholeheartedly the principle of equality of opportunity for women.' (Mr Connolly);[30] 'we have decided not to oppose it because of our deep commitment to the concept of equal opportunity in employment.' (Mr Howard);[31] 'There is little doubt that every member of this chamber would be very seriously committed to the principle of equal opportunity in employment.' (Mr Adermann);[32] 'Equal opportunity for women is a much valued principle.' (Mr McGauran).[33] This was to be a pattern followed by subsequent speakers for the Opposition in the House of Representatives and in the Senate. Nobody wanted to be outside the group that wanted Australian women to have a fair go. Politicians were uniformly particular in pointing out that they supported the overarching principle of equal opportunity and that their objections focussed on 'the machinery the Bill establishes'.[34]

Not only did this consensus frame the debate on the bill, it framed the process of its development. All the 'hidden agendas' of the bill that caused so much concern later on were pre-empted and addressed directly by the Prime Minister, Bob Hawke, with the release of the 1984 Discussion Paper (Department of Prime Minister and Cabinet 1984). These issues included: equating affirmative action with quotas, interference in the private sector, overturning the principle of merit and reducing industry efficiency. At the outset, the use of the term 'affirmative action' in the Australian context was differentiated from the use of the term in the US context. According to the Prime Minister, 'Our approach is not one that relies on the experience of other countries. We have explicitly rejected the American model with its system of court-imposed quotas. . . . Put quite simply, equal employment opportunity is our objective, and affirmative action is the way to achieve it.'[35] He went on to say that 'the Government strongly believes that all jobs should be awarded on merit . . . and that affirmative action programs will only achieve long term benefits, for women and the economy, if they are regarded as employment policies designed to improve the skill, efficiency and mobility of the work force.'[36] Finally, he expressed confidence in business, stating that what was needed was 'a self-determined, industry specific approach'[37] and concluded on the note of consensus: 'The proposals in this paper have been widely discussed between the government, business, and unions. I repeat how grateful my Government is for the very substantial support we have already received from these quarters. To that I now add the indication of support from the Opposition.'[38]

The consensus, while Hawke's trademark, did not come to fruition without a support base. This base comprised women in the community, activists and femocrats, a base recognised more narrowly by Wendy Fatin in her tribute to her fellow politician, Susan Ryan, and the head of the Office of the Status of Women, Anne Summers,[39] and more broadly by Peter Duncan: 'Women's groups have kept up the pressure, have kept us informed and have continued the struggle for women's rights. . . . One of the fortunate results . . . has been the recognition by the Government of the need for this legislation.'[40]

The pressure was indeed due to the efforts of many women over a decade or more who brought their organisations into co-operative alliances (Ronalds 1990). Together they advanced the feminist agenda through the setting up of a policy machine in the bureaucracy where women were appointed to provide specialist knowledge on women's issues (femocrats). Hester Eisenstein (1990; 1996), Marian Sawer (1990) and Anna Yeatman (1990) have provided insightful accounts of the achievements and tensions between Australian femocrats and women's organisations. These analyses recognise the fine line walked by femocrats between their open commitment to feminism and their institutional loyalties. In walking this line, they often disappointed those women on the outside who had pinned their hopes for change on them. In spite of these tensions, femocracy is an example of putting in place interlocking implementation chains. Eisenstein explains how such chains work: 'As leader of OSW [Office of the Status of Women], Anne Summers reported formally to her department head, but because of her political connections and her friendship with Susan Ryan, could occasionally gain direct access to the Prime Minister.' (1996: 47). In an earlier work, Eisenstein (1990) commended the power that femocrats can evoke by forming alliances with traditional bureaucrats whose interests run parallel to their own. Forming an alliance with the Prime Minister must be seen as the implementation of Eisenstein's principle at the commanding heights.

Hawke's strategy from the beginning was to build and keep the consensus and co-operation between business, government, opposition, women's groups and trade unions through proposing a piece of gentle and loose legislation that took care of everyone's needs and worries. In so doing, he linked unlikely actors together in a co-operative exercise and made it possible for joint action by people with different underlying motives.

The compromise involved in taking care of everyone's needs does seem to lead inevitably to 'an affirmative non-action Bill'.[41] The legislation has a major redeeming feature, however. A second type of consensus was embedded in the bill, the consensus that the workplace should be empowered. Employers were given the freedom to identify their own problems and solutions as long as they did so in consultation with employees, particularly women.[42] The legislation mandated the kind of consultation that was happening among an elite at government level should be duplicated in every workplace in Australia. This was to be the key to changing workplace culture.

In summary, at the highest level of government, traditionally conflicting interest groups were brought together as members of an elite group to guide the introduction of affirmative action into Australian workplaces under the consensus umbrella of equal opportunity. While the tensions and strains of the group are not to be underestimated (Ronalds, 1990; Sawer, 1990), different players were given a voice, co-operation was maintained, legislation was drafted and the disparate interests of conflicting groups were heard. To the disillusionment of many feminists, the Affirmative Action Bill did not cut across the goals of the business community. The bill had a dual function: to increase social justice and profit through helping business make better use of women in the workforce. The legislation was packaged to achieve a new and somewhat controversial goal (gender equality), at the same time as reinforcing a widely held and established goal (better business practices). In this way, the bill succeeded in rendering opposition to anti-discrimination measures on business grounds irrelevant. The outcome was that an Affirmative Action Bill was enacted by parliament with bipartisan support. This latter strategy illustrates the principle of institutional redundancy: that is to say, that if an institution is multi-purposed, each purpose can serve as a backup for the other. Under such circumstances, newly designed institutions can find a wide support base and have some protection against being prematurely dismantled.

The AAA did not provide answers for workplace discrimination. It mandated the asking of questions, but this was not going to happen without strategically placed pressure from outside organisations and well distributed informational bases for finding and implementing solutions. What was offered to those wishing to see workplace reform through this loose, gentle and weak legislation were four important levers for implementing social change:

1 spreading the message through the community that there was a *consensus* among politicians, business representatives, trade union officials and women's groups that workplaces in Australia should support equal employment opportunity practices. As Senator Baume

noted: 'One of the requirements for the success of this legislation is that it receive community acceptance.'[43] Consensus at the more abstract level of the overriding principle of equal opportunity provides a sufficient base for acceptance. With such an umbrella, members and groups in civil society have (a) a reason to engage in the change process, (b) a comfort zone for expressing disagreement and engaging in dialogue with each other, (c) a basis for linking practices across institutions, and (d) a rationale for sharing ideas across disparate groups.

2 paving the way for the *empowerment* of civil society to voice concerns and propose their own solutions. The legislation gives employers, employees, trade unions and women's groups an opportunity to participate actively in changing their own workplace culture. Political theorists' notions of communicative democracy (Young 1990) and deliberative democracy (Dryzek 1990) are given practical expression in this aspect of the legislation.

3 using the *redundancy* principle to provide multiple reasons, preferably both conservative and liberal, for changing work practices that are unfair to women. Institutions need to be set in place that serve a number of purposes and that advance new agendas while reinforcing old, uncontroversial ones. When different interest groups are guaranteed a voice in policy development and implementation, courses of action can be negotiated that produce win-win solutions. There is no reason to assume that one agenda (for example, economic efficiency) will drive out the other (for example, social justice). Building momentum for change depends on harnessing multiple agendas to one unified course of action.

4 nurturing alliances between key groups in civil society so that knowledge and understanding of discriminatory practices can be spread along and across interlocking implementation chains. The secondment of staff from the business sector to the Affirmative Action Resource Unit exemplified this process.

Implementation issues

The time of the passage of the Affirmative Action Bill through the Senate was the time for commencing the orchestration of the implementation of the legislation. This did not happen to the extent necessary to capitalise on the opportunities created by the consensus of the parliament. This message should have been shared with civil society, those that made up the business community, the employees, trade union members and citizens. Instead the co-operation and commitment among the key players disappeared from public view. At a time when resources should have been directed toward informing the public of a new program of workplace reform, the task of engaging civil society was left to the initiative of the media.

The role the media performed was to disperse cynicism and fear through the community by means of reports of dissension. Fewer than half a dozen stories appeared in the *Age*, the *Sydney Morning Herald*, the *Australian*, the *Australian Financial Review*, and the *Canberra Times* in the week either side of the passing of the AAA and all conveyed stories of fears, conflict and resistance. The centrally important story, that the government and the Opposition believed that women were not getting a fair go in the workplace and that they supported the legislation for this reason, was notably absent. As a consequence, the security and the sense of involvement that civil society needed to play its role in workplace reform was non-existent. People were left ignorant, confused and dis-interested. Five years later, they were still ignorant and confused. Managers did not understand the legislation, many did not recognise a problem, and employees didn't know the legislation existed (Braithwaite 1992; Powell and Russell 1993; Victorian Trades Hall Council 1993).

The second lever of institutional redundancy was better implemented due to the efforts of the Affirmative Action Agency and its director. Women's traditional roles have been kept intact for so long by a multi-tude of institutions all pushing in the same direction of subservience and dependency: the family, the workplace, education, religion, marriage, even the romantic novel. It makes sense, therefore, that to change both women's and men's behaviour, chances of success are higher if there are a host of institutional reasons for doing so. The consensus forged between government and business allowed the link to be made between good business practice and affirmative action. Maintaining the links between these institutions was the success story for the Affirmative Action Agency in its first five years of operation (Braithwaite 1993). Where strong human resource management practices were in place so too were embryonic affirmative action programs. Where they were not, affirmative action remained on the shelf as a report to be filled out for the government once a year.

The principles of consensus on equal opportunity, empowerment of civil society and institutional redundancy imply homogeneity in attitudes and actions that is neither intended nor deemed desirable. The model that is being proposed is one that tolerates, indeed encourages, diversity under the umbrella of equal opportunity. The important principle for the transmission of a new culture is that different groups interlock with other groups and not that they are so identical that they overlap. Mark Granovetter (1973) represents this idea as the strength of weak ties. Those on the fringe of a group can be of greater value than those who are central players because they are often influential in other groups and provide a bridge to such groups. Interlocking implementation chains may bring together, for instance, radical feminist groups with a radical environmental group to share their ideas on how work can be organised more fairly for women. Radical environmental groups may share their understandings with mainstream environmental groups. These, in turn, may influence private industry and, ultimately, the most conservative organisations in the country. The notion of interlocking implementation chains is not that radical feminists will share their vision directly with conservative CEOs, but rather that the ideas will percolate across this seemingly impenetrable divide through intermediaries that have the trust and respect of groups that are closer to them in outlook and identity.

The usefulness of these principles was examined empirically through interviews with a random sample of 153 EEO contact persons in 1992 (Braithwaite 1992). One of the goals of the study was to identify pockets of success where the legislation was being used to achieve substantive compliance. These cases were contrasted with those in which compliance was procedural (mandated steps were in place but no workplace change had occurred) and where the legislation was being ignored (a report was lodged revealing little activity of any kind).

Compliance of a procedural and substantive kind was found in companies which professed a commitment to the spirit of the legislation and which believed the legislation could produce favourable business outcomes. In contrast, companies which had reported little activity of any kind saw the legislation as something to be resisted at all costs and as having nothing to offer business. These data demonstrate that the principle of redundancy, appealing to both profit and social justice in the legislation, was a factor in moving companies beyond the posture of resistance. Needless to say, moving beyond procedural compliance to substantive compliance involved a concern about sex discrimination that went beyond the profit motive.

One path to substantive compliance was based on an ideological commitment to affirmative action within the company, mainly on the part of the EEO officer. Not surprisingly, these EEO officers perceived themselves to be more committed than management, but the fact was that change was taking place and management was not obstructing the change completely. The EEO officers tended to be well connected, particularly with staff in the Affirmative Action Agency. This was a story of a group of highly committed women, sharing an ideology of equal opportunity which had been legitimated by legislation (value consensus). Furthermore, the legislation had empowered them to bring equal opportunity to their workplace. Their links with the staff of the Affirmative Action Agency were personal and often strong. Under the directorship of Valerie Pratt, the Affirmative Action Agency acted constructively to strengthen ties with co-operating companies through sponsoring, with the *Business Review Weekly*, annual awards for best practice (Affirmative Action Agency 1992a). Employers were thereby rewarded for doing the right thing and supporting their EEO officers. Furthermore, some businesses carried their citizenship responsibilities further, advising other companies on various aspects of their affirmative action programs. Legitimation through value consensus, empowerment, and interlocking implementation chains were all evident in these high profile, centrally located workplaces, as was institutional redundancy. Institutions of good business practice and of affirmative action had become so intertwined that competition was rife for having a workforce that properly valued and retained its female workforce. It is here that we see innovation. These companies are the pathfinders for the rest of the business community.

The second way to substantive compliance was interesting because it did not involve high commitment to either the Affirmative Action Agency or the legislation. These links were irrelevant to implementing change. The principles that emerged to explain progress were value consensus and employee empowerment. Taking this path were work-places where there was a belief that equal employment opportunity should be prioritised and that the women themselves knew how to do it. Change was rising out of grassroots support and peer networks. There was no evidence that management was particularly knowledgeable about such matters nor were they concerned. Of considerable importance was the management style in these organisations. There was a commitment to having good employee relations and open communication in the business. In other words, these organisations were managed with the intention of being open to new ideas. Management could, of course, squash any of the activities of the women if they so desired, but there appeared to be trust that the women would not hurt the company. In this sense, the redundancy principle seemed to be at work in that equal opportunity was not regarded as incompatible with the organisation's goals. An interesting lever for change for this group of women remained unrecognised by them. The Affirmative Action Agency should have been able to help them influence or consolidate their work with senior management. Unfortunately, the women did not feel affiliated with the agency. Their networks were local, and in their view, agency staff visited only to talk with the 'boys upstairs' (Braithwaite 1992).

Future directions

In spite of these success stories, I am not claiming here that dramatic progress has been made as a result of the AAA, but rather that opportunities for change are there for those who can mobilise co-workers to reconsider the ways in which work is done. The need for women to find their footing in workplace negotiations has loomed large with the demise of Australia's central wage-fixing system. Concerns have already been voiced about the way in which 'the move to individualise and re-privatise work relations will exacerbate gender inequities in the workplace and re-inforce work-home relations oppressive to women' (Bennett 1995: 142). Such fears may be realised, but strategies are available and progress has been made toward setting up the apparatus that is needed so that women's voices can be heard and accommodated.

Least used for building support for change has been consensus on equal opportunity. Too often it has been dismissed as empty rhetoric, rather than as a framing device for bringing people together to decide upon a workplace action plan. It remains the most compelling argument for getting the Australian workforce, men and women alike, engaged in the debate and in the change process. In the case of women working at the grassroots level, the message of consensus surrounding equal opportunity has been shown to work well. But it should have worked better. Recently, we have seen greater efforts on the part of the Affirmative Action Agency to sell its programs and promote its consensus-based activities. In addition to co-operative ventures with the business sector such as the Business Council of Australia, the Confederation of Australian Industry, EEO practitioner associations, human resource management groups and business schools (*Affirmative Action Agency Annual Report 1991–92*), there are increasing examples of efforts to reach a broader cross-section of women and men in the community. The agency has devoted considerable efforts to developing closer relationships with the media to increase exposure to ideas for workplace change (*Annual Report 1994–95*; *Canberra Times* 5.12.1995). Magazines, such as *New Woman*, carry regular features on women and work, which set out reasons for the need for change, suggesting options for organising workplaces so that they are more gender-friendly and productive, and empowering women to be pro-active in the change process. Such steps to engage women and men who are not part of corporate elite groups are long overdue. Contrary to legislative intent, both women and men have been left in a state of ignorance about the legislation. Yet it is difficult to see how any meaningful change can be accomplished without their inclusion and participation.

Selling the message of national commitment to equal opportunity is one way of bringing employers and employees together to discuss an agenda for change, and the argument presented in this paper is that it still has not been done well enough to capture the imagination of most Australians. What has been done exceptionally well, however, is setting up the interlocking implementation chains at elite levels through the principle of redundancy: implementing the affirmative action legislation is not only being fair to women, but is good management practice. The first five years of the operation of the act saw affirmative action programs being hitched to the cart of good management practice, so much so that some were critical that social justice concerns were being compromised too much (Burton 1991; Poiner and Wills 1991; Bacchi 1994b; Braithwaite 1994). Undoubtedly, there remains some truth in these criticisms. But a radical agenda for workplace change is of limited usefulness if supporters are not signing up to implement it. The actions of the Affirmative Action Agency were strategic, given their small numbers and their insecure future, and they have paid off handsomely. More recently, the influential Karpin Report (Industry Task Force on Leadership and Management Skills 1995), a comprehensive industry-based three-year review of leadership and management skills, presented a surprisingly critical and frank account of Australian managers' performance. Management was accused of poor leadership and lack of vision, of ignoring problems of discrimination and not making the most of the diversity of its workforce. The release of such a report, which has confirmed concerns about the poor implementation of the AAA, shows the potential power of both principles of redundancy and interlocking implementation chains. As a result of linking competent management with affirmative action initiatives, the traditional naming of non-compliant companies in parliament assumes new significance. The message that has been given out since the Karpin Report is not a nostalgic one about a few remaining bastions of male chauvinism. Instead, being named for non-compliance conveys a public message about bad management and poor leadership.

To this point in the legislation's brief history, the major achievement has been the setting up of chains of influence that can serve as carriers of social change. What is carried along these chains, however, remains to a considerable extent bereft of input from the majority of men and women whom the legislation was meant to serve. Enterprise bargaining offers the first major challenge to men and women to co-operate in a push for family-friendly work provisions[44] and for a workplace that allows women to contribute their special skills from the lowest to the highest levels. The task for the next decade is to ensure that the Affirmative Action legislation is understood, used and owned by Australian citizens from a broader base. While it is guarded protectively by elites, it can never achieve its potential for cultural change in the workplace.

Notes

1 Special thanks to Moira Gatens, Deborah Mitchell and Joan Eveline for their helpful comments and constructive criticisms on earlier drafts of this manuscript, and to Janine Bush for her research assistance.
2 Commonwealth Parliamentary Debates (CPD), House of Representatives, HR, 10 April 1986, vol. 147 at 1979.
3 CPD, HR, 10 April 1986, vol. 147 at 2071.
4 CPD, Senate, S, 20 August 1986, vol. 116 at 126.
5 Mr Slipper referred to the naming in parliament of companies that refused to go along with the government's plans as shades of McCarthyism (CPD, HR, 10 April 1986, vol. 147 at 2066). Senator Knowles expressed the view that being named in parliament was another example of 'big brother creeping into our daily lives' and it would be a 'brave employer who dares defy the government' (CPD, S, 20 August 1986, vol. 116 at 183); and Senator Short asserted that the business community did not support the sanction of being named in parliament, a sanction which was non-trivial because it impacted on one's standing in the community (CPD, S, 22 August 1986, vol. 116 at 366).
6 CPD, S, 20 August 1986, vol. 116 at 177–178.
7 CPD, S, 20 August 1986, vol. 116 at 128.
8 CPD, S, 20 August 1986, vol. 116 at 129.
9 CPD, S, 22 August 1986, vol. 116 at 316.
10 CPD, HR, 10 April 1986, vol. 147 at 2067.
11 CPD, S, 22 August 1986, vol. 116 at 379.
12 CPD, S, 22 August 1986, vol. 116 at 378.
13 CPD, S, 22 August 1986, vol. 116 at 378.
14 CPD, S, 22 August 1986, vol. 116 at 338.
15 CPD, S, 22 August 1986, vol. 116 at 309.
16 CPD, S, 22 August 1986, vol. 116 at 337.
17 CPD, S, 22 August 1986, vol. 116 at 317.
18 CPD, S, 22 August 1986, vol. 116 at 317.
19 CPD, S, 22 August 1986, vol. 116 at 317.
20 CPD, S, 8 December 1992, vol. 157 at 4362.
21 CPD, S, 22 August 1986, vol. 116 at 366.
22 CPD, S, 12 June 1986, vol. 115 at 3839.
23 CPD, S, 12 June 1986, vol. 115 at 3839.
24 CPD, S, 22 August 1986, vol. 116 at 375–377.
25 CPD, S, 22 August 1986, vol. 116 at 406.
26 CPD, S, 22 August 1986, vol. 116 at 399–403.
27 CPD, S, 22 August 1986, vol. 116 at 339.
28 This is not to suggest that more reasonable accounts did not appear in the press. For example, The *Sydney Morning Herald* (2.6.84) reported the business community's recognition that it was in their interests to make greater use of their female workforce and the *Australian Finanical Review* (25.6.84) reported 'no "big stick" approach to affirmative action'. Such stories, however, were dominated by accounts of disruption and conflict.
29 CPD, HR, 9 April 1986, vol. 147 at 1930.
30 CPD, HR, 9 April 1986, vol. 147 at 1925.
31 CPD, HR, 10 April 1986, vol. 147 at 1976.
32 CPD, HR, 10 April 1986, vol. 147 at 1981.
33 CPD, HR, 10 April 1986, vol. 147 at 1987.

34 CPD, HR, 9 April 1986, vol. 147 at 1930.
35 CPD, HR, 5 June 1984, vol. 137 at 2870.
36 CPD, HR, 5 June 1984, vol. 137 at 2872.
37 CPD, HR, 5 June 1984, vol. 137 at 2872.
38 CPD, HR, 5 June 1984, vol. 137 at 2874.
39 CPD, HR, 9 April 1986, vol. 147 at 1928.
40 CPD, HR, 9 April 1986, vol. 147 at 1933.
41 Senator Baume attributed this description to Senator Haines, CPD, S, 22 August 1986, vol. 116 at 376.
42 Senator Baume stated: 'It is our belief that the appropriate people with whom consultations should be carried out are the employees.' CPD, S, 22 August 1986, vol. 116 at 399.
43 CPD, S, 22 August 1986, vol. 116 at 376.
44 *Age*, 1.11.1997.

PART THREE

Reshaping Citizenship:
Class, race and nation

CHAPTER 8

Being Civil and Social:
The proper study of womankind

Lenore Coltheart

Introduction

The relation of the social to the civic as a contemporary problem of institutional design is explored here by first tracing the delineation of the social as a field of systematic inquiry, and uses of the metaphor of 'woman's sphere', in nineteenth-century Britain. By the end of the century the boundaries of the social and understandings of the civic were recharted: just as urbanisation changed the landscapes of Britain, the configurations of 'civic' and 'social' reshaped the political and economic terrain of citizenship. In sketching women reformers' advocacy of 'socialism' and 'social science' this chapter highlights the possibilities they perceived in redesigning their relation to the state. These aspirations are then contrasted to the twentieth-century practice of women's citizenship which, through a redefinition of the civil and social virtues, was institutionalised within a microrealm where civic responsibility was equated with domestic values and, most particularly, hygiene. Finally, there is the question of what it means to be 'civil' and 'social' a century later, in a so-called new world order of globalising institutions.

In this discussion 'civil' and 'civic' are taken as synonymous. They are allied by their common origin, the Latin *civis* for citizen, conveying classical associations of rights and duties of membership of a body of citizens, synonymous with the political, the public. In liberal democracies like Britain, the USA and Australia there developed a sense almost the opposite of the Latin meaning, with polite and courteous associated with the private realm where morality or manners are learned. In this sense 'civil society' can seem a tautology, 'civil war' an oxymoron. While for Foucault civil society is 'the great fantasy' of a universality of wills, in the post-Cold War world there is a new emphasis on civil society as that category of institutions mediating between person and state, distinguishing private, civic (professional, socially participatory) and political selves (Shotter 1993: 131; Gellner 1994).

This summary does not of course exhaust the semantic possibilities, but rather indicates an instability of meaning, so that in contemporary discourse it is 'not clear whether "citizenship" and "civil society" are competing ideas' (Turner 1993: viii–x). Whereas we seem to know exactly what 'society' is.

The origin of the social

In contrast with our times, however, in Britain and Europe in the early nineteenth century 'the social' was a radical concept. The British view of the Australian continent as a *terra nullius* required a contrast between people in civil society and those in barbarous community. Though profound in its Australian effect, this was an expedient of little import in Britain. There the reigning distinction was the one between nobility and clergy, the 'civil state' of English law, and the rest of the population of a legally united kingdom. The corollary of a view of human suffering as God's will was that its alleviation was God's work – if earthly ills were not decreed by an omnipotent deity, then they could be removed or redressed by human action, if those with a will to do this had political power. Just as Newton had provided the foundations for science for a secular explanation of the physical world, Enlightenment arguments for reason rather than faith as the means of understanding human institutions provided a new political optics. In arguing that the origin of human suffering could be found in structures of society, early socialist thinkers identified a terrain of human inquiry and activity in which the privileged position of political and ecclesiastical regimes was no longer shielded by a divine justification. The French Revolution, and responses to it in England and north America as well as in Europe, proclaimed a new problem: that of securing political obligation among free and equal citizens. We should not need to remind ourselves that when the British occupied Australia the concept of 'social problems' was new, even if two hundred years later it has produced academic and professional institutions.

Among the socialist ideas prominent in France before Marx arrived was that of a social system based on investigation and experiment, an applied science of society. The term 'la science sociale' was used in the 1790s as synonymous with the earlier '*l'art social*' of the Physiocrats – that is, as a rational basis for social reform and public policy, an attractive idea in a post-Revolutionary era of democratic vision. It is indeed an idea full of potential in opposition to government designed from above, where law and policy is neither informed nor influenced by the experiences and views of those affected. Robert Owen and Charles Fourier, among other early socialist thinkers developed a radical conception of 'the social' as the ultimate end of moral and economic inquiry, the basis for the development of a systematic method of investigating and redesigning social structures to remedy or remove problems (Corcoran 1983: 3–5).

The dawn of social science

Characteristics of early French socialism included a concern to communicate with 'the people', the role of science in opposing industrial capitalism and reshaping economic relations and an idea of overcoming class division in harmonious community. While in English usage 'socialism' was contrasted to 'capitalism', in France the antonym was 'individualism', a disorder opposed to the wellbeing of a polity based on reciprocal relations. The aims of abolishing the institutions of private property, and reshaping those of religion, education and the family created an opportunity for women reformers who pressed with vigour the idea of a regeneration of humanity through the emancipation of women. Among the proposals in the first half of the nineteenth century were the end of the 'sex-slavery' of marriage, a common standard of morality for men and women, divorce on request, birth control assistance and communal living. 'Les dissidentes Saint-Simoniennes' of the 1830s included women journalists in France who developed and publicised ideas for new social relationships and proclaimed themselves 'new women' whose time had come for '*La république est morte d'avoir exclu les femmes*' (The republic is dead because it excluded women). Flora Tristan's *L'Union ouvrière* pamphlet, a popular call for an international union of working women and men, was published the year Marx arrived in Paris, having just begun his reading of socialist writers. Even for later women socialists, however, it was Fourier rather than Marx who was the vital source of ideas on women's place in society. (Zeldin 1973: 346–347; Evans 1977: 153–155; Adler 1979: 19, 166; Corcoran 1983: 1–2, Ch. 10).

In the late eighteenth century Jeremy Bentham had promoted statistics as an instrument of judicial and legislative reform. The purpose of collecting population data is implied in the name 'statists', used for the nineteenth-century statisticians. The first national census in Britain was held in 1801 and education and crime statistics were soon utilised in campaigns for the 'moral improvement' of the 'lower orders' (Cullen 1975; Eyler 1979: 20–21). After his appointment to the newly established Register Office, medical statistics were substantially refined by William Farr, whose maxim that disease was 'the iron index of misery' made public health a field of social inquiry for reformers as well as insurers. The office bought Babbage's calculating machine in an attempt to reduce the time taken for the compilation of the life tables based on Farr's improved calculations of birth, death, and fertility rates. Under the 1836 legislation registration of deaths, and cause of death, was compulsory, but pressure from the Church of England meant that births were still recorded by each parish rather than in the national office (Eyler 1979: Ch. 4; Cullen 1975: 1, 12–15, 30).

Statistical inquiry was 'the passion of the times' (Young 1963: 32). The London Statistical Society, formed in 1833, proclaimed

> The Science of Statistics differs from Political Economy, because, although it has the same end in view, it does not discuss causes, nor reason upon probable effects; it seeks only to collect, arrange, and compare, that class of facts which can alone form the basis of correct conclusions with respect to social and political government. (*Journal of the Statistical Society of London* 1833, quoted Eyler 1979:15)

In England the new doctrine of political economy occupied the prominence that socialism held in France, drawing on the influential ideas of Adam Smith, Malthus, Jeremy Bentham and David Ricardo. The challenge of a political economics was considerable and when Ricardo in the House of Commons 'led the way through the tangle of rent, profit, price and wages, members of Parliament fell in behind him with immense relief' (Bosanquet 1927: 41–42).

Among those who saw the potential of the new science was Harriet Martineau, who became a firm advocate of political economy in her fiction, her journalism and her outlook. She adopted the 'cardinal conception' that self-interest is necessary for the common welfare, while an uninformed benevolence stems from 'the impulse of the heart' and thus is not susceptible to rational inquiry into causes and effects. Martineau was an effective broadcaster of ideas through popular tales and expositions, such as her *Illustrations of Political Economy* published in 1832. Her stories were read by British, French and Russian royal families – until she wrote about equality and subscriptions were rapidly cancelled. In Britain other opponents confined themselves to ridicule in the conservative *Quarterly Review* where, in 1833, she was likened to the 'She Politician':

> Tis my fortune to know a lean Benthamite spinster
> A maid who her faith in old Jeremy puts,
> Who talks with a lisp of 'the last new Westminster',
> And hopes you're delighted with 'Mill upon Gluts'.

Though Robert Owen rejected Martineau's benevolence leavened by reasoned self-interest as 'rampant individualism', in her view this was a 'lovely impulse', moving freely between private and public selves and rising above the polarisation of socialist and Liberal principles in contemporary England. Florence Nightingale observed in 1851 how socialism had become in Victorian England 'a convenient word, which covers a multitude of new ideas and offences', and was no longer a topic men discussed with women in polite society (Nightingale 1852; Bosanquet 1927: 43–44, 70–71; Webb 1960).

More respectable was the new 'positive philosophy' of Auguste Comte. Positivism advocated the scientific collection and analysis of social data, with the aim of identifying laws directing social life. In England John Stuart Mill was among influential proponents of Comte's work, as was G. H. Lewes, who proclaimed in his *History of Philosophy from Thales to Comte*, published in 1880:

> A new era has dawned. For the first time in history an explanation of the World, Society and Man is presented which is thoroughly homogenous, and at the same time thoroughly in accordance with accurate knowledge. (quoted in Willey 1949: 187; Head 1982: 115–116; Evans 1977)

In the 1840s Martineau had been equally optimistic about Comte's work. She saw positivism as the scientific system which could provide what the practice of benevolence lacked – the knowledge of causes and effects that many other political economists still saw as the sole province of God (Bosanquet 1927: 45). She undertook the huge task of translating into English, and condensing into one volume, Comte's *Cours de Philosophie Positive*, the six books of dense and rambling lectures he published during the 1830s and 1840s. Martineau's edition of Comte not only popularised his work in England, but also in France, for at his request it was re-translated and published there as the official – and readable – version.

Women's participation in early socialism can be more readily understood than this enthusiasm for Comte. His ideas on the role of women had more in common with an era of political oppression considered by many to have terminated in 1789. A chapter entitled 'The influence of Positivism upon women' in his 1848 *Discours sur l'ensemble du positivisme* has an epigraph

> Women represent the affective element in our nature, as philosophers and people represent the intellectual and practical elements. (Comte 1851: 151)

Comte suggested 'positivism holds out to woman a most important sphere of public and private duty' (1851: 180), identified in the 1851 edition in a quotation from the novel *Lucie*:

Surely the true sphere of woman is to provide man with the comforts and
delights of home, receiving in exchange from him the means of subsistence
earned by his labours. (1851: 197)

Comte achieved an apparent closure of a torrent of questions about
human society and human capacities unleashed by Enlightenment
thinkers, by Mary Wollstonecraft, by the early socialists and in the work of
Harriet Taylor and John Stuart Mill. Mill pointed to Comte's view of the
role of women as one of the reasons for terminating their collaboration
and his enthusiasm for Comtean positivism. Martineau, however, saw no
necessity for positivism to dissect a social from a broader political and
economic sphere, nor to assume the confinement of women therein.
Instead, she advocated positivism as the means of drawing up sound institutional foundations for a society in which capacity for full participation
could be demonstrated and utilised.

In 1851, when Martineau was absorbed in the immense task of
translating and condensing Comte's volumes, she had to decline an
invitation to attend a women's rights convention in Massachusetts, but
wrote a letter to be read to the gathering, saying

> there can be but one true method in the treatment of each human being of
> either sex, of any colour, and under any outward circumstances – to ascertain
> what are the powers of that being, to cultivate them to the utmost, and *then* to
> see what action they will find for themselves . . . till it is done, all debating
> about what women's intellect is – all speculation, or laying down the law, as to
> what is women's sphere, is a mere beating of the air. *A priori* conceptions have
> long been found worthless in physical science . . . Whether we regard the
> physical fact of what women are able to do, or the moral fact of what women
> ought to do, it is equally necessary to abstain from making any decision prior
> to experiment. (quoted in Graham Yates 1985: 75)

The Massachusetts gathering drew up a resolution based on this
argument, later affirmed by Harriet Taylor Mill, who pointed out the cost
to society of a 'proper sphere of women' where 'qualities which are
not permitted to be exercised shall not exist' (Goldby 1990: 243–244).
Martineau's conviction that social science could demonstrate the abilities
of women and overturn justification by political or religious doctrine –
and fill the gap in Comte's work – remained unshaken in her advocacy of
social experiment and measurement as the means to overturn the
rationale for a separate, limited sphere for women.

Thirty years later, when US feminist Elizabeth Cady Stanton read
Martineau's edition of Comte her interest was qualified by finding

> the part on woman most unsatisfactory. He criticises Aristotle's belief that
> slavery is a necessary element of social life, yet seems to think the subjection of
> women in modern civilization a matter of no importance. (1898: 394–395)

When Cady Stanton and her colleague Susan B. Anthony met 'some Positivists' during a stay in England and Scotland in 1882 they found these men

> though liberal on religious questions, were very narrow as to the sphere of woman. The difference in sex, which is the very reason why men and women should be associated in all forms of activity, is to them the strongest reason why they should be separated. (1898: 425)

What had happened to the promise of the ungendered foundations for social institutions Martineau saw social science providing? A clue lies in the contrasting meaning of 'women's sphere' as used by Comte and by the women theorists. In the mid-nineteenth century the 'new women' who succeeded the early socialists saw an expanding sphere as the only means of achieving a scientifically sound basis for society. They themselves comprised the kind of experiment Martineau had in mind.

Societies of 'new women'

Perhaps the most prominent London group of 'new women' in the 1850s was the Langham Place Circle formed by Barbara Leigh Bodichon to support the removal of laws denying married women the right to their incomes and property. This was one of the groups pursuing legal and penal reforms which merged to form the National Association for the Promotion of Social Science (SSA) in 1856 (Goldman 1986: 98). Many members of the SSA had been prominent in the early statistical societies, in decline in the 1850s, and the SSA promoted scientific techniques of social investigation and also acted as a body of 'volunteer legislators' providing expert advice to the paid legislators. The SSA was a 'parliament of social causes', its founders including prominent reform parliamentarians from both Houses, including John Stuart Mill, who sat on its governing council, civil servants like the government statistician William Farr, and professional and lay experts. The association took the radical steps of appointing a woman as assistant secretary and of admitting women not only as participants in discussion but as authors and very soon presenters of papers. Among the most prominent papers on hospital statistics and the science of public health were four prepared by Florence Nightingale, and those of her mentor, doctor and statistician William Farr, president of the SSA's Health Section.

The SSA was a training ground for investigative studies of many kinds, and an advisory platform for policy recommendations by women as well as men. At the third conference in Bradford in October 1859 delegates proposed ways for the 1861 national census to yield information on social and economic conditions in the country. Women's contributions at this meeting gave an impetus to questions of female employment and the following year at the Glasgow conference Emily Faithfull read her own paper on the all-woman Victoria Press and Bessie Rayner Parkes gave her account of 'A year's experience in woman's work'. These papers were published in Barbara Bodichon's *Englishwoman's Journal* and in the editor's view helped to reveal the extent of the destitution of working women of limited education. The *Journal* argued that the Glasgow SSA conference

> forced the public to put prejudice aside, and to test the theory hitherto so jealously maintained, that women were, as a general rule, supported in comfort and independence by their male relatives. The press then took up the question . . . with a zeal and honesty which aided considerably in the partial solution of a problem in which is bound up so much of the welfare and happiness of English homes during this and future generations. (p. 26)

This argument for an empirical base for the formulation of social policy was precisely that put forward by Martineau and by Harriet Taylor Mill twenty years before. The gender dimension of the SSA was widely acknowledged: in 1858 women comprised one third of the 1,500 participants, while at the 1860 Glasgow conference newspaper reports noted that the numbers of women taking part added 'a certain warmth and humanity to the scene'. In all the cities hosting annual conferences 'everyone was caught up with social science', thousands of people attending discussions in the meeting rooms, or at grand dinner parties in private houses, or at the public soirées, or listening to sermons (Smith 1982: 134; Goldman 1987: 136). If socialism was not a topic for civil discourse, the space was filled with what Martineau had anticipated: men and women discoursing on social science. The participation of women in the work of the SSA made middle-class domestic environments a locus of intellectual work and political discussion, not an enclave of morals and manners preserved from political and economic realities. The SSA members all saw themselves as part of politics, as informed policy advisers. Their activity constituted a form of citizenship both active and associative – parent to the institutionalised lobbying of parliamentarians by business, professional and community groups today.

When the prominent Adelaide writer Catherine Helen Spence spent twelve months in Britain in 1865–1866, leading participants in the SSA among the contacts arranged for her by Caroline Clark in Adelaide included Rosamund and Florence Hill, Barbara Bodichon, and Frances Power Cobbe, whose *The Philosophy of the Poor Laws* had been published the previous year. Spence met John Stuart Mill, who led the discussion after Thomas Hare spoke on proportional representation at the 1865

SSA conference. Both had read with approval Spence's own pamphlet on the topic, and she spoke of this paper as her passport into these circles. The SSA helped to secularise the reformist movement in the sense that Spence was able to participate in far wider circles than a woman visitor from the Australian colonies might otherwise enjoy in her own right. This example also serves to show the close connections between political reformers in the colonies and in Britain – closer than between Britain and the USA, where the social science association followed a more European form without the close links to legislators (Goldman 1987: 147; Magarey 1985: 89, 96–101).

In Britain the SSA functioned as an 'outdoor parliament' – in fact it provided women with their first opportunity to occupy seats in the House of Commons when in the summer of 1862 the SSA held a soirée for eight thousand people at Westminster. The *Spectator* recorded 'the legislative fortress was taken by storm and in rushed the stream of Social Science' (Goldman 1986: 112; 1987: 137, 161). The model was adopted by the 'new women' who were beneficiaries of the struggle to have women admitted to university lecture halls. For instance, in their new college at Cambridge, Newnham students formed a 'political debating society' explicitly to practice as an 'outdoor parliament'. Bodichon's close involvement in the establishment of Girton meant that SSA activities were followed with interest there and this bold venture in women's university education was of as much interest to her SSA contacts.

The SSA was organised like the government, its separate 'departments' linking members of parliament to different interests – with industrialists and business people in the Department of Social Economy, with doctors in the Department of Health, with lawyers in the Department of Jurisprudence, with the 'aristocracy of labour' in the Department of Labour and Capital. Every department had its complement of educated, liberal, and usually young, women and men, often fired by Comtean positivism and Christian socialism. This forum of 'brains and numbers' lent considerable strength to the emergent Gladstone Liberal Party, but many conservatives also participated in the work of the departments and in the annual conferences. (Goldman 1987: 138–139).

While urbanisation was dramatically changing the landscapes of Britain, the practice of an active and associative citizenship was incrementally reshaping relations between women and the state. Women's sphere was conceived as co-extensive with society, not as a sub-set of the whole, a polite and private sphere quite distinct from a political and powerful one. What forces reversed this trend so that British women did not win the franchise for half a century after the Newnham students began to prepare themselves for a place in parliament? While male resistance to female emancipation is all too evident, it is not sufficient explanation as to why women themselves apparently failed to seize their moment and why institutional change effected the Comtean delineation of women's sphere roundly dismissed by reformers.

A sanitary sphere

While the SSA began to decline in influence in the later nineteenth century, the political influence of statisticians burgeoned. The success of the SSA reformers in bringing to political centre stage the role of education and of public health in alleviating social problems and social costs was itself a factor as governments increasingly sought statistical facts to strengthen arguments both for and against reform proposals. The cloak of objectivity was just that. For a start, assumptions were built into the very design of data collection, as well as forming the framework of analysis. Even professional statists, like Farr and his colleague in the Register Office Edwin Chadwick, did not deduce their theories of causal links between insanitary living conditions, poverty and disease from their data. Rather, they modelled their investigations on the premise of a necessary link between domestic environments and disease in urban areas. Farr initiated the use of female rather than male mortality rates, not for gender comparison but on the presumption that this would minimise the effect of occupation and produce a more distinct picture of the 'contaminated atmosphere' of cities (Eyler 1979: 125. 130–131). Despite the inbuilt choices and assumptions, the status of the official returns derived from the twin authorities of government and of empirical method so that 'in that rationalist dawn of the social sciences Farr could foretell the future on the basis of laws supposedly as immutable as those of Kepler or Newton' (Cullen 1975: 39).

Overcrowding and lack of sanitation were obvious problems in Victorian Britain, where the number of towns almost doubled between 1851 and 1871, while the urban population leapt from nine million to fourteen million. As Alison Mackinnon demonstrates in the next chapter, reproduction and public health remained closely linked by reformers, with insanitary conditions and improvidence seen as causes of the morbidity and mortality of the poor. In attributing the high mortality rates of the urban poor to hygienic, not economic, causes, statisticians designated a social rather than a political arena for their solution. Governments might be called on to regulate overcrowding and municipal bodies to provide water supply and sewerage facilities, but political reponsibility ended at the front door of the Belgravia mansion and of the slum tenement alike.

Criticisms of the Register Office's ranking of districts by mortality rate had led Farr to refine this tool by including age and gender in the

1849–1853 report, and for the first time the mortality rate of women of childbearing age was identified in a supplement to the 1851–1860 report. Even more importantly, this supplement showed that infant mortality accounted for 80 per cent of the difference in the overall rates between 'healthy districts' and the thirty large towns. Industrialists disputed the necessary connection between urbanisation and ill health and pointed to the inadequacy of birth figures. Once this problem was overcome – when registration of births and marriages was wrested from religious to 'civil' officials – infant mortality became the cardinal indicator of public health. This was the key to Chadwick's well-publicised pressure for urban sanitation, in particular municipal sewerage and refuse disposal (Eyler 1979: 142). Both the Register Office and the SSA emphasised hygiene and infant mortality in establishing the case for the Sanitary Commission of 1869–1871, thus directing the reform focus to the role of women. In marshalling domesticity to ameliorate the effects of industrialism and urbanisation, the responsibility of legislators, industrialists and civil servants was shifted to women. In this policy formulation, women were institutionalised as civil servants of a particular kind and 'new women' caught back into a private domain, their citizenship circumscribed by virtue of their sex. Thus statistics, the 'science of the arts of civil life', was influential in reconstructing an older civic space into a newer social space, so that 'woman's sphere' remained a satellite of the world of social science and of institutional design (*Journal* 1840, quoted in Eyler 1979: 16; Folbre 1991).

This statistical reinforcement of gender roles was a powerful counter-force to the potential of social science: it eliminated the possibility Martineau envisaged of an empirical basis removing gender prejudice in institutional design. The correlation of poor hygiene and infant mortality problematised the home, not the economic and political decisions behind rapid urbanisation, not only in Britain but also in the USA and in Australia where Timothy Coghlan, the influential New South Wales government statistician, was a persuasive exponent of the infant mortality indice (Deacon 1989: 135–136). This dimension of statistical analysis is of profound importance in the redefinition of the domestic as women's sphere at a time when the sickness and deaths of small children in inner city areas were so feared and so familiar. Ladies' Sanitary Associations were formed, in Britain in the 1850s and then in the Australian colonies, to improve the management of poor households, though in Australia at least, the associations also saw their role as exerting influence on governments to provide adequate water supply, sewerage and drainage. Public health was a contestable terrain for 'the notion of cultivating health according to what we now call the laws of life is very modern indeed' (*Englishwoman's Journal* 3, 14, 1859). Women's agency in the policy and commodity aspects of water supply and sanitation is an intriguing issue I must turn from here in order to examine another social response to this privatisation of responsibility for urban problems.[1]

The new women's sphere

While Elizabeth Cady Stanton was pointing to the gender problem of positivist social science in England in 1882, she and Susan B. Anthony were initiating with British colleagues a group which became the International Council of Women (ICW), the second international organisation of women. The first was the Woman's Christian Temperance Union (WCTU) established in the USA, the Pacific, Southeast Asia, India and Australia during the 1880s. Both have been criticised as 'maternalist' in their reform agendas in that alcohol abuse, poor health and hygiene, family violence, and the need for free kindergartens in poor urban areas are linked with campaigns for suffrage and education for women. While temperance in Britain has been distinguished from the European and Scandinavian movement in its emphasis on moral improvement rather than on government regulation, this analysis is clearly contradicted when the work of the WCTU is included. In Australia as in Britain and throughout its worldwide branches, this organisation pursued legislative change, including suffrage rights, as well as lobbying governments for a broad range of reforms, the 'do every-thing' strategy whereby Frances Willard, American social reformer and world leader of the WCTU, made women's sphere co-extensive with the social and the civil.

The idea of moral improvement as appropriate work for women lent respectability to the temperance cause – Willard's rhetoric was that women were 'translated out of the passive and into the active voice on this great question of the protection of their homes' (Willard 1879; Harrison 1971: 150–160, 363).

Moral reform was a key principle of the WCTU but in practice the worldwide WCTU relied less on moral suasion than on targeting governments on a range of political and social reforms. The British SSA 'outdoor parliament' model was adopted by the WCTU which worldwide was organised in 'Departments', some identical in purpose and name to those of the SSA. Under Frances Willard's 'do everything' policy members could work in a Suffrage Department, a Department of Labour and Capital, a Department of Peace and Arbitration and departments of physical culture, and of rational dress reform. A resolution passed in an Australian union in 1890 argued that 'what is good for the home is also good for the State' (Tyrrell 1991: 33, 208; Oldfield 1992: 139).

The rhetoric of woman's sphere strategically deployed by the WCTU was in tension with the actual political work of the branches worldwide. Harriet Martineau had observed that religion was American women's occupation; if piety were their tool, then among the useful works they produced, the home was the most valued. In this culture temperance work functioned as an agent in transforming the home from workplace to sanctum, as machinery was moved out and manufactured furnishings were moved in. Woman's skill in shaping this retreat was the means for directing her husband's steps from work homewards rather than saloonwards (Bordin 1981: 4). Urbanisation shaped much more complex spatial relations than a gendered public/private dichotomy suggests: women workers in factories might desire the very home confinement that newly educated middle-class women deplored, and the 'new women' of the Victorian era used the rhetoric differently from the earlier generation. The voluntary organisations pursuing political goals of establishing the conditions for women's citizenship were also part of this reshaping.

Interpretation of the metaphor of 'woman's sphere' reveals this variety of discursive positions. In the post-Revolutionary era in both America and Britain a reactionary theme is common in 'attempts to cloak woman's public activity with the aura of woman's sphere' (Matthews 1992; 95). In 1837 Martineau's friend Maria Weston Chapman satirised this in 'The times that try men's souls':

> Confusion has seized us, and all things go wrong
> The women have leaped from 'their spheres'. . .
> (quoted in Graham Yates 1985: 120)

In Victorian England the idea of the minisphere was increasingly embedded in middle-class culture, in a development running parallel to the exertions of women in expanding their political influence. During the 1850s the London *Times* editorialised against women's political organisations, arguing the greater influence of women in the 'sacred circle' of the home. John Ruskin extolled this role in 'Of Queen's Gardens' and the enduringly popular *Sesame and Lilies* in 1865 (Davidoff and Hall 1987), while the household magazine *Good Words* trumpeted the special role of girls as a 'vestal sisterhood'. Women's own ideas were as vigorously and skilfully expressed. Bodichon's *Englishwoman's Journal* could not resist a lengthy satirical piece on the new sentiment of domesticity mounting on this wave. The writer reviewed Coventry Patmore's 'The Angel in the House' as entirely conventional, a poem which could have been so well received at no other time and at no other place: 'Here, simply and exquisitely expressed, is the instinct which makes the poor beaten creature in our police-courts beg off the offender at any risk' (*Englishwoman's Journal* 1, 1, 1858: 59).

Ruskin presented copies of his books to the Girton College library as did Tennyson, whose 'The Princess' was there seen as a 'fairy tale' of a women's college, with a moral which 'did not, could not, ought not to work'. In 1852 Florence Nightingale had written

> Why have women passion, intellect, moral activity – these three – and a place in society where no one of the three can be exercised? . . . Nothing can well be imagined more painful than the present position of woman, unless . . . she keeps herself within the magic sphere, the bubble of her dreams . . . [Women] teach themselves to dramatise 'little things', to persuade themselves that domestic life is their sphere and to idealise the 'sacred hearth'. (*Cassandra* (1852) quoted in Goldby 1990: 252)

The first Girton students wrote their own sonnets to the college where they 'came sick to the soul for larger scope' and 'Felt the world widen round, saw clear Horizons stretch' (cited in Constance-Jones 1913: 12). Florence Nightingale argued that women desired 'a great sphere of steady, not sketchy benevolence, of moral activity, for which they would fain be trained and fitted'. In the Australian colonies the 'sphere' was as constant a motif from all who contributed to the question of women's citizenship. South Australian suffragist, WCTU member and Methodist missionary Serena Thorne Lake wrote: 'we recognize that the home is the centre of our sphere, but not its circumference'. Students at the Presbyterian Ladies College in Melbourne followed the debate in their school magazine:

> Woman's sphere, it is said, is in the home. Truly; but we cannot consent to have the radius from a vital centre arbitrarily limited; and further, we know that harsh necessity drives multitudes daily from their 'sphere' to outside labour . . . The sphere is a circle of chalk which the tide of necessity and the steps of these noble ones are obliterating. (*Patchwork* (October 1885) quoted in Bomford 1993: 8)

One of these students, Vida Goldstein, started the suffragists' paper *Woman's Sphere* – with the suffrage won, this became the *Woman Voter* (Bomford 1993: 8). The assignment to women of a role in keeping a hygienic home not only delimited this sphere, but also devalued the associative citizenship practised in order to fight for citizenship for women.

A global society

The rise of international organisations of women in the late nineteenth century re-delineation of a civil and social sphere can be seen as a domestic supplement of liberalism. Nonetheless these constituted 'outdoor parliaments', where citizenship was exercised by disenfranchised women. These campaigns for political equality were developed in international fora – the conferences, conventions, executive meetings, publications and networks of the various organisations – but until the establishment of the League of Nations in 1919 they were directed only to national governments. The significance of this internationalisation and of the nature of the citizenship formulated in these campaigns is too readily overlooked if these organisations are dismissed as handmaids to liberalism or imperialism. More importantly, understanding the nineteenth-century sources of late twentieth-century globalism provides opportunities for institutional redesign which might address the contrived limitations on women's political participation.

For instance, international organisations such as the WCTU and the ICW can be seen as forerunners, with the Red Cross, of the modern non-government organisations (NGOs) that now mediate the relations of states, citizens and official international organisations such as the United Nations (UN), the International Labour Organisation and the World Trade Organisation. Some central characteristics of the citizenship practised by the early women internationalists is replicated in modern NGOs with an international structure and transnational political aims – most importantly the associative nature of this form of political participation. Membership of the organisations repositions an individual in relation to the state and to the UN, its agencies, and to all other supra-national bodies. Current globalising trends, including the establishment of large regional economic federations, indicate the need for new theorising about these relationships in liberal democracies. Redesigning participatory citizenship might now include an appreciation of the practice and experience of feminist internationalism and of the context of institutional change in which it emerged.

The relation of 'social' to 'civil' at the end of the eighteenth century had become very different a hundred years later. As Ruth Bloch argues, the communal and selfless values associated with male citizens in the 'classical' republican notion of virtue shifted into 'woman's sphere': home, church, and voluntary societies. Gender conventions, supplemented by law and policy, functioned to relocate as 'nonpolitical the communal values republicanism defined as quintessentially public', that is, to relocate the civic from a public (political, male) sphere to a private (domestic, female) sphere (Kerber 1980; Bloch 1987; Zagarri 1992). This dimension of the defining of the social and of a social science influenced the shaping of liberal democratic institutions and still underlies the distinction between citizenship based on individual legal rights and a civics of mutual social responsibilities. In the 1920s and 1930s this assignment was contested by women internationalists involved in the

legislative and administrative functions of the League of Nations, but the
development of international institutions has not followed the form they
proposed. The slippage of civics from a political to a social activity
construed women's citizenship as non-political; a process assisted by
arguments of the nineteenth and the twentieth century for a 'different'
citizenship. These issues – whether citizenship for women is necessarily
different from the male model; whether there can be a social space
immune from politics; and whether citizenship can be human and states
humane – remain problems for the twenty-first century. For Australians,
a new opportunity to deal with these issues is offered in the process of
moving towards a republic as Chilla Bulbeck's chapter (10) shows.

Contemporary discourses of 'civil society' are of vital significance to
institutional design in a context of twentieth-century globalisation rather
than nineteenth-century urbanisation. For instance, to Ernest Gellner
civil society is fundamental to liberty and cannot exist in the totalitarian
state. It is 'based on the separation of the polity from economic and
social life' and comprises 'intermediary' institutions: trades unions, pressure groups, clubs 'which fill the gap between family and state'. While
Gellner sees civil society losing its 'natural' supports in an emergence of
any global political authority, to Geoff Mulgan the new importance of
civil society heralds a 'post-political' age when many influences of social
and economic life are beyond the reach of old institutions of national
government (Gellner 1994; Mulgan 1994). Both accounts fail to recognise the potential of associative citizenship by confining it to a terrain
outside economic and political institutions, perhaps because of what
Phillip Pettit has referred to as the 'mesmeric dichotomy' of the liberal-
communitarian debate (Pettit 1994).

The splitting of the civil from the political which posits the former as
social and the latter as individual institutionalises the inequalities which
women as women experience in their relations to the state. A social
science predicated on this split reinforces such institutions. The political
practices of the first women's international organisations were formulated to address the resulting problems, recognised by early women
socialists and social scientists. It is not accurate to identify that work as
not political; and attempting to do so by containing it within the borders
of 'civil society' makes that very term a political instrument. In proposing
the women's international organisations as forerunners of modern
NGOs I am suggesting a similar effect is entailed in the categorisation of
all voluntary associations as institutions of civil society. This has now
become common; not only Gellner and Mulgan, but United Nations
officials contribute to this discourse, and so do many of the NGOs
themselves. The identification of NGOs as institutions of civil society was
a motif at the UN Fourth World Conference on Women in 1995, where

several of the original international women's organisations were represented among the 2,750 organisations from 184 countries participating in the NGO forum at that conference in Beijing. It was also the emphasis of former Secretary-General Boutros Boutris-Ghali's opening and closing addresses, and of the World Bank-sponsored workshop 'Reclaiming civil society in the global south'. It was the theme at Hiairou, where representatives of hundreds of NGOs took a pledge as 'organizations of civil society' and the veteran USA political activist Bella Abzug proclaimed

> Women, organized as never before, and represented here in the myriad of . . . NGOs attending, are the emerging progressive force of civil society. (Beijing conference email news list, October 1995)

The problem of the 'residual' definition – that institutions which are not part of formal government structures are part of civil society – is all too familiar to feminist theorists. It is a bad definition in contemporary industrialised and urbanised liberal democracies because political power exercised other than by formal institutions of government is always a bit player, an unofficial visitor, an any-other-business item on the political agenda. It is also a dangerous definition if globalisation entails the transfer of political power offshore because then we need to focus on the possibility of political participation shifting from individual citizens to international associations of non-government and, I hope, uncivil associations.

Characterising citizens as free and equal meant giving everyone a reason to be governed. This process has taken two centuries so far and has produced the concept of universal human rights and contributed to the idea of a global society. Associative citizenship in an international sphere, acting on institutions exercising international and regional power as well as on national governments, is one way of addressing the new problem of political obligation posed by the current redefinition of society as global. But just as the power of associative citizenship was circumscribed by relegating this activity to a social as distinct from a political sphere, so its contemporary manifestations are weakened when institutionalised within a sphere of civil society defined as non-political. There is a need to distinguish lawn bowls from political activism, and membership of a local choir from, for instance, the campaigns of Greenpeace and the lobbying of the International Alliance of Women. Indeed, it is pointless to promote the former as the lifeblood of liberal democracy – bowlers and choristers are going to associate anyway. It is far more important to design institutions of citizenship, not of civility, and critical to do so when it is far from obvious to most citizens that they can make a scrap of difference to the politics that govern their lives.

This is not an argument for replacing the modern concept with the classical republican idea of civil society – both had a built-in separate sphere for women. Rather it is an observation about being civil and social if these are institutionalised as non-political. It is also a warning about how this served to circumscribe women's political participation, about the consequences of an imprecise political language in theorising on institutional design and, possibly most of all, about hearing the voices history has stilled.

Notes

1 A relevant study on the significance of urban sanitation in colonial politics is Shirley Fitzgerald *Rising Damp: Life and work in Sydney 1870–1890*, Melbourne, Oxford University Press, 1986.

CHAPTER 9

Redesigning the Population:
Narratives of sex and race

Alison Mackinnon

The question of population is fundamental to key institutions of our society. So central indeed that population questions are addressed in a variety of competing voices, political, moral, economic, demographic and social at the very least. Rarely do those voices come together, leaving a strange disjunction between those examining population from an historical perspective, a demographic perspective or indeed a policy approach. The voices of women are the least audible in this confusion. For most of the twentieth century a growing population has been critical in providing 'manpower' for the industrialising world's insatiable appetite for factory workers and for war. These imperatives are still salient in some parts of the developing world. In the developed world, however, debate about the size of the population has for the moment given way to debate about the constitution of the population with issues of race, ethnicity, ageing and levels of immigration increasingly to the fore. How are these population questions expressed? And what connections can be found between current debates on population and those of earlier times? One is reminded here of French philosopher Michel Foucault's preoccupation with 'the processes of recuperation, of the distillation of earlier discursive imprints, remodeled in new forms' (Stoler 1995: 68). How are the 'discursive imprints' of population configured today – and what implications do they have for gender relations?

At the heart of many national concerns about population stands the citizen mother, prepared (or expected) to do her duty for the state, a symbolic figure deployed in the early part of the twentieth century by both men and women, the latter in the interests of gaining access to citizenship (Grimshaw et al. 1994: 192). Within much population debate, both academic and popular, a common motif can be discerned – the reduction of women's bodies to the status of a national resource. Barry

Maley, for instance, in a paper for the Australian Family Association, writes of the nation 'failing to reproduce itself'. His title was explicit: 'Babies – a National Resource' (Maley 1990). The use of such language places fertility change firmly in the category of the natural, something to be 'managed' for the good of the nation. Yet at the same time it is intensely political. This tension between the language of fertility as apparently natural, yet at the same time intensely political, is central to my essay.

In the late twentieth-century developed world the imperative of population growth is no longer strong. Indeed the opposite is most often the case. In the interests of global survival it is accepted that lower levels of population growth are desirable. What then in a low growth society is the role of citizen mother? Of women released from the imperative of motherhood? There are vast implications here for the institutions of marriage, of heterosexual monogamy and of gender relations generally. For, arguably, the expectation of motherhood has been the major defining aspect of women's lives throughout history.

In this chapter I discuss three narratives circulating around issues of population, one from history, one from demography, one drawing on social policy. Through these narratives, and the embedded issues of race and gender, I tease out some of the implications for institutional design. I tap into one of the major arguments in population studies: How does population change occur? Specifically, why does fertility decline? I allude deliberately to the term 'narratives', seeking to illuminate the ways in which they construct women as bearers of children and, implicitly, as the means of favouring certain racial groups at the expense of others. Within a range of disciplines narrative has increasingly occupied a central place. Researchers in political philosophy, psychology, legal theory, feminist theory, anthropology and medical sociology are claiming that social life is storied, 'that stories guide action, that people construct identities (however multiple and changing) by locating themselves or being located within a repertoire of emplotted stories, that experience is constituted through narrative' (Somers and Gibson, cited in Joyce 1994: 153). As an historian, part of a discipline which has always told stories, I welcome this development. But narratives are more than stories, than particular constructions of the world told for academic and popular audiences. They provide the material on which policy-makers frequently depend. There is much at stake, then, in whose narrative is heard. The American demographer Sheila Ryan Johansson suggests that as long as advice is contested, as academics compete for intellectual dominance, bureaucrats will be able to shrug their shoulders and pursue self-interested policies (Johansson 1991). There is much competition for dominance in population studies: even more confusion as to policy.

The institution of population is a fruitful field for issues of gender and race. Fertility concerns are a powerful element in the symbolic order of nations, causing industrialising nations at the turn of the last century to speak of race suicide; causing French demographers in the early 1990s to misrepresent population figures in the national interest and creating massive controversy at the 1994 Cairo conference on population. Feminists ask why women rarely appear as active agents in scientific discourses on demography (Mackinnon 1995). When not completely invisible in the fertility literature, women are often portrayed as either lacking decision-making ability or, when recognised as decision-makers, as responsible for poor or selfish decisions. In development literature they are frequently viewed as problem overproducers; in developed societies they underproduce (Hicks 1978; Watkins 1993). There are strange contradictions in a debate which recommends raising the status of women in developing countries as a means to lowering fertility while deploring the below-replacement fertility of middle-class groups in developed countries.

Institutions and population

Given the breadth of activities and structures described as institutions (the institution of the family, of the labour market, of education, for example) it is useful to examine attempts at defining them. Demographer Geoffrey McNicholl talks of institutions as 'clusters of behavioural rules governing (or, to put it more neutrally, regularities describing) human actions and relationships in recurrent situations' (McNicholl 1994: 201). McNicholl advocates an awareness of the historical nature of institutions, claiming that 'they persist, generating a society's distinctive patterns of social organization and the texture of social life' (201). Echoing that notion of historical embeddedness, the political philosopher Robert Goodin speaks of institutions as 'ossified past practices' (Goodin 1996). A distinction can be made, McNicholl argues, between 'organic' and 'pragmatic' institutions (1994: 201), that is those that are inherited from the past, that have emerged 'without a common will' and those that are consciously designed as part of efforts to plan, remedy or reform. Yet, as he notes, institutional design of the latter type may easily be subverted. As J. S. Mill wrote in 1848, '[T]hough governments or nations can in some measure determine what institutions shall be established they cannot arbitrarily determine how those institutions shall work (Mill (1848), quoted in McNicholl 1994: 201). Population might well be seen as one of these.

   Another distinction developed by McNicholl is that 'institutions have both material and cultural antecedents' (1994: 201). Some institutions, such as those of economic development, appear to be largely material.[1]

Some, such as the institutions of political development, share both aspects. Others, however, such as the sexual division of labour, are multi-faceted:

> [t]he sexual division of labour is, like all fundamental institutions, multi-faceted. Within any particular society, it is an integral part of the ideological system, economic organization, daily family life and often the political structures as well . . . In any one case all these dimensions reinforce each other, so that the current structure seems both heavily overdetermined and ultimately mysterious since it is difficult to assign weight to one factor over another (Guyer 1980, cited in McNicholl 1994).

This complex notion of institutions has a greater usefulness for my analysis. Recent feminist theory resists the notion of binary oppositions, such as pragmatic or organic, material or cultural, seeing within such dualisms a tendency for them to shape up on male/female lines with the female inevitably assigned to the less significant side of the divide. The recognition that institutions are often multi-faceted, that they carry the weight of past historic practices and that they may often be subverted or distorted by those acting within or upon them, provides part of the the context for the discussion in this essay. National aims for population growth, for example, are frequently confounded by those who are expected to provide the increase: behaviours normally proscribed (illegitimate births, for instance) can be given leeway in periods of national crisis.

But we need to go further, I believe, than acknowledging institutions as multi-faceted; to look at the use of language in relation to institutional discourses. Foucault's insight that the discourse of sexual development becomes constitutive of the social reality it portrays is particularly useful here as is his notion of recuperating earlier discursive imprints (Foucault: 1978). New discursive regimes bring into existence the very phenomena they purport to describe. Foucault claims that one of the great innovations in the techniques of power in the eighteenth century was the emergence of 'population' as an economic and political problem. The articulation of a population as opposed to subjects or merely 'people' led to a fascination with such phenomena as birth and death rates, life expectancy, fertility, health and a range of other issues including 'the precocity and frequency of sexual relations' (Foucault 1978: 25).

Anthony Giddens argues that power/knowledge does not just operate in one direction, as Foucault implies, but that it is constantly in motion. Discourse is a basic structuring element of social activity in modern settings and 'it is reflexive in the sense that terms introduced to describe social life routinely enter and transform it', not mechanically but 'because they become part of the frames of action which individuals or groups adopt' (Giddens 1992: 28–29). This 'institutional reflexivity' is a useful tool for analysis of institutions and their reshaping. What is not clear, however, is the way in which the terms may work to the advantage of some groups rather than others.

In examining some of the narratives of population and fertility, an area which links into and affects a broad range of institutions, I argue that the discourses used reveal the extent to which relations between men and women, a neglected area in institutional design, intersect with and shape a broad range of institutions and institutional policy. Conversely, institutional policies impact upon relations between men and women, often with unintended results. The process is ongoing, unfinished, and reflexive. Work in this area reveals the inadequacy of any theoretical separation of public and private. At times of population crisis, for example, the most intimate and private decisions between men and women become a major focus of national inquiry and often, of national anxiety (see, for instance, Royal Commission into Health 1926; National Health and Medical Research Council Report 1944). Extensive changes in relations between men and women in developed societies, changes categorised by Giddens as 'a transformation of intimacy' (1992), reveal even more starkly the impact of the purportedly private domain of gender relations on the world of public policy. Let us look briefly then at three narratives which circulate around the issue of population.

Narrative 1. Population and national survival – from
'race suicide' to The Camp of the Saints

The nations are rising from the four corners of the earth and their number is like the sand of the sea. They will march up over the broad earth and surround the camp of the saints and the beloved city . . . (Jean Raspail, 1973, cited in Connelly and Kennedy 1994: 61)

In an article provocatively titled 'Must it be the Rest against the West?', Matthew Connelly and Paul Kennedy raise fundamental questions about population trends in the late twentieth century (1994). In particular the authors confront the growing population imbalance between the birth-limiting nations of the developed world and the population rich but materially poor nations of the developing world. They hark back to Jean Raspail's 1973 book, *The Camp of the Saints*, which depicted 'a world of two "camps", North and South, separate and unequal, in which the rich will have to fight and the poor will have to die if mass migration is not to overwhelm us all'. The book describes the pilgrimage of a million desperate Indians who set off in an armada of decrepit ships for the French Riviera. As disturbing as the pilgrimage itself is the reaction of the French population to the impending arrival of the multitude.

Raspail's book, rejected in the more progressive seventies as a racist tract, has a certain grim relevance twenty years later as armadas of refugees stream from Albania to Italy, from China to the United States, to Australian shores from Southeast Asia. Talk of national survival in the face of mass immigration has resurfaced in developed countries in the less liberal climate of the late twentieth century. In the affluent nations of the developed world a painful consciousness of the needs of the populous developing world translates into anxiety about guest-workers, extremist right-wing racism and a tendency to close doors to new arrivals. While Australia in the early 1990s prided itself on its unique multi-culturalism and rejoiced in slogans of cultural diversity, by 1997 it had tightened immigration policies, obstructed the settlement of particular groups of refugees and witnessed an outburst of anti-Asian feeling seemingly legitimated by the inflammatory words of the Independent MP, Pauline Hanson. In this it is entirely in accord with western Europe's increasing hostility to asylum-seekers (*Australian*, 16 January 1996). What is most at issue in many Western countries is the fact that growth is led by net immigration rather than by natural growth, leading to recurring anxieties about national identity (Winter and Teitelbaum 1998).

The questions raised here are both moral and political. They are but the latest in a long line of anxieties (discursive imprints?) underpinned and given urgency by the study of population statistics. Australia has always been prey to such anxieties. In turn-of-the-century Australia the declining birth rate caused massive apprehension, resulting in the 1903 New South Wales Royal Commission into the Decline of the Birthrate (RCDB). In that year Dr Yatsima, a Japanese social scientist, visited the Australasian colonies, wishing to acquaint himself with the vital statistics of the population (Mackellar, in RCDB, 1904: 249, para. 6593). Why, he pondered, was a country progressing in wealth and comfort 'cursed with a decreasing birth-rate'? 'This is the riddle of the Sphinx', declared Dr Yatsima, 'which faces all progressive nations'. The problem, Yatsima believed, was the universal law expressed in the Persian proverb 'A full belly, a bed of roses, and an empty cradle'. Where a high standard of comfort prevails, and there is an abundance of food and leisure, 'the rose of fatness bears the thorn of sterility'. Yatsima viewed the waning birth rate as 'a sure sign of racial decay'. The great British nation, in his view, was doomed by the worm of luxury which bore into its vitals. When the 'ascendent star' of the British nation had set, he warned, the hardened sons of his nation would set their faces towards the empty nation to their south.

> You look upon us as barbarians unfit for admission into your country, but the sons of my nation, hardened by war and adversity, and tempered in the fires of poverty, are even now gazing forward to the time when your ascendent star shall have set. (RCDB: 1904: 249)

Yatsima's comments in 1903, Raspail's novel seventy years later, remind us that issues around fertility and immigration provide two of the poles through which race and gender are institutionalised. Fear of invasion from the north (of being 'swamped by Asians') was a sub-theme of the 1903 Royal Commission, one rarely invoked directly but always understood: the decline of white fertility, on the other hand, was central and continuously invoked. In their findings, findings which echoed thinking in a range of countries, the commissioners identified women's love of luxury and pleasure, their dislike of the discomfort of child-bearing, their selfishness in fact, as major reasons for steeply declining birth rates. The focus on selfish women was not new. In late eighteenth-century France, in mid nineteenth-century America, in almost identical language women's love of luxury and pleasure was also blamed for declining birthrates. Thus the most intimate aspects of life – sexual pleasure, personal autonomy, relationship with others – were inextricably linked with one of the most public, national, indeed global, concerns. Relations between men and women, constructions of gender and gender-linked behaviour were inextricably linked with the imperative to provide sufficient numbers of the 'right' children.

Fear of any dilution of the Anglo-Saxon 'race' was a dominant motif in turn-of-the-century Australia, producing an institutionalised racism which underpinned the virtual genocide of the original Aboriginal inhabitants. Alfred Deakin, a leading federationist, argued that 'the question of white Australia touches all colonists' instinct for self-preservation'. No motive force was as powerful in leading to the linking of the disparate colonies in one federation as 'the desire that we should be one people, and remain one people, without the admixture of other races' (Grimshaw et al. 1994: 192). Central to the maintenance of a strong white Australia was a continuing supply of healthy white babies, the best guarantee against invasion from the populous north. Women's major task as citizens in the newly federated nation of Australia was as mothers, as producers of the next generations. The alternative was 'race suicide'.

The discourse of race suicide can be found in the political, educational and medical literature of several continents (Hicks 1978; Dyhouse 1981: 91ff; Palmieri 1995: ch. 13). Anxiety about the falling birth rate was not just explained in terms of its decline but that it was falling relative to the Asiatic and negroid races. In the early 1900s declining fertility struck fear into the hearts of all who wished to see the continuing dominance of the Anglo-Saxon race. In America President Roosevelt was quoted as saying:

Do you know that there are fewer descendents of the revolutionary forefathers living today than there was fifty years ago? . . . We must either alter our ways or we must make way for the other races, Asiatic or whatever they are, that will certainly replace us (cited in Finch 1993: 109–10).

As worrying as the issue of overall fertility decline was the fact of differential fertility: the upper classes were producing fewer babies than the prolific working class. Medical men stridently argued that highly educated women lost their ability to reproduce. Using the language of social Darwinism, they firmly reduced women to their biology (Zschoche 1989). A century ago Karl Pearson, a leading British social Darwinist, wrote 'If childbearing women be intellectually handicapped, then the penalty to be paid for race predominance is the subjection of women' (cited in Lewis 1984: 84).

In England the 'scary prospect of "race suicide" . . . was revived time and again before World War 1 and, though often with more subtlety and with greater sophistication, in the interwar years as well' (Soloway 1990: xv). Others, such as the Canadian dominion statistician George Johnson, stated less hysterically that the decline in the birth rate was 'due to the spread of education which enables females to become better wage earners and therefore less interested in marriage' (Prentice et al. 1988: 159). The concern culminated in Australia in the New South Wales Royal Commission into the Decline of the Birth-Rate which produced a narrative of selfish women, their voracious sexuality unleashed.

As we approach the end of the twentieth century the discursive trope of a declining and decadent West again reverberates through Western societies. Worried commentators talk of 'babies going out of fashion' and write books with alarmist titles such as *The Birth Dearth: What Happens When People in Free Countries Don't Have Enough Babies?* (Wattenberg 1987; see also Wattenberg 1998: 14–16). Population experts point out in carefully muted language, mindful of the hysteria of the past, that 'there is a clear gradation downwards in the number of children as family income increases' (Hugo 1993: 3–4). Further, more women in higher income families are childless. An Australian policy analyst claims that the spectre of depopulation which last arose in the 1930s was dispelled by the baby boom of the 1940s, 50s, and 60s, but has now returned to haunt us. Again, the protectors of society's moral values are raising their voices in protest, speaking of selfishness and doom. Women are being asked to shoulder the responsibility for those changes. To prevent a possible 'empty' Australia, the writer suggests that we apply 'effective measures to encourage Australian women to have two-plus . . . children on average' (Blandy 1994: 11). Speaking of a 'demographic winter' a Catholic archbishop calls for Australia's population to be increased to 50 million (Pell 1997: 1).

Now the discourse of race suicide takes on a global dimension as the 'developed' elite, failing to replace itself, is outbred by the millions of the developing countries. In the cultural uncertainties of post-Cold War Europe, strict border controls are being placed around national identity, and fear of boundary-crossing leads to heightened national and racial antagonism. In European war zones it is claimed that women's bodies were appropriated by invading troops to obstruct the reproduction of an alien ethnic group.

There is no room for doubt in this historical and political narrative that women's role is that of citizen mother, her body to be given freely, in extreme circumstances taken by force in the pursuit of national or ethnic purity. Her selfishness when she limits births is noted with alarm: her role is visible and active. In the second narrative, however, her very visibility is at stake.

Narrative 2. 'Population shrinkage', 'fertility decline' and 'a drop in the crude birth rate' – is anyone responsible?

The language used by demographers to describe the changing numbers of babies born is frequently detached, apparently (seductively) 'scientific'. We hear, for instance, of 'population shrinkage', of 'fertility decline' or, more starkly, of 'a drop in the crude birth rate'. Let us consider the term 'fertility decline'.[2] It is strangely named as the term is totally disembodied, indicating – as several feminist historians have pointed out – some type of transhistorical, elemental and natural force akin, perhaps, to the ebb and flow of the tide rather than the historically specific refusal or unwillingness of considerable numbers of women to continue to have large numbers of babies (Mackinnon 1990; Grimshaw 1991; Allen et al. 1992). Furthermore it has strong overtones of the biological, indicating a fundamental shift in some unidentifiable quantum or essence necessary for the perpetuation of the species. Did men become less potent, some might wonder; did women find it more difficult to conceive?[3] The term 'fertility decline' is a constructed category and operates to ground contemporary issues in a natural universe uncontaminated by social change.

How has 'fertility decline' come to be a characteristic of populations rather than of persons, we might ask? How has it come to have an apparently unitary and seamless meaning? What meanings have collected around the term, and how has it come to be so central in explanations of social change? The apparent objectivity of such terms as 'population shrinkage', or 'drop in the crude birth rate' operates in a manner which masks the social and sexual relations of men and women, the changing social expressions of desire, the changing social positioning of those who conceive and bear children?[4] As the historical sociologist Wally Seccombe writes, after surveying the literature on population change over the centuries, there is very little recognition of changing relations between men and women. 'Sexual desire and conjugal power are absent from the standard paradigms', he claims, 'it as if the demographers believed in the Immaculate Conception – for everyone' (Seccombe 1993: 157).

The use of scientific discourse obscures vitally important moments in the changing relations between men and women, masks the fact that the issue of declining or increasing birth rates is intensely personal and political. Yet the very production of those purportedly objective statistics has been shown to depend on political motives. Simon Szreter demonstrates that the demographic study of fertility even before the 1950s, was 'thoroughly influenced by policy considerations', particularly the need of US economic planners and strategists to export American liberal democratic political and economic practices to those countries in the process of decolonisation (Szreter 1993; see also Demeny 1988).

We cannot throw out population statistics, however. On the contrary, we can 'read' changing fertility patterns imaginatively as sites of contestation where relations between men and women were undergoing fundamental change. Two such critical moments are the the decades at the turn of the last century, when completed family size in all developed countries dropped significantly, and our own *fin-de-siècle* decades. Both periods can be characterised as times of massive change in relations between men and women and by the existence of significant numbers of single and independent women.

Much of the demographic literature, both historical and contemporary, assumes a harmony of interest between men and women within the family in relation to fertility decision-making. As the feminist economist Nancy Folbre argues, 'The family is not a static, unchanging institution, a decision-making black box. It is', she maintains, 'a group of individuals who make collective, but not necessarily consensual decisions. It is prone to conflict and compromise, to domination and resistance' (Folbre 1983). Folbre saw the failure to incorporate any considerations of changing power relations between men and women into discussions of fertility decline as a critical omission. We must deconstruct the black box that is the conjugal couple, she claims, and examine the differing investments men and women have in deciding to have children. This is entirely in keeping with feminist insistence that women's actions must be recuperated for the official record.

The potential for major change indicated by the falling birth rate was clearly understood by late nineteenth-century/early twentieth-century observers. The anxiety focussed on the declining birth rate among the middle class and the propensity of the working class to produce larger families. The decades surrounding the last century's end were also categorised as a period of crisis in marriage, particularly for the new well-educated professional women who often chose an independent life and the chance to employ their education in a professional career (Mackinnon 1997). Contemporary observers, such as the Royal Commissioners into the Decline of the Birth-rate in 1904, were convinced that women's selfishness in refusing to bear large families, in preferring 'a life of luxury and pleasure' was at the heart of the matter. Further, the forward movement of women (the commissioners' way of describing those who supported women's emancipation) was deeply implicated in fertility decline. The significance of the period as one in which women were attempting to redefine their position – to enter the professions, to gain economic independence – was not lost on their contemporaries.

It is strange, then, to turn from such historical evidence to the large-scale modern studies which have attempted to explain the demographic transition. Here we find a distinct demarcation between those who would explain change in economic terms and those who apply cultural explanations. A broad consensus existed among demographers in the 1950s and 1960s which went by the name of 'demographic transition theory' (Notestein 1945; Davis 1963). In its simplest terms this elegant schema posited a three-stage transformation – from high mortality and high fertility through lower mortality with high fertility and finally, as numbers of surviving children became impossible to support, a necessary adjustment to low fertility and low mortality. As Sheila Ryan Johansson points out, 'In some versions this theory was a complex story about demographic change in response to modernization, including mortality change and increased migration' (Johansson 1991: 387; see also Greenhalgh 1995: 5–7). However, over time it was reduced to a tendency to link fertility decline to increasing industrialisation and urbanisation. Simon Szreter comments on the amazing ability of this model of fertility change 'to survive a continuous stream of contradictory findings that would long ago have killed off more mortal entities'. He concludes that the 'continuing currency of the idea of demographic transition, albeit as merely a descriptive term in the eyes of most of its users', is hampering progress in the study of fertility change (Szreter 1993: 661). Perhaps we are now ready to discard the notion altogether as one which imposes a falsely unitary universalism on a very disparate set of social relations. Yet an idea of demographic transition 'relatively untouched by conceptual developments' (Greenhalgh 1996: 27) continues to underpin much population policy.

Narrative 3. The emancipation of women and the birth rate: towards a policy narrative

Let us turn to a narrative that again places women rather than mathematical constructs at the centre. The realm of the personal has changed dramatically over the last century. Women in developed countries have, after considerable struggle, removed themselves from the inevitability of motherhood. This goal, one that a small number of women achieved in the past by removing themselves to women's communities such as those of the church, is now available to many more. The hard won (and always precarious) acceptance of birth control has severed the link between reproduction and sexuality. The continuing unease which accompanies a general acceptance of birth control underlines the significance of the break. Sexuality, no longer inevitably linked to reproduction, has become part of personality: in many ways in late twentieth-century urban societies a life-style choice. Sexuality for women is no longer 'mired in nature' but is also part of cultural expression, 'intrinsically bound up with the self'. Sexuality is 'a prime connecting point between body, self-identity and social norms' (Giddens 1992: 15). A century on, women's awareness of their sexual identity, their sexual autonomy has major implications for the reshaping of relations between the sexes, for fertility and, hence, for the population. And, as younger women have fewer babies, anxiety that the burden of supporting an aging society will fall on too few shoulders becomes palpable.

Norman Ryder believes that 'our past success at population replacement, throughout all of human history, has been conditional on the discriminatory treatment of women' (1993: 81). Historian Carl Degler acknowledges that point in his aptly-titled book *At Odds: Women and the family in America from the revolution to the present* (Degler 1980). Degler points out, 'The central values of the modern family stand in opposition to those that underlie women's emancipation. Where the women's movement has stood for equality, the family historically has denied or repudiated equality' (1980: 473). This is a critical point in a climate where politicians, particularly those on the right, hark back nostalgically to family values. Degler concludes of our era, 'After two hundred years of development, both the future of the family and the fulfillment of women as persons are at odds as never before' (1980: 473).

The 1997 *Australian Women's Year Book* provides a familiar set of statistics demonstrating again that women are marrying less, marrying later, starting childbearing later and having fewer children than the cohorts of the 1950s and 1970s (McLennan and Goward 1997). Does this mean that we are revisiting a period in which women and families are 'at odds'? Has the forward movement of women (to use the language of 1904) helped to create a climate of increased education and employment opportunities for some women, providing them with choices which make commitments to families problematic? Australian demographer Peter McDonald has argued that more than a quarter of the generation born in the 1960s will not marry and that professionals will be disproportionately represented in that percentage (McDonald 1988).

Is this state of disjunction between women's needs for autonomy and the needs of families inherently and for all times 'at odds'? Will women always be forced to choose between embracing family-oriented values and hence compromising autonomy – or embracing autonomy and forgoing family involvement? Will it always be a choice between 'Love and Freedom' (Mackinnon 1997)? We can read the population statistics as a barometer of the degree of that disjunction. Population statistics constitute a set of texts through which we can track the relative reproductive autonomy of women, their attempts to assert themselves against the dominant narrative of the family and of the citizen mother.

Echoing Degler's notion of women's autonomy and family needs as 'at odds', the Swedish demographer Eva Bernhardt asks if the emancipation of women inevitably leads to a situation where too few children are born (Bernhardt 1993: 80)? This, of course, was precisely the question that exercised observers at the turn of the century. Concern over the possible negative effect of a too far-reaching emancipation of Western women on the birth rate has come to predominate both in academic and non-academic debates. Several demographers have recently pronounced that '[l]ow fertility is the ultimate natural outcome of gender equality' (see, for instance, Keyfitz, cited in Bernhardt 1993: 81). Proponents of the self-defined 'culturally conservative' Australian Family Association are also vocal exponents of this concern, fearing that feminism will lead to a collapse of the family. In a paper to a Liberal Party seminar, Mary Helen Woods claimed that 'the damage that has been done to the social fabric in the name of "justice" for women, is inestimable' (Woods 1994: 7).

Is it possible to achieve equality between the sexes and 'sufficient' fertility? Offered access to a wide range of alternative options in the workplace, women will not generally choose to have large families. This choice is shaped by the typical Western conflict between work and family commitments. Summing up the 1994 Cairo conference on Population and Development, Susan Heschel claims that if a woman has a life of her own, she is satisfied to create just one or two more lives (Heschel 1995: 16).

Interestingly, Bernhardt points out that in a society such as Sweden, where government policy has moved further towards a pattern of social responsibility for parenting than elsewhere, where there is high labour force participation by women, and where there have been conscious efforts on the part of government to promote equality of the sexes, birth rates are not as low as in comparable countries. In a general context of below-replacement fertility in Western societies, Swedish fertility has remained relatively high and is near replacement level, despite all the factors that would seem to encourage the contrary (Bernhardt 1993: 103; see also McDonald 1995). This runs counter to the fears of conservatives who claims that the size of welfare spending is inversely related to fertility and that this relationship holds across a variety of cultures at various levels of development (Maley 1990: 27). Bernhardt illuminates the way in which the social organisation of parenting can operate in a pro-natalist fashion in practice, if not in theory or intent (Bernhardt 1993: 101–102). Thus the social organisation of parenting, in a context of increased education and labour force participation for women, is of fundamental importance to women and societies alike. The case of Sweden demonstrates that women's emancipation and the family, then, do not always have to be 'at odds'. Is this what Blandy has in mind when he states that we must apply 'effective measures to encourage Australian women to have two-plus . . . children' (Blandy 1994: 11)?

Conclusion: Population, institutional design and policy

There are several other population narratives that could be developed here (the moral/ethical/religious, for example). But space does not allow. However, we can draw several inferences from those three sketched above. What can be concluded in relation to institutional design? Can we apply any notion of design to the unweildy concept of the population? While demographers search for elegant mathematical patterns in population trends the messiness of politics and policy continues to shape human behaviour in ways that cannot be neatly modelled. Stephen Linder and Guy Peters identify two major traditions in institutional design, the decisional and the dialogic (1995). The decisional is more instrumental, typically averse to politics. A contemporary referent is rational choice theory. Much is made in this variant of institutional design theory of the notion of rational choice, of preference, in human behaviour. How does this notion stand up to a study of the literature of fertility? Much of neoclassical economic demography places the analytic focus on 'the household's derived demand for children as a function of privately formed parental tastes, household income levels , and the relative costs of children' (Johansson 1991). But little is said of individual women's preferences – or the context in which those preferences are shaped.

Given the context of national imperatives and of policy straightjackets it would appear that structural/institutional elements severely constrain individual choice. In both turn-of-the century Australia and Sweden of the 1990s broader influences affecting population shaped the outlines of fertility decline and growth. Yet within those parameters men and women, harmoniously or in conflict, used those wider changes to meet their own needs. Further if we accept that 'history matters', the narrative of population reveals a long struggle between women and men, between women and the state, both within the household and within the arena of local and international politics, for the right to determine reproductive futures (see Siedlecky and Wyndham 1990, for example).

If moral and political issues are acknowledged, say Lindner and Peters, the decisional becomes 'too thin', too instrumental. We turn then to the second tradition: the dialogic. This approach, linked in our time to critical theory, creates a public space, has a communal base in politics, is concerned with open deliberations about facts and values. It draws from public dialogue meeting universal requirements for open discourse and equal participation (Linder and Peters 1995: 136ff). Here there is room for all participants, for reflexivity, for political struggle, not just the policies proposed by technical experts. Institutions reflect the bargaining power of the relevant interests: the negotiating currently under way between men and women is revealed in the instability of relations between the sexes, the changing shape of the family, an institution constantly represented as being in crisis.

We live at an unprecedented moment in the demographic history of the developed world. In Europe the pattern of low fertility, the fact that in many countries growth is led by net migration rather than natural growth, has led to the resurgence of issues of national identity and ethnic conflict (Winter and Teitelbaum 1998). It is hard to imagine that individual preference could prevail in the face of the political uncertainties generated by these trends. In countries with strong fundamentalist religious regimes fertility is still part of women's duty to the state. Yet at the same time individual preferences by women to undertake paid work in the face of few gender equity policies has led to some of the lowest birth rates of all time in Italy and Germany, for example (McDonald 1997).

How, then, does institutional change proceed in relation to the population? It is at the same time evolutionary and pragmatic, the result of both struggle and of design, of politics and policies evolved by technical experts. One of the major mechanisms fuelling population change is the transformation of relations between men and women. Not only are women aware of the critical link between their autonomy and their reproductive futures, that they are central actors in shaping the population. United Nations policy now accepts that educating women in the developing world, for instance, is central to lowering fertility, although this position is contested (Knodel and Jones 1996). Cross-country econometric studies show that an extra year of schooling for girls reduces fertility rates by about 5–10 per cent. Universal female enrolment over the next fifteen years is viewed by the United Nations as a highly desirable outcome, one which can be achieved with political will and determination (United Nations Development Program 1995: 110–111). Cynics might wonder why educating girls for fertility decline seems more compelling than educating girls for their own benefit.

Should we attempt to redesign the population, to demand an Australian population policy as we approach the twenty-first century? As Geoffrey McNicholl has argued, population policies are virtually non-existent in industrialised countries with slow rates of population growth. This he believes is partly due to the compartmentalisation of political interests related to population growth so that, for example, debates about reproduction are unrelated to sensitive debates about immigration or environment. Equally the three narratives described above occupy different discursive realms, different policy arenas: they rarely meet. McNicholl further argues that modern democratic states find it virtually impossible to engage in discussions about long-term population objectives because the immediate policy implications have the potential to restrict the freedom of individuals and groups. This tendency to relegate population issues to 'being a byproduct of all our other decisions' is, he claims. 'bizarre helplessness' (McNicholl 1995: 111).

In Australia such reticence has not always been the case. As in other countries whose fertility began to decline in the late nineteenth century, Australia's leaders first responded with moral fervour and pronatalist policies. As in other countries, these were largely ineffective; their impact overwhelmed by antinatalist consequences of other policies in associated domains, such as education, which were not seen to have a relevance to population (Johansson 1991). But the fact that the policies were not effective does not negate the fact that population size was seen as an issue of major concern, and a large increase in the white population a 'keystone of a national policy of defence and development' (Grimshaw et al. 1994: 207). Even in mid-century, works such as *Women and Children First: An outline for a population policy for Australia* (Wallace 1946) advocated a higher fertility rate for Australian women of British or Nordic 'stock' whilst rejecting broader immigration initiatives. 'White Australia' underpinned Wallace's ideal society.

Recently the fear of an ageing population and declining fertility has raised the spectre of a 'culture of death', leading the then Australian Labor Party's spokesman on immigration affairs to propose the development of a formal population policy (McKenzie 1997). It is that fear of the burden of an ageing population which may well propel us towards such a policy. Peter McDonald points out that it is future fertility which will determine the extent of the ageing of the population. And future fertility, he argues, depends specifically on the levels of gender equity and intergenerational equity which prevail in a specific country (McDonald 1997). Countries with the lowest fertility rates in the world, such as Italy, Spain, Germany, Austria, Greece and Japan, are those which are socially conservative or familistic, provide work disincentives to married women, and unfriendly workplace conditions for women. In

English-speaking and Nordic countries, by contrast, where greater gender equity prevails, higher fertility rates are seen.

In Australia we have a mixed model of social service provision, as Deborah Mitchell argues in Chapter 2. Some institutions support a notion of equality between the sexes (education and the labour market, for instance), while others (family and industrial relations and the tax-transfer system) hark back to the male-breadwinner model. A first step towards a population policy demands coherence in provision of service and entitlements, some recognition that women want access to both paid work in family-friendly workplaces and to the choice to bear children.

But is this the narrative we wish to prevail – one which has certain resonances with the 'populate or perish' slogans of mid-century? In a context of lower fertility globally we may expect to see a resurgence of pronatalist policies, perhaps attempts to limit access to medical abortion, or to paid employment for women with children. My aim here is not pronatalist – rather a concern that women who wish to undertake paid work and to have children should be offered compatible policies rather than mixed messages from a fragmented and often contradictory policy arena. Australia could equally well avoid an ageing population by encouraging significant levels of immigration of younger people. There are several paths emerging, paths which will have quite different political and gendered consequences, some of which are more politically sensitive than others. Echoes of the discursive imprint of 'race suicide' are still heard: the shadow of the 'selfish middle-class woman' neglecting her duty, is still occasionally recuperated. It is time to re-examine the varied narratives of population and to write another drawing upon history, demography and public policy. A wide public debate amongst demographers, social policy makers and representatives of women's groups might well begin to tell us a new story. Such a rich narrative of population might very well shape the twenty-first century in new and exciting ways.

Notes

1 However, as McNicholl points out, if one looks far enough for an explanation, one finds aspects of beliefs and ideologies. In relation to Western capitalism, for example, one could cite the importance of the protestant work ethic as an explanatory device.

2 Some also refer to the fertility transition or population decline in a similar manner. Both are part of the vast social transformation known as the demographic transition, that period in which high fertility and high mortality were replaced by low fertility and low mortality.

3 Interestingly, biological arguments still constitute an element of the debate today. Recently medical science has claimed that men's sperm count is declining due, perhaps, to the increasing amount of oestrogen in the environment which is passed to male babies in the womb.

4 Foucault suggests that the 'hysterization of women', the thorough medicalisation of their bodies and their sex, was carried out as part of population management, as was the 'socialization of procreative behaviour' (1978: 104–105).

CHAPTER 10

Treating Ourselves to a Republic

Chilla Bulbeck

Introduction[1]

On 7 June 1995, the then Prime Minister, Paul Keating, unveiled his proposals for an Australian republic in Parliament. The Prime Minister focussed on an Australian head of state ('Each and every Australian should be able to aspire to be our head of state'), whose powers would be similar to those of the Governor-General, and who would be elected by a two-thirds majority of a joint sitting of both houses of parliament. These proposals would be put to Australians in a referendum in 1998 or 1999, following 'extensive consultations with the people of Australia'. A Constitutional Convention was proposed the following night by the then Leader of the Opposition, John Howard, who became the Prime Minister in 1996.

Besides unnamed members of the public, of the fourteen people who spoke on the two Australian Broadcasting Commission programs dedicated to this debate (7 and 8 June 1995), five were women. The academic lawyer Professor Cheryl Saunders claimed that the head of state's powers should be spelled out. The political historian Dr Helen Irving called for 'indicative referenda'[2] as a way of gauging people's responses to various constitutional questions. Pat Turner, from the Aboriginal and Torres Strait Islander Commission (ATSIC) and a member of the Constitutional Centenary Foundation, suggested nation-wide consultations instead of indicative referenda. She also stated that the Constitution should have a preamble recognising Australia's history and the status of indigenous people. The then leader of the Australian Democrats, Senator Cheryl Kernot, argued for a people's petition of 20,000 to 40,000 signatures, through which a short-list of candidates could be put to parliament, the head of state then elected in the manner

Keating had proposed (*Canberra Times* 13 March 1995). Professor Mary Kalantzis stated that 'if these dull depressing men lead the debate we haven't got a hope'. Instead, we need to 'harness the energies' of indigenous and immigrant communities and their 'sense of vision of where we might go'. Kalantzis recommended a series of conventions to achieve dialogue.

Several of the female commentators referred to the need to recognise the diversity of Australian culture and people in the republican process. Most also called for a more participatory and multi-layered passage along the republican road than that envisaged by the two male political leaders. Generally speaking, too, the arguments put by these women were not picked up for further comment, either by the compere, Paul Lyneham, or the male speakers. Thus Kernot's proposal for popular involvement in choosing a head of state was not put to Keating or any other speaker.[3] The debate over consultation continued to be framed in terms of a referendum or a people's convention, although Irving's proposal for indicative referenda 'attracted widespread interest at the Constitutional Centenary Foundation conference in May 1995' (Saunders 1996: 3).

Howard's proposal for a ten-day people's convention on the Constitution was legislated in August 1997 and held in February 1998. The Constitutional Convention comprised 152 delegates, of whom 76 were appointed by the government (including 40 federal and state parliamentarians) and 76 were elected on the basis of the population in each State. There were a number of young people and seven indigenous Australians while 35 per cent were women (*Weekend Australian* 14–15 February 1998: 20). As the first Aboriginal magistrate in Australia, Pat O'Shane, said, 'There is an obvious sweetness about being here, given that neither women nor Aborigines were allowed to participate in the Constitutional Convention of a century ago' (*Weekend Australian* 7–8 February 1998: 33). On its first day the Convention adopted gender balance in its own proceedings (Mary Kelly, 'Women for a Just Republic' posting to ausfem-polnet@postoffice.utas.edu.au).

The original proposal that the convention was to consider not only the republic, but also four-year fixed parliamentary terms, a bill of rights, Aboriginal reconciliation and other constitutional issues was reduced almost entirely to consideration of the Australian head of state and a republican form of government. Indeed the Constitutional Convention did not even form the 'clear majority' the Prime Minister had demanded before a republican model would be put to a referendum. The proposal 'That this convention supports the adoption of a republican system of government on the bipartisan appointment model in preference to there being no changes to the Constitution' was carried with 73 voting yes, 57 no and 22 abstaining (*Weekend Australian* 14–15 February 1998:

18). The Prime Minister decided that this 'clear view' justified him in taking the proposal to a referendum (*Weekend Australian* 14–15 February 1998: 17). The Convention voted that gender and community diversity were issues to be taken into account in the composition of the committee responsible for shortlisting the presidential candidates (Marian Sawer, posting to ausfem-polnet@postoffice.utas.edu.au, 14 February 1998).

Discussion of broader issues like Aboriginal reconciliation and a bill of rights found their way into proposals for a new preamble to the Constitution. However the preamble was 'not to be used to interpret any other provisions of the Constitution' (Mary Kelly, ausfem-polnet@postoffice.utas.edu.au, posting 19 February 1998); in effect, it was not to have any legal force. The Convention supported a preamble which should acknowledge 'original indigenous occupation and the recognition of cultural diversity, environment and the system of democracy' (*Weekend Australian* 14–15 February 1998: 18). However, a proposal that the 'equality of women and men' be included in the preamble was rejected (Marian Sawer, posting to ausfem-polnet@postoffice.utas.edu.au, 14 February 1998). Instead the Convention accepted that 'gender equality be considered [later] by parliament for inclusion' along with equality of all people before the law and recognition that indigenous Australians have continuing rights by virtue of their status as Australia's indigenous people. While being unable to stomach the equality of men and women, the Convention did vote by a majority that if the republic referendum was successful, a two-thirds elected convention should be held within five years to consider a number of further issues, including the rights and responsibilities of citizenship, a Commonwealth environmental power, proportional representation and equal representation of men and women in parliament (Marian Sawer, posting to ausfem-polnet@postoffice.utas.edu.au, 14 February 1998).

A number of women who participated in the Constitutional Convention met on 29 and 30 January 1998 for a Women's Constitutional Convention, organised by Australian Women Lawyers, the Constitutional Centenary Foundation (ACT Chapter), the National Women's Justice Coalition, the Women's Electoral Lobby, Women into Politics and the YWCA of Australia. The Women's Constitutional Convention reached a majority position that Australia should become a republic in which constitutional changes include 'full recognition of Indigenous Australians'; 'gender equity' in the processes and outcomes of constitutional change; 'respect for diversity, including cultural, religious and sexual diversity' and 'the need to ensure that social cohesion, political stability and our democratic culture are promoted'. This Convention felt that a new preamble should, *inter alia*, acknowledge Aboriginal and Torres Strait Islander occupation, rights and culture; include a statement of regret for past injustices; affirm Australia's multicultural society and commitment to equality, including between men and women and racial equality. The Convention also recommended civic education and a constitutional bill of rights to protect substantive equality for women, to contain special measures to address women's inequalities and recognise rights in relation to sexual orientation and education ('Outcomes', posted to http://www.peug.org.au/other/wel/issues/constit/index.htm). How were these broad claims voiced in the Women's Constitutional Convention narrowed and cut to fit the less visionary cloth of the Constitutional Convention which succeeded it?

Carole Pateman claims that women in the political sphere are required to be 'indistinguishable' from men in politics, that they are forced to don the 'political lion skin', 'mane and all' (1989: 6, 14). In terms of the republican debate, however, it would appear that women's political speech is different, but at a cost: women's voices are there in the republican debate, but they are marginalised, both in terms of numbers[4] and lack of integration into men's speech. Male citizenship and nation-building is normative; women's politics is subordinate. The differences which marginalise women's voices can be captured in a different notion of citizenship, focussing more on connection and protection than individual self-interest and rights.

Women's difference is not only from men, but also from each other. Along with other female commentators, I argue that to meaningfully accommodate the differences between women, the new Australian republic must be imagined as a process rather than an accomplishment, as 'a discourse of projection' (Morris 1993: 154) which accepts that 'compromise and negotiated outcomes' will be required because of people's differences (Cox 1995: 61). In this process, women and men will hammer out complex deals which understand both rights and responsibilities, both independence and connectedness, both similarities and differences. I use the concept of a treaty to contrast this vision with the minimalist constitutional changes which form the generally agreed agenda for 2001. Australian women's experiences in suffrage and femocracy provide a ground from which we might consider their voices in the republicanism debate.

Suffragists and femocrats

Suffrage, won at the turn of the century[5], extended a male public right to women. Even so, for some campaigners, suffrage was understood in terms of women's difference: newly enfranchised women believed they might 'sow the seed now of the sort of civilization women of all countries dream about' (Lake 1994a: 32). The ways in which women have sought to stretch the meaning of citizenship to encompass their particular concerns for bodily autonomy in relation to health, reproductive autonomy and freedom from violence are discussed by Mackinnon and Coltheart in the preceding chapters of this volume. However, women's struggle for rights peculiar to their needs – for female bodily integrity – has made little headway, especially when compared to the gains made in education and income, for example. Thus Australia apparently remains one of the most violent countries in the world.[6]

Femocrats have also had more success in achieving an extension of men's rights to women than they have had in redefining rights and citizenship to encompass women's needs. It is possible that Australian feminism gave the world the term 'femocracy' (Eisenstein 1991: 12), a term which combines feminist, bureaucrat and aristocrat (or a position of influence) (Eisenstein 1996: 69). Thus the femocrat is appointed to a senior position within the bureaucracy on the basis of her expertise in advising governments on how to meet the special needs of women.

The success of femocracy in Australia has been attributed to a combination of 'representative bureaucracy', a commitment to a 'fair go' and pragmatism (Eisenstein 1996: 3–8; Sawer 1993: 3). Representative bureaucracy means that segments of the population expect their interests to be expressed in the state, for example in the Industrial Commission or an Office of Multicultural Affairs. Thus former femocrat Sara Dowse notes, 'When I want something done I look to just that arena [the state]. My expectations are low, but my directions are clear' (in Leech 1994: 85). The notion of a 'fair go' is an Australian vernacular (and limited) translation of 'liberty, equality, fraternity', an expression of antipodean egalitarianism. The pervasiveness of this rhetoric is suggested by the early suffrage victory for women, the development of industrial arbitration (Sawer 1993: 2–3) and debates in New South Wales Parliament early this century concerning the right of single women to public service employment (Deacon 1993: 53–56). The ideal of a 'fair go' was enacted in equal opportunity legislation, strongly supported by 75 per cent of respondents in a 1987 survey in New South Wales, Victoria and South Australia (Sex Discrimination Commissioner 1992: 15). Femocracy is also an expression of 'pragmatic willingness to settle for half a loaf rather than no bread at all' (Anne Summers in Sawer 1993: 4) by avoiding the paralysis of abstract debates concerning the inherently patriarchal or capitalist nature of the state (Sawer 1993: 3, 5). Instead women rolled up their sleeves, entered the state and worked to achieve whatever reforms they could.

Femocrats have shown not only a pragmatism in working in the state for change but also an ability to trim their demands to prevailing ideological winds. Michael Pusey (1991) charts the invasion of top public service jobs in Canberra by economic rationalists or 'econocrats' (1991: 87), mostly young men trained in Australia's elite private schools and then in economics departments of the universities. Econocrats 'have no coherent concept of society (except as both protoplasm and shell for the market)' (1991: 173). In this climate, femocrats have been forced to become 'ideologically bilingual' as this is called in New Zealand, 'speaking one language (managerialism and economic rationalism) while thinking another' (Sawer 1993: 17). As an example, Te Ohu Whakatupu in the Ministry of Women's Affairs did not argue that job creation reduced unemployment but that establishing Maori women as business entrepreneurs would contribute to New Zealand's goal of developing an enterprise culture and export-oriented businesses (Tahi 1995: 71).

In Australia, femocrats have maintained some programs by focussing on the costs of non-intervention; for example, on the economic costs of domestic violence. Thus the Women's Policy Unit in Queensland commissioned a tellingly named study, 'Who Pays: The Economic Costs of Violence Against Women' (Mason 1994: 14), which discovered that the cost of domestic violence is $557 million per year and the cost of rape and sexual assault $63 million per year (Office of the Status of Women 1995: 31). Australian women have become a resource in free market restructuring; violence perpetrated against them is wrong not because it hurts and causes death but because it stops them participating in the workforce[7]; equal employment opportunity programs, re-training for the emerging multi-skilled occupations and mathematics for girls at school are no longer issues of equity but of efficient use of women as members of the labour force.

This tactic has imposed costs on Australian women, for example in the previous Labor government's attempt to force all women into the workforce and thus reduce the costs of welfare (Bryson 1994a: 297, 301) or to provide subsidised child-care and training only to women who are working or training to enter the workforce, rather than considering women's wishes to participate in sports or education for personal growth (Keating and Fatin 1992: 67, 79; Cox, 1995: 77). The costs of economic rationalism are becoming more visible under the present Coalition government which has cut the budgets for a number of government functions intended to meet the particular needs of women. Both James Walter (1996) and Eva Cox (1995) suggest that the needs of people as citizens and social members have become subsumed to the presumed needs of the economy.

Eva Cox discusses this issue through the notion of social capital, a neglected fourth kind of capital in addition to financial, physical and human capital (1995: 15–16). Social capital 'refers to the processes between people which establish networks, norms and social trust and facilitate co-ordination and co-operation for mutual benefit'. Economic rationalism – or 'fiscal anorexia' – starves social capital, for example, in the lack of time available to participate in groups which extend trust, because people are required to work longer hours in the name of productivity; expansion in home-based work, due to outsourcing production processes, which removes people from daily interaction with other workers; the development of a 'legitimate sense of injustice', which may become racist resentment when welfare spending is so far reduced that people lose any sense of economic security (Cox 1995: 50, 23, 39, 46, 65). According to Walter (1996: 69), the Labor Party lost the 1996 election because it lacked a comprehensive social vision and failed to address the daily conditions of people 'pinched hard by economic reform' and 'their efforts to make ends meet'. Citizenship, learned in civil society, reminds us 'we are social beings before we are either political or economic beings' (Walter 1996: 110). Let me turn, then, to the meanings of citizenship for women.

Ideas about citizenship

When I studied Politics I at the University in Adelaide in 1969, the message was that women were politically ignorant and inactive, lacking the capacity or inclination to be good voters because they relied on emotional responses to candidates rather than making rationally-calculated decisions about candidates' policies. More recently a discussion of citizenship and republicanism, contained in the report of the Civics Expert Group (1994a) chaired by Stuart MacIntyre, accepts that the blame lies not so much with women as the nature of political processes. Women, especially those engaged in home duties or part-time work, do indeed perceive themselves to know less about citizenship than men (Civics Expert Group 1994a: 134). But women 'especially' also report alienation from government (Civics Expert Group 1994b: 7). Parliament was described as 'two parties yelling at each other and calling each other names'; 'They can't come to a decision, they're just like children'; 'It's just that you feel so useless. You have no power' (Civics Expert Group 1994a: 21–22).

In 1992 focus group discussions with 224 women from 'middle Australia'[8] drew these comments:

> 90% of men in parliament are older men who have been brought up to be spoilt . . . they are a boys' club for men 40 plus and they think women should stay at home . . . any women they have there are tokens.

> [I]t's all superficial . . . they get into power and don't care about anything except winning votes (in Riley-Smith 1992: 61, 63).

Thus the indifference of women is not only ascribed to the ignorance of women but also to an understandable alienation from politics, from a 'boys' club' of 'children' 'calling each other names'. Responding to this analysis, the Civics Expert Group extended the definition of citizenship to include women's high levels of voluntary association involvement. They quoted with approval Marian Sawer's claim that women's 'ethic of care' 'should enrich our notions of citizenship' beyond rights to include 'the duty of care and concern for the vulnerable members of society' (Civics Expert Group, 1994a: 101).

But 'our' notions of citizenship which should be thus enriched seemed to be those of the writers of the report rather than the survey respondents who were asked what made a good citizen. The three main answers, covering two-thirds of the responses, were 'obey laws', 'care and consideration for others' (e.g. help others, treat others equally, live and let live), and community involvement and community activities (Civics Expert Group 1994a: 155). Citizenship was not so much about individual rights like a vote – mentioned by only five per cent of respondents (Civics Expert Group 1994a: 155) – but about consideration for others in the community. Respondents were more likely to come to an understanding of citizenship from their personal or community experiences (38 per cent of weighted responses) when compared with how they came to understand issues like the Constitution or the republic, where they relied more on formal sources like education, the media and books (85 per cent of weighted responses for the Constitution and 73 per cent for the republic, compared with 61 per cent for citizenship) (Civics Expert Group 1994a: 159). The small change of citizenship is enacted daily: 'We pause to let a car join a line of traffic, we walk a little further across a park to put our rubbish in a bin, enjoy giving at fund-raising functions' (Cox 1995: 80).

That citizenship involves both rights and obligations is captured by the franchise: adult citizens have both the right to vote and the obligation to do so (Walter 1996: 106). In the Application for Citizenship form (DILGEA 1992), three responsibilities and privileges are paired: enrol as a voter and receive the right to 'help elect Australia's governments'; obey the laws and receive the rights the law affords; defend Australia should the need arise and have the right to enlist in the defence forces and hold other government jobs. Overseas born Australians, who choose Australian citizenship rather than having it thrust upon them, reflect this pairing (Marsden 1993). While mundane matters like acquiring a passport, especially if a refugee, or not paying taxes were mentioned by some, a recurrent theme was more noble: 'my duty to give allegiance to the country which has given me the privilege of residency' (Edith Colbeck, from the Philippines in Marsden 1993: 8); 'I have the right and responsibility to this country' (Khan-Tuong Pham, from Vietnam in Marsden 1993: 10); 'in a sense lay down my life for the things I'm prepared to take from it' (Sim-Hee Neoh from Malaysia in Marsden 1993: 13).

The Republic – making a man out of Australia?

Frankly, when Paul Keating made his speech in Parliament about the British selling out Australia in the War, my heart stopped. I was profoundly moved . . . as though anything might be possible. It was heart-stopping in the same way as the ending of terra nullius and the destruction of the Berlin Wall. (Meaghan Morris 1993: 155–156)

Meaghan Morris goes on to note that her 'republican enthusiasm is not significantly feminist' (1993: 156). Even so, it appears that the then Prime Minister, Paul Keating, had a place for women in his vision of the Australian republic:

What won the [1993] election for Labor? The things we stood for won it for us. The social policies, Medicare, the rights of Aboriginal Australians, the rights of women, the central place of the arts, the republic. We won it with our vision for Australia. (Prime Minister Paul Keating at the ALP national conference 1994: 'Sensitive New-Age Keating', *Australian* 10 October 1994: 9)

This is typical of the former Prime Minister's statements, which collected together policies which accepted and celebrated diversity (economic, cultural, sexual and so on) as hallmarks of a good and unique Australian nation. Speaking of CEDAW's[9] praise of Australia's role, Keating stated that Australians should be proud of feminist advances: 'Nowhere in the image we present to the rest of the world – nor I suspect in our self-image – is there a reflection of that fact' (Curthoys and Muecke 1993: 186–188).

Why then did women not echo the voice that even Keating sought to give them? Instead of an easy echo, some women have taken the harder path of asserting their own and different ideas about what a republic might mean. While citizenship is about care and connection, the republic is consistently seen to be about 'greater independence' (as well as changes to the head of state) (Civics Expert Group 1994a: 152).[10] To the respondents in the Civics Expert Group's survey (1994a: 154), independence was both the chief advantage (22 per cent) and disadvantage (11 per cent) of a republic. In contrast, the women from 'middle Australia' 'require understanding: they want a feeling of empathy from the government, almost a sense of caring' (Riley-Smith 1992: 90). As I have argued elsewhere (Bulbeck 1993: 93), republicanism can make a man of Australia as it renounces the mother country and her female monarch, cuts the apron-strings of empire. Furthermore, the republic most commonly presented to Australians contrasts the possibility of a formal role, in which a politician is appointed by other politicians, with the domestic motif of the Royal Family (Connors 1996: 74). It is thus not surprising that men are more attracted to the idea of a republic than women.[11]

Similarly, in response to the suggestion that Australia should include in its republican constitution a bill of rights, some feminists argue that a bill of rights reflects individualist rights-based discourses rather than shared obligations and needs. Thus Carol Bacchi and Vicky Marquis (1994) suggest caution, based on Canadian women's decade-long experience with such a Charter of Rights.[12] Even though women intervened to affect the terms of the charter, it has still been used to limit women's access to rights and resources, rather than to expand them. As with legislation in the United States,[13] men have more often been litigants than women and this has led in some instances to 'equalising down', or the erosion of women's welfare gains. Indeed the litigants in Canada have mostly been people challenging the legality of breath-testing or perceived economic discrimination, producing comparative categories like 'fishpersons with long boats versus those with short boats' or 'steel pop can manufacturers versus aluminium pop can manufacturers' (Bacchi and Marquis 1994: 99). Bacchi and Marquis note that those with resources are best placed to launch expensive court cases and question that a privileged white male judiciary will even comprehend the interests of disadvantaged groups (1994: 102).

As a partial counterweight to this scenario, Rosemary Hunter (1996: 63–64) notes that the National Women's Justice Strategy provides funding for test cases of particular importance to women. As interveners or 'friends of the court', women's groups could place before judges issues of wider concern than those represented by two litigants. The Australian Law Reform Commission (ALRC), under the presidency of Justice Elizabeth Evatt and including Hilary Charlesworth, Regina Graycar and Jenny Morgan, produced the impressively feminist *Equality Before the Law: Women's Equality* (1994). Noting that every democratic industrialised society except Australia has legal protection of rights in one form or another (ALRC 1994: 58), the commission advocates an Equality Act, with entrenchment in the constitution as a long-term goal (ALRC 1994: 63). While agreeing that experience in Canada was initially uninspiring for women, the commission suggests inequality is now examined in context, thus addressing issues wider than formal equality (ALRC 1994: 65). Thus, as an example, instead of the formal equality of equal distribution upon divorce of resources to the partners of a marriage, if it can be shown that marriage systematically disadvantages women and advantages men, an unequal distribution of resources following divorce may be a more equal outcome. This notion of equality of result, rather than input or formal equality (Mahoney 1993) has been given some legitimacy in Canada since the Andrews case in 1989.

The concerns of Bacchi and Marquis relate to the historically limited nature of a legal rights rhetoric in the face of women's systemic inequality and positional difference. The law has been inept at seeing system-wide discrimination or oppressive structures, focussing as it does on the individual claimant and his (or, with more difficulty, her) bundle of individual rights, like freedom of speech, freedom to make contracts and so on. Thus so-called 'first generation' political and civil rights fit more neatly into legalistic discourse than second-generation economic and social rights, such as rights to freedom from poverty or to participate in the cultural life of one's nation. Bacchi and Marquis are also concerned that a legal discourse designed with men in mind cannot be readily adapted to the needs of women. For example, surveys of Australian women consistently report that sexual violence is their paramount concern.[14] However, Justice Evatt's inquiry advocated that 'violence is an integral part of the inequality of women in Australia' (ALRC 1994: 71) and this should be represented in the Equality Act. A minority report went even further, advocating an Equality Act specifically for women, which would also allow women to challenge private relations (ALRC 1994: 333–334).

Women are speaking about 'their' republic, 'their' rights, 'their' view of citizenship as encompassing both caring and independence, even if they are not always heard by the men in power. Are women also effectively speaking about how to accommodate their differences from each other?

The Hard Yakka Republic: dealing with women's differences

In 1994, Helen Irving (1994: 24) bemoaned a 'colonization of the republicanism debate by men', while Senator Cheryl Kernot (*Age*, 18 February 1995; Kernot 1996: 83–84) then leader of the Australian Democrats, claimed that 'the republican debate has failed to capture the imagination of women', largely because of its narrowness and alienation inspired by 'the two-party juggernaut' which failed to address issues like an environmental head of power in the Constitution, recognition of prior Aboriginal occupation and equity between women and men. Even so in August 1994, some 530 women 'crushed into a Sydney meeting' on the republic. They heard the young Aboriginal singer Brenda Webb call for a head of state who was 'native to this country and preferably a woman'. Chief executive of the legal firm Price Brent, Wendy McCarthy, wanted a head of state who used 'our words, our idiom'. Associate Professor Elaine Thompson claimed that in the past 'the fair go' had been limited to Anglo-Saxon males but 'a republic could be the beginning of a new era for Australian women'. The Aboriginal actor Lydia Miller hoped for a republic which could recognise and value the different cultures and individuals within Australia (*Sydney Morning Herald*, 5 August 1994: 2). For more than five hundred women, then, the republican dream is utopian or maximalist, rather than the minimalist position suggested by the Australian Republican Movement. Instead of asking, 'What is the least we need to do to make Australia a republic?' many women are asking, 'What do we need to do to make Australia a better place for women in all their diversity?' This requires a lot more than crossing out 'governor-general' wherever it appears in the Constitution and writing in 'president'.

Let me turn now to the issue of a multicultural multi-vocal republic. Just as undifferentiated women tend to be flattened into the male mould of worker-citizens, policies for 'different' women, women from Aboriginal, Torres Strait Islander or non-English-speaking backgrounds, are contained within policies for their menfolk. Thus in the *National Agenda for a Multicultural Australia* (Department of the Prime Minister 1988), the main document had only one table comparing men and women and only one mention was made of women in the text (Cox 1993: 26). In its 1991–2 budget, ATSIC allocated $1.3 million of its $158 million budget to the indigenous women's initiatives program. Of ATSIC's senior policy-makers in 1991, seven per cent were indigenous women, seventeen per cent were indigenous men, and 59 per cent were non-indigenous men (Moreton-Robinson 1992: 8, 6). In Community Development Employment Programs, administered by regional Aboriginal and Torres Strait Islander Councils, women represented only 20 per cent to 36 per cent of workers in most schemes, and as few as four per cent in some cases (Johnston 1991: 435).

But 'mainstream' femocrat agencies also neglect the differences among women. In Australia's Second Report on Implementing the United Nations Convention for the Elimination of Discrimination Against Women, paragraphs 95 to 130 ostensibly dealt with women of non-English speaking background, but women were not differentiated until paragraph 107 (Cox 1993: 39). The House of Representatives Standing Committee's inquiry *Half Way to Equal* (1992) only allocated non-English-speaking background women two out of 280 pages (Cox 1993: 26). Eva Cox summarised the government's response as an attempt to incorporate 'women with special needs' into the prevailing system: 'Nowhere is there any assumption that the system will change to accommodate women in their diversity' (Cox 1993: 39).

Beyond the femocracy, difficulties – indeed differences – over difference are also apparent. Aboriginal women writers like Jackie Huggins (1994: 74) suggest that 'colonialism is alive and well in the women's movement', differing little from former attitudes of missionaries' wives who sought to 'raise up' indigenous women to their levels of consciousness. Similarly, women of non-English-speaking background have noted a patronising attitude among Anglo-Australian feminists, who appear to believe only white women are not victims of barbaric practices or excessive commitment to families and so have an agency capable of resisting oppression (Martin 1991: 122; Vasta 1991: 163).

Black Australian Roberta Sykes criticises the exclusion of indigenous women from women's funding bodies because Aboriginal women do not think to work separately from men (Sykes 1990: 183). She also attacks white lesbians on the basis that they want to claim a lesbian culture 'so that it can be given the same status as Aboriginality, and training on the theme of lesbianism increased to the level of Aboriginal culture, where such training is available' (Sykes 1990: 184). Irene Moss, of Chinese descent and a former Race Discrimination Commissioner, has said that 'Australia must work through its identity crisis. It is an Asian nation with a European heritage'. The Aboriginal elder Shirley Smith (Mum Shirl) responded:

> This is not part of Asia, Race Discrimination Commissioner Irene Moss needs to understand this. Your continuing failure over the past 200 years to treat with us as equals will condemn you, all of you, as a community of thieves in the eyes of your children's children, and the rest of the world. We are your only true connection to this continent, to this entire region. We are the land, and we are here forever. (quoted in Curthoys 1993: 19)

On the other hand, Aboriginal magistrate Pat O'Shane commended Irene Moss's time as Federal Race Discrimination Commissioner: 'Aboriginal people feel emboldened by her stance and enormously grateful to her for highlighting those problem areas where, before NIRV [her National Inquiry into Racist Violence], few dared to tread' (1994: 2).

Paul Keating addressed the Global Cultural Diversity Conference in Sydney (26 April 1995) with the joint claim that we must make 'cultural diversity less of an impediment to human progress and more of a means to it' and that Australians must accept 'the basic principles of Australian society, including the rule of law'. Just prior to this announcement, Social Justice Commissioner Mick Dodson asserted that indigenous people needed social and economic rights more than political rights, and might be wary of a 'rule of law' which had just denied the women of Hindmarsh Island their freedom of expression and protection of their religion (*Australian* 13 February 1995). Following the election of the Coalition government and Pauline Hanson as the independent Member for Oxley in 1996, an intense debate has emerged concerning indigenous rights, racism and multiculturalism (see also Mackinnon, Chapter 9).

Thus a rainbow republic will be so much 'hard yakka'. How then might Australian women take up this challenge? Keating provided the beginnings of an answer himself. He suggested that we could not have comprehended the institutional changes required to produce a multi-cultural Australia out of the isolationist society of the 1950s. More significantly, 'we could not have conceived of the necessary changes in ourselves'. Whereas Keating thinks we have now arrived, feminists are more likely to claim that in the process of politics one never arrives (see, for example, Eva Cox's criticism of Prime Minister Bob Hawke's 'naive assumption' that consensus is possible (1995: 60)). Thus political citizenship is not pre-given, 'derived from blood or land, class or gender', but as 'a political identity' is a 'conversation piece', an ongoing process (Walter 1996: 108). While the conversations of citizenship are 'never static', neither are they only provisional, given that they derive from the sedimentation of material institutions and ideas from our past (Walter 1996: 108, 117).

Conclusion

The idea of growing a treaty, as opposed to the imposition of a revised Constitution or a bill of rights in the year 2001, refers to three issues which should preoccupy women in their 'institutional design' of a republic: a focus on process as well as goals, a focus on groups and sociality as well as individuals and independence, and an acceptance of the particularistic differences between concrete human beings rather than the construction of an abstract universal (but non-existent) self-interested actor. Instead of the political deals favoured by institutional design theorists (see the critique by Moira Gatens in Chapter 1), we need ongoing conversations and shifting coalitions. Aboriginal societies, more so than white nations, understand the journey as being at least as important as arrival. Mary Graham contrasts the attempt by Europeans to reach an ideal (which 'seems to put enormous pressure on people and their relationships') with Aboriginal commitment to 'growing peace' (you cannot make it) (in Kouwenberg 1993: 8). Her focus is on process not goals, on infinite games ('caring for the land') rather than finite games.

How might this treaty be grown? The Civics Expert Group[15] recommended 'education', meaning this to include both understanding how the system works and learning about the benefits of participation and opportunities for doing so (1994a: 92). The group focussed on schools as the main vehicles for education, followed by higher and other adult education, including information sources like the Electoral Commission, the Constitutional Centenary Foundation and service organisations like Rotary (1994a: 83–92). This focus on formal educational sites seems to neglect the fact that understandings of citizenship are renewed by

Australians among their friends and families. Civics education should be instilled in pubs and clubs and committees and associations where 'we learn the importance of connecting with others, and of responsibility', and where 'we find the networks that give life meaning' (Walter 1996: 109). The trust required to develop the tolerance needed to deal with conflicts and different interests is based on working together in 'civic' groups, voluntary associations like Rotary, parents and citizens' groups, environmental groups (Cox 1995: 17).

Like Walter and Cox, I have in mind something much more pro-active, much more widespread, much more related to women's daily experiences than what is normally understood by civics education or what has hitherto passed for the republicanism debate. I am imagining that time be set aside in families, associations, factories and schools to debate issues and produce concrete results: for example letters to newspaper editors, a new anthem or flag, proposals for the head of state or a revised (but provisional) constitution. What would be the benefits and costs of institutionalising the annually renewed demands for equal pay, child care, freedom from bodily violation and so on within a treaty? Rather than a fixed constitution, should Australians 'grow' their treaty, changing or confirming it in a national referendum every generation? These grassroots discussions, not only envisaged by Malcolm Turnbull but apparently already happening,[16] can flow into wider rivers through the channels of consultation proposed by female commentators on the republicanism debate: indicative referenda, constitutional conventions and petitions to parliament. As Lisa Hill says, 'the strength of the constitution is upheld by the integrity of an active, factious, fractious and equally endowed citizenry' (1996: 593). This is not to deny that my vision is utopian, if not visionary: 'Popular debates, in which people in all walks of life talk and argue on an everyday basis about a complex shared concern, are quite rare' (Morris 1993: 164).[17]

Australians will need to meet sometimes in their homes and sometimes beyond them. As Berenice Johnson Reagon put it, 'home', like nationalism, is a nurturing but 'little barred room' (1983: 358). It enables identity-formation and establishes shared interests. But it also produces xenophobia. For a long time, middle-class white feminists thought all-women gatherings were home gatherings until some 'other' women – women of colour, women with disabilities, working-class women and so on – sought entrance. This proved that what women do together is coalition work and not nurturing work: 'Coalition work is not work done in your home. Coalition work has to be done in the streets. And it is some of the most dangerous work you can do' (Reagon 1983: 359).

Coalition work is the product of accepting differences between women as well as similarities. The differences demand that we recognise multiple and purposive alliances. The similarities make it possible to speak to each other at all, however fraught with misrecognition that process might be.

The good news for women with a pragmatic bent is that coalition work is done with the sleeves rolled up and the nose to the ground, not with the head in the clouds. It enables women to transform grandiose republican ideals into practical outcomes. Coalitions will require us to accept that to eliminate poverty means that the wealthy must give up some of their wealth; to reduce rape and domestic violence means that men must give up some of their notions of masculinity and male rights; to respect other cultures might mean learning another language and accepting different practices; to have a treaty means that we must all seek a balance between our rights and our responsibilities. A republican treaty, like citizenship, is not a 'magic pudding capable of providing benefits for whoever claims a slice' (Civics Expert Group 1994a: 15).

Given the vitriol of antagonisms noted above, is it possible to produce a set of goals which allows all women to see their needs expressed? Australian women have shown their capacity for 'ideological bilingualism' in the political sphere. They have demanded their needs both as carer-citizens and as worker-citizens. Australians, with their commitment to a welfare state and a fair go, are well placed to understand that connection is as necessary to humanity as independence. Indeed, our understanding of citizenship reveals this. Such understandings, however, are often seen to lie outside 'real' politics, as Lenore Coltheart's discussion of associative citizenship in this volume and Cox's (1995) analysis of social capital suggest.

Women's debate about republicanism must continue to assert that 'real' politics includes 'real' men and women in all their diversity. This means it will be an often anguished process of coalition-building. Women have already imagined a republic which breaches the minimalist boundaries that powerful white men have erected. They took that imagination to Canberra and hammered some aspects of it out in the Women's Constitutional Convention which met prior to the Constititional Convention. The women's convention was supported by a website which included recommended reading as well as papers presented to the delegates; women across Australia communicated with the delegates and each other through lists like ausfem-polnet. Although women delegates to the Constitutional Convention were unsuccessful in placing the word 'women' even in the preamble to the Constitution, they did win the right to fight another day. Resolutions were carried that 'gender equality be considered by parliament for inclusion' and that another two-thirds elected convention should be held within five years to consider wider issues, such as the meanings of citizenship and equal representation of men and women in parliament. Feminists are developing 'a specifically feminist republican model' (Irving 1996a: 97). Australian women have a history of 'conjunctive, not additive, pluralist politics – feminism *and* labour relations, feminism *and* immigration policy, feminism *and* human rights' (Morris 1993: 167) – in which they generate pro-feminist outcomes within the political context. In these ways, women usually enter the republicanism debate with 'at least three terms of discussion . . . in play' (Morris 1993: 163), that is as members of actual or potential coalitions:

> Connection and coalition are bound to sometimes painful structures of accountability to each other and to the worldly hope for freedom and justice. If they are not so bound, connection and coalition disintegrate in orgies of moralism. (Haraway 1997: 47)

Notes

1 My thanks to Carol Bacchi and Marilyn Lake for their helpful dialogue in writing an earlier version of this chapter; and to the other contributors to this volume who provided crucial suggestions for the development of my ideas, especially Lenore Coltheart, Joan Eveline and Alison Mackinnon who read earlier drafts of this chapter.

2 By 'indicative referenda' Irving meant they would not be binding on the government but would indicate national opinion.

3 Although he later stated 'I don't necessarily believe that the Parliament is so bereft of view or acknowledgement [sic] that there has to be some extra process of nomination' (*Weekend Australian* 10–11 June 1995: 21).

4 In the clippings file held by the Department of Politics, Research School of Social Sciences, Australian National University, for December 1994 to May 1995, only four articles on republicanism reported the views of women: Professor Cheryl Saunders, Jocelynne Scutt, Helen Irving and Cheryl Kernot (*Age*, other details missing; *Age*, 18 February 1995; *Australian*, 14 March 1995: 15; *Canberra Times* 13 March 1995). Similarly, of the 85 articles indexed by the *Sydney Morning Herald* on the issue during 1994, only five reported the views of women.

5 And linked to women's contributions to the constitutional debates according to Irving (1996b: 42–45).

6 For example, see the National Committee on Violence (1990) and the 1989 International Crime Survey which discovered that Australian women reported the highest rate of overall sexual victimisation, including both sexual incidents and sexual assault. Of course, high reporting rates also indicate a willingness by women to claim that violence is unacceptable (Standing Committee on Social Issues 1993: xvii).

7 In Queensland the first government policy on violence against women released in 1992 (Office of the Status of Women 1992: 55) claimed that 'The Queensland Government will strive to realise a vision of a Queensland society in which women are empowered to participate actively and equally in all forms of social, economic and community life unimpeded by the incidence or threat of violence in their homes, on the streets, in residential, health or educational institutions or in their workplaces' (Women's Policy Unit 1992: 5).

8 Defined as having a personal income of $35,000 or less and household income of $60,000 or less.

9 CEDAW (the Committee for the Elimination of All Forms of Discrimination Against Women, a UN committee) acclaimed the women's budget statement provided by Australian femocrats 'as the most comprehensive breakdown of the gender effects of government activity anywhere in the world' (Sawer 1988/9: 18).

10 Forty-six per cent of respondents answered in terms of 'self-reliance', 'maturity', 'cut ties with Britain', while 31% referred to changes in the head of state and 11% to symbolic changes like the flag, national anthem and the currency (Civics Expert Group 1994a: 152).

11 In March 1995, 34% of men polled and 22% of women were strongly in favour of a republic, while 51% of men and 44% of women were in favour. In June 1997, 45% of women and 54% of men were in favour of a republic (*Australian* 15 March 1995: 6; Newspoll reported in the *Australian* 2 July 1997). As age is a significant variable (24% of those over 50, as opposed to 30% of those from 18 to 34 years old being strongly in favour of a republic), this may contribute to the gender gap (*Australian* 15 March 1995: 6).

12 The bill of rights in Canada and in New Zealand reproduces in essence Article 26 of the United Nations International Covenant on Civil and Political Rights which disallows discrimination on the basis of colour, race, ethnic or national origins, sex, marital status, religious or ethical belief, but allows measures in good faith to assist or advance persons disadvantaged for these reasons (Electoral and Administrative Review Commission 1992: 153).

13 Kathleen Lahey (1987) draws a parallel between equality claims brought by black and female litigants. From 1868 to 1911 only 28 of the 604 cases heard by the United States Supreme Court related to black interests and blacks lost 22 of those cases. In the 65 years following legal emancipation of slaves, 99% of cases reproduced and reinforced racial privilege enjoyed by non-blacks (Lahey 1987: 74). Similarly male complainants were making and winning ten times as many equality claims as women (Lahey 1987: 82).

14 For example, in the Australian Council of Women's (1995: 33) consultations, the issue of violence was reported by 40% of respondents in one survey (N=725).

15 Members of the group were the historian, Professor Stuart MacIntyre, Dr Ken Boston, director-general of the New South Wales Department of School Education, and Susan Pascoe, consulting chair (Policy) of the Catholic Education Office, Melbourne. They were to 'provide the government with a strategic plan for a non-partisan program of public education and informa-tion on the Australian system of government, the Australian constitution, citizenship and other civic issues'; then to monitor the implementation of the program and contribute to its evaluation.

16 On the ABC programs discussing republicanism (referred to in my introductory paragraphs) Malcolm Turnbull, the chair of the Australian Republican Movement (ARM), agreed with the need to 'promote discussion at the grassroots of society'. He noted that community groups sent dozens of requests for materials to the ARM every month. He proposed government-funded factual and objective material, which could be supplemented by organisations making their own cases.

17 Who goes on to suggest that the debates surrounding Mabo are/were one of these rare events, 'a vast and intricate mesh' (Morris 1993: 164).

References

ABS 1980 *Labour Force Status and Other Characteristics of Families*, Cat. No. 6224.0, Canberra.

ABS 1993a *Women in Australia*, Cat. No. 4113.0, Canberra.

ABS 1993b *How Australians Use Their Time*, Cat. No. 4153.0, Canberra.

ABS 1994a *Focus on Families: Demographics and family formation*, Cat. No. 4420.0, Canberra.

ABS 1994b *Labour Force Status and Other Characteristics of Families*, Cat. No. 6224.0, Canberra.

ABS 1994c *Focus on Families: Education and employment*, Cat. No 4421.0, Canberra.

ABS 1994d *Focus on Families: Demographics and family responsibilities*, Cat. No. 4422.0, Canberra.

ABS 1994e *Australian Women's Year Book*, Cat. No. 4124.0, Canberra.

ABS 1995a *The Labour Force Australia July 1995*, Cat. No. 6203.0, Canberra.

ABS 1995b *Renters in Australia 1994*, Cat. No. 4138.0, Canberra.

ABS 1995c *Focus on Families: Income and housing*, Cat. No. 4424.0, Canberra.

ABS 1995d *Australian Social Trends*, Cat. No. 4102.0, Canberra.

Acker, J. 1989 *Doing Comparable Worth: Gender, class and pay equity*, Philadelphia: Temple University Press.

Adler, L. 1979 *A L'aube du Féminisme: Les premières journalistes (1830–1850)*, Paris: Payot.

Affirmative Action Agency 1990 *Taking Steps: Employers' progress in affirmative action*, Canberra: Australian Government Publishing Service.

Affirmative Action Agency 1992a *Annual Reports (1991–92)*, Canberra: Australian Government Publishing Service.

Affirmative Action Agency 1992b *The Final Report of the Effectiveness Review of the Affirmative Action (Equal Employment Opportunity for Women) Act 1986*, Canberra: Australian Government Publishing Service.

Affirmative Action Agency 1995 *Annual Reports (1994–95)*, Canberra: Australian Government Publishing Service.

Allen, K. 1996 'The Politics of Survival: The effects of gendered institutional practices in Australian universities', unpublished Ph.D. thesis, Adelaide: Flinders University.

Allen, J., Ferres, K. and Reekie G. 1992 'Sexual Patternings and Sexual Cultures: An Australian and comparative regional study 1870–1970', in *Australian Feminist Studies* 15.

Anderson, L. S., Chiricos, T. G. and Waldo, G. P. 1977 'Formal and Informal Sanctions: A comparison of deterrent effects', *Social Problems* 25: 103–114.

Anderton, N. and Lloyd, C. 1991 *Housing Australia: An analysis of the 1986 census*, AGPS, Canberra.

Australian Council for Women 1995 'Report on Consultations with Non-Government Organisations and Australian Women February to September 1994', Canberra: Office of the Status of Women, Prime Minister and Cabinet.

Australian Institute of Health and Welfare 1994 *Public Housing in Australia*, AIH&W, Canberra.

Australian Law Reform Commission (ALRC) 1994 *Equality Before the Law: Women's equality*, Sydney: Commonwealth of Australia.

Australian Urban and Regional Development Review 1995a *Creating Jobs: Where they are needed, when they count*, Discussion Paper No. 3, Canberra.

Australian Urban and Regional Development Review 1995b *Urban Australia: Trends and prospects*, Research Report, No. 2, Canberra.

Australian Urban and Regional Development Review 1995c *Investing in Infrastructure*, Proceedings of a Conference organised by Australian Urban and Regional Development Review, August 1994, Workshop Papers No. 5, Canberra.

Ayres, I. and Braithwaite, J. 1992 *Responsive Regulation: Transcending the deregulation debate*, New York: Oxford University Press.

Bacchi, C. 1991a 'Survey Examines Staff and Student Attitudes to Affirmative Action', *Lumen*, University of Adelaide magazine, 20(2): 8–11.

Bacchi, C. 1991b 'Every Man for Himself', *Lumen*, University of Adelaide magazine, 20(5): 3, 7.

Bacchi, C. 1991c 'Discrimination and Justice', *Lumen*, University of Adelaide magazine, 20(6): 3, 6.

Bacchi, C. 1992 'Sex on Campus – Where Does "Consent" End and Harassment Begin?' *Australian Universities' Review*, 35 (1): 31–37.

Bacchi, C. 1993 'The Brick Wall: Why so few women become senior academics', *Australian Universities' Review*, 36(1): 36–41.

Bacchi, C. 1994a '"Consent" or "Coercion"? Removing conflict of interest from staff–student relations', *Australian Universities' Review*, 37(2): 55–61.

Bacchi, C. 1994b *From Antidiscrimination to Managing Diversity: How did we get here from there?* unpublished paper, Department of Political Science, Research School of Social Sciences, Australian National University, Canberra.

Bacchi, C. 1996 *The Politics of Affirmative Action: 'Women', equality and category politics*. London: Sage.

Bacchi, C. and Jose, J. 1994 'Dealing with Sexual Harassment: Persuade, discipline, or punish?' *Australian Journal of Law and Society*, 10: 1–14.

Bacchi, C. and Marquis, V. 1994 'Women and the Republic: "Rights" and wrongs', *Australian Feminist Studies*, 19, 93–113.

Baldock, C. 1988 'Public Policies and the Paid Work of Women', in Baldock, C. and Cass, B. (eds) *Women, Social Welfare and the State*, Sydney: Allen & Unwin: 20–53.

Baldock, C. and Cass, B. (eds) 1988 *Women, Social Welfare and the State in Australia*, Sydney: Allen & Unwin.

Baldwin, P. 1995 *Beyond the Safety Net: The future of social security*, mimeo, Canberra: Parliament House.

Barclay, L., Johns L., Kennedy P. and Power K. 1991 *Speaking of Housing: A report on a consultation with Victorian women on housing for the Minister for Planning and Housing*, Joint Project by the Ministerial Advisory Committee on Women and Housing and Women in Supportive Housing (WISH), Melbourne, Victoria.

Barrett, M. 1980 *Women's Oppression Today*, London: Verso.

Barrett, M. and McIntosh, M. 1982 'The Family Wage', in Whitelegg, M. et al. (eds) *The Changing Experience of Women*, Oxford: Blackwell: 71–87.

Baxter, J. 1993 *Work at Home: The domestic division of labour*, Brisbane: University of Queensland Press.

Baxter, J. 1994 'Why Don't Men Do More Housework?': 37–39. *Eureka Street* 4 (9).

Baxter J., 1997 'Gender Equality and Participaton in Housework: Cross-national perspective', *Journal of Comparative Family Studies* 28 (3): 220–247.

Baxter, J., Gibson, D. with Lynch-Blosse, M. 1990, *Double Take: The links between paid and unpaid work*, Canberra: Australian Government Publishing Service.

Baxter, J. and Western, M. 1998 'Satisfaction with Housework: Examining the paradox', *Sociology* 32(1): 101–120.

Beechey, V. and Perkins, T. 1987 *A Matter of Hours*, Cambridge: Polity.

Beggs, J. and Chapman, B. 1988 'The Foregone Earnings from Child Rearing in Australia', *Centre For Economic Policy Research, Discussion Paper*, Australian National University, Canberra.

Bem, S. and Bem, D. 1973 'Does Sex-Biased Advertising "Aid and Abet" Sex Discrimination?' *Journal of Applied Psychology* 3 (6).

Benhabib, S. 1987 'The Generalised and the Concrete Other', *Feminism as Critique*, S. Benhabib and D. Cornell (eds), Minneapolis: University of Minnesota Press.

Bennett, L. 1995 'Women and Enterprise Bargaining: The legal and institutional framework', in Thornton, M. (ed.), *Public and Private: Feminist legal debates*, Melbourne: Oxford University Press.

Berk, Sarah Fenstermaker 1985 *The Gender Factory*, New York: Plenum Press.

Bernhardt, E. 1993 'Changing Family Ties, Women's Position, and Low Fertility', in Nora Federici, Karen Oppenheim Mason and Sølvi Sogner (eds), *Women's Position and Demographic Change*, Oxford: Clarendon Press.

Bittman, M. 1991 *Juggling Time: How Australian families use time*, Canberra: Australian Government Publishing Service.

Bittman, M. 1995 'Changes at the Heart of Family Households', *Family Matters* 40 (Autumn): 10–15.

Blackmore, J. 1993 'Towards a "Post Masculinist" Institutional Politics', in Baker, D. and Fogarty, M. (eds), *A Gendered Culture: Educational management in the nineties*. Melbourne: Victoria University of Technology: 75–89.

Blair, S. L. and Johnson, M. P. 1992 'Wives' Perceptions of the Fairness of the Division of Household Labor: The intersection of housework and ideology', *Journal of Marriage and the Family* 54 August: 570–581.

Blandy, R. 1994, 'Why an Ageing Australia Needs to Support Bigger Families', *Australian* December 6.

Blau, F. D. and Ferber, M. A., 1990 *Women's Work, Women's Lives: A comparative economic perspective*, Washington: National Bureau of Economic Research Working Paper No. 3447.

Bloch, Ruth 1987, 'The Gendered Meanings of Virtue in Revolutionary America' *Signs* 13 (1): 37–58.

Boggiano, A. K., Barrett, M., Weiher, A. W., McLelland, G. H. and Lusk, C. M. 1987 'Use of the Maximal-Operant Principle to Motivate Children's Intrinsic Interest', *Journal of Personality and Social Psychology* 53: 866–879.

Bomford, J. 1993 *'That Dangerous and Persuasive Woman': Vida Goldstein*, Melbourne: Melbourne University Press.

Bordin, R. 1981 *Women and Temperance: The quest for power and liberty, 1873–1900*, Philadelphia Penn.: Temple University Press.

Bosanquet, T. 1927 *Harriet Martineau: An essay in comprehension*, London: Frederick Etchells & Hugh Macdonald.

Bradley, H. 1989 *Men's Work, Women's Work*, Cambridge: Polity.

Braithwaite, J. 1989 *Crime, Shame and Reintegration*, Cambridge: Cambridge University Press.

Braithwaite, V. 1992 *First steps: Business reactions to implementing the affirmative action act. Report to the Affirmative Action Agency*, Canberra: Research School of Social Sciences, Australian National University.

Braithwaite, V. 1993 'The Australian Government's Affirmative Action Legislation: Achieving social change through human resource management', *Law and Policy* 15: 327–354. (A version of this paper appears as Administration, Compliance and Governability Program Working Paper No. 11).

Braithwaite, V. 1994 'Beyond Rokeach's Equality-Freedom Model: Two dimensional values in a one dimensional world', *Journal of Social Issues* 50: 67–94.

Braithwaite, V. 1994 'EEO and HRM: Compatible positions, different interests', in Davis, E. M. and Pratt, V. (eds), *Making the Link 5: Affirmative action and industrial relations*, Canberra: Australian Government Publishing Service.

Braithwaite, V. 1995 'Games of Engagement: Postures within the regulatory community', *Law and Policy* 17: 225–255 (A version of this paper appears as Administration, Compliance and Governability Program Working Paper No. 26).

Braithwaite, V. and Blamey, R. 1996 'Value Consensus and Difference: Compatible and complementary goals', (unpublished paper).

Braithwaite, V., Braithwaite, J., Gibson, D. and Makkai, T. 1994 'Regulatory Styles, Motivational Postures and Nursing Home Compliance', *Law and Policy* 16: 363–394 (A version of this paper appears as Administration, Compliance and Governability Program Working Paper No. 5).

Brant, Clare and Too, Yun Lee (eds) 1994 *Rethinking Sexual Harassment*, London: Pluto Press.

Brehm, S. S. and Brehm, J. W. 1981 *Psychological Reactance: A theory of freedom and control*, New York: Academic Press.

Brennan, D. 1994 *The Politics of Australian Child Care: From philanthropy to feminism*, Cambridge: Cambridge University Press.

Brennan, F. 1995, *One Land, One Nation*, Brisbane: University of Queensland Press.

Brenner, Johanna and Ramas M. 1984 'Rethinking Women's Oppression', *New Left Review* 144: 33–71.

Brett, Judy 1996, 'From Monarchy to Republic: Into the symbolic void?', in Hoorn and Goodman (eds) *Vox Reipublicae: Feminism and the republic, special edition of the Journal of Australian Studies*, Bundoora: La Trobe University Press.

Bryson, L. 1992 *Welfare and the State: Who benefits?* London: Macmillan.

Bryson, L. 1993 'Women Within a Gendered Management Culture', in D. Baker and M. Fogarty, M. (eds) *A Gendered Culture: Educational management in the nineties*, Melbourne: Victoria University of Technology, pp. 93–105.

Bryson, L. 1994a 'The Welfare State and Economic Adjustment', in Stephen Bell and Brian Head (eds) *State, Economy and Public Policy in Australia*, Melbourne: Oxford University Press.

Bryson, L. 1994b *Dealing With a Changing Work Environment: The issue of sexual harassment in the ADF (Australian Defence Forces)*, Report prepared for the Assistant Chief of Defence Force Personnel, Headquarters, Australian Defence Force, Canberra.

Bryson, L. 1994c 'Women, Paid Work and Social Policy' in *Australian Women: Contemporary feminist thought*, Melbourne: Oxford University Press, 179–193.

Bulbeck, C. 1993 'Republicanism and Post-Nationalism: What are the boys up to now?', in David Carter and Wayne Hudson (eds) *The Republicanism Debate*, Kensington: University of New South Wales Press.

Burton, C. 1991 *The Promise and the Price: The struggle for equal opportunity in women's employment*, Sydney: Allen & Unwin.

Burton, C. with Hag, R. and Thompson, G. 1987 *Women's Work: Pay equity and job evaluation in Australia*, AGPS: Canberra: Australian Government Publishing Service.

Butler, J. 1990 *Gender Trouble*, New York: Routledge.

Butler, J. 1993 *Bodies that Matter*, New York: Routledge.

Cady Stanton, Elizabeth 1898, *Eighty Years and More*, New York: Europe Publishing.

Calasanti, T. M. and Bailey, C. A. 1991 'Gender Inequality and the Division of Household Labor in the United States and Sweden: A socialist-feminist approach', *Social Problems* 38(1) February: 34–53.

Cass, B. 1986 'Women, Income Distribution and Housing Policy', *Journal of Australian Social Work* 39 (2) June: 5–14.

Cass, B. 1991 'The Housing Needs of Women and Children', Discussion Paper for The National Housing Strategy, Australian Government Publishing Service, Canberra.

Cass, B. 1993 'Sole Parent Family Policy in Australia: Income support and labour market issues', *New Zealand Social Policy Journal* (1) November: 3–16.

Cass, B. 1995 'Overturning the Male Breadwinner Model in the Australian Social Protection System', in P. Saunders and S. Shaver (eds), *Social Policy and the Challenges of Social Change*, Social Policy Research Centre Reports and Proceedings no. 122, University of New South Wales, Sydney.

Castleman, T., Allen, M., Bastalich, W. and Wright, P. 1995 *Limited Access: Women's disadvantage in higher education employment*, South Melbourne: NTEU.

Castles, F. 1985 *The Working Class and Welfare: Reflections on the political development of the welfare state in Australia and New Zealand, 1890–1980*, Wellington: Allen & Unwin.

Castles, F. and Mitchell, D. 1992 'Identifying Welfare State Regimes: The links between politics, instruments and outcomes', *Governance* 5, (1).

Chadeau, A. 1992 'What is Household Non-market Production Worth? *OECD Economic Studies* (18), Spring, Paris: 85–103.

Civics Expert Group 1994a *Whereas the People . . . : Civics and citizenship education*, Canberra: Australian Government Publishing Service,

Civics Expert Group 1994b *Whereas the People . . . : Civics and citizenship education*, Summary Report, Canberra: Australian Government Publishing Service.

Cockburn, C. 1983 *Brothers: Male dominance and technological change*, London: Pluto Press.

Cockburn, C. 1985 *Machinery of Dominance: Women, men and technical know-how*, London: Pluto Press.

Cockburn, C. 1991, *In the Way of Women: Men's resistance to sex equality in organizations*, London: Macmillan.

Cockburn, C. and Ormrod, S. 1993 *Gender and Technology in the Making*, London: Sage.

Coltrane, Scott and Ishi-Kuntz, M. 1992 'Men's Housework: A life course perspective', *Journal of Marriage and the Family* 54 February 43–57.

Commonwealth of Australia 1994 *Working Nation: White paper on employment and growth*, Australian Government Publishing Service, Canberra.

Commonwealth of Australia 1995 *Community and Nation*, Australian Government Publishing Service, Canberra.

Comte, A. 1851 *A General View of Positivism*, (trans. J. H. Bridges 1865), London: W. Reeves.

Connell, R. 1987 *Gender and Power*, Sydney: Allen & Unwin.

Connelly, M. and Kennedy P. 1994 'Must it be the Rest against the West', *Atlantic Monthly*, December.

Connors, J. 1996 'Betty Windsor and the Egg of Dukemburg: Men, women and the monarchy in 1954', in J. Hoorn and D. Goodman (eds) *Vox Reipublicae: Feminism and the republic*, special edition of the *Journal of Australian Studies*, Bundoora: La Trobe University Press.

Constance-Jones, E. E. 1913 *Girton College*, London: Adam & Charles Black.

Corcoran, P. 1983 *Before Marx: Socialism and communism in France, 1830–48*, New York: St Martins Press.

Coverman, Shelley 1985 'Explaining Husband's Participation in Domestic Labor', *Sociological Quarterly* 26(1): 81–97.

Cowan, Ruth Schwartz 1984 *More Work for Mother*, New York: Basic Books.

Cox, E. 1988 ' "Pater-Patria": Child rearing and the state', in Baldock, C. and Cass, B. (eds) *Women, Social Welfare and the State*, Allen & Unwin, Sydney: 190–204.

Cox, E. 1992 *Superfudge or Subterfuge? Options for equity*, Sydney: Women's Economic Think Tank.

Cox, E. 1993 'Policy Contest: Immigrant women on a flat playing field', *Australian Feminist Studies* 18: 25–48.

Cox, E. 1995 *A Truly Civil Society*, 1995 Boyer Lectures, Sydney: Australian Broadcasting Corporation.

Cullen, M. J. 1975 *The Statistical Movement in Early Victorian Britain: The foundations of empirical social research*, New York: Harper & Row.

Curthoys, A. 1993 'Feminism, Citizenship and National Identity', *Feminist Review* 44: 19–38.

Curthoys, A. and Muecke, S. 1993 'Australia, For Example', in W. Hudson and D. Carter (eds) *The Republicanism Debate*, Kensington: University of New South Wales Press.

Dahlerup, D. (ed.) 1990 *The Nordic BRYT–Project*, Final Report (May). Copenhagen: Nordic Council of Ministers.

Daly, Anne 1995 'Employment and Social Security for Aboriginal Women', in Edwards and Magarey (eds), *Women in a Restructuring Australia: Work and welfare*, Sydney: Allen & Unwin.

Davidoff, L. and C. Hall 1987 *Family Fortunes: Men and women of the English middle class 1780–1850*, London: Hutchinson.

Davies, B. 1982 'Discrimination, Affirmative Action and Women Academics: A case study of the University of New England', *Vestes* 25, (2): 15–22.

Davis, K. 1963 'The Theory of Change and Response in Modern Demographic History', *Population Index*, 29: 345–366.

De Swarte Gifford, C. 1987 *The Ideal of 'The New Woman' According to the Woman's Christian Temperance Union*, New York: Garland Publishing.

de Beauvoir, S. 1949 *The Second Sex*, Harmondsworth: Penguin.

Deacon, D. 1989 *Managing Gender*, Melbourne: Oxford University Press.

Deacon, D. 1993 'Reorganising the Masculinist Context: Conflicting masculinities in the New South Wales Public Service Bill debates of 1895', in Susan Magarey et al. (eds) *Debutante Nation: Feminism contests the 1890s*, Sydney: Allen & Unwin.

DEET (Department of Education, Employment and Training) 1993 Higher Education Series, *Female Academics*, Report No. 18, August.

Degler, C. 1980 *At Odds: Women and the family in America from the revolution to the present*, New York: Oxford University Press.

Demeny, P. 1988 'Social science and population policy', *Population and Development Review* 14 (3).

Department of the Prime Minister and Cabinet 1984 *Affirmative Action for Women. Volume 1. Discussion Paper*, Canberra: Australian Government Publishing Service.

Department of the Prime Minister and Cabinet 1989 *National Agenda for a Multicultural Australia*, Canberra: Australian Government Publishing Service.

Department of Social Security (DSS) 1992 *Rent Assistance reforms 1989–90: Evaluation report*, Social Policy Division, DSS, Canberra.

Department of Social Security (DSS) 1993 *Income Support and Housing Assistance: Submission to the inquiry on public housing by the Industry Commission*, DSS, Canberra.

Devlin, P. 1965 *The Enforcement of Morals*, Oxford: Oxford University Press.

Dryzek, J. 1990 *Discursive Democracy: Politics, policy, and political science*, Cambridge: Cambridge University Press.

Dryzek, J. 1996 'The Informal Logic of Institutional Design', in R. Goodin (ed.) *The Theory of Institutional Design*, Cambridge: Cambridge University Press.

Dyhouse, C. 1981 *Girls Growing Up in Late Victorian and Edwardian England*, London: Routledge and Kegan Paul.

Dzeich, B. W. and Weiner, L. 1984 *The Lecherous Professor: Sexual harassment on campus*, Boston, Mass.: Beacon.

Economic Planning and Advisory Council (EPAC) 1995, *Income Distribution in Australia: Recent trends and research*, Commission Paper No. 7, EPAC, Canberra.

Edelman, M. 1988, *Constructing the Political Spectacle*, Chicago: University of Chicago Press.

Edwards, Anne 1983 'Sex Roles: A problem for sociology and for women', *Australian and New Zealand of Sociology* 19(3) November: 385–412.

Edwards, A. and Magarey, S. (eds) 1995 *Women in a Restructuring Australia: Work and welfare*, Sydney: Allen & Unwin.

Ehrenreich, Barbara and English, Deidre 1979 *For Her Own Good: 150 years of the experts' advice to women*, London: Pluto.

Eisenstein, H. 1990 'Femocrats, Official Feminism and the Uses of Power', in S. Watson (ed.) *Playing the State: Australian feminist interventions*, Sydney: Allen & Unwin.

Eisenstein, H. 1991 *Gender Shock: Practising feminism on two continents*, Sydney: Allen & Unwin.

Eisenstein, H. 1996 *Inside Agitators: Australian femocrats and the state*, Sydney: Allen & Unwin.

England, P. 1993, 'The Separative Self: Androcentric bias in neo-classical assumptions', Ferber, M. A. and Nelson, J. A. (eds), *Beyond Economic Man*, Chicago: University of Chicago Press.

Englishwoman's Journal 1858, 1, 1.

Englishwoman's Journal 1859, 3, 14.

Esping Andersen, G. 1990 *Three Worlds of Welfare Capitalism*, Cambridge: Polity Press.

Evans, R. 1977 *The Feminists: Women's emancipation movements in Europe, America and Australasia 1840–1920*, London: Croom Helm.

Eveline, J. 1989 'Patriarchy in the Diamond Mines', unpublished honours thesis, Murdoch University, Perth, WA.

Eveline, J. 1994a 'The Politics of Advantage: Managing work and care in Sweden and Australia.', unpublished PhD thesis, Murdoch University, Perth, WA.

Eveline, J. 1994b 'The Politics of Advantage', *Australian Feminist Studies* 19 (Autumn): 129–154.

Eveline, J. 1994c 'Normalisation, Leading Ladies and Free Men', *Women's Studies International Forum*, 17 (2–3): 157–168.

Eveline, J. 1995a 'Stories of Heavy, Dirty and Limp: Protecting the institution of men's work', Administration, Compliance and Governability Program Working Paper No. 27, Australian National University.

Eveline, J. 1995b 'Surviving the Belt Shop Blues: Women miners and critical acts', *Australian Journal of Political Science* 30 (1) March: 91–107.

Eveline, J. 1995c 'The Politics of Advantage', *Political Theory Newsletter*, Canberra: Australian National University.

Eveline, J. with Booth, M. and Chadwick, R. 1989 *A Tiger by the Tail: Report to the workers at ADM on their interviews on women in the workforce*, Perth: Murdoch University.

Eyler, John M. 1979 *Victorian Social Medicine* Baltimore, Md.: Johns Hopkins University Press.

Fairclough, N. 1992 *Discourse and Social Change*, London: Polity.

Falkingham, J. and Hills, J. (eds) 1995 *The Dynamic of Welfare: The welfare state and the life cycle*, London: Harvester-Wheatsheaf.

Farley, L, 1978 *Sexual Shakedown: The sexual harassment of women on the job*, New York: McGraw-Hill.

Ferber, M. A. and Nelson, J. A. (eds) 1993 *Beyond Economic Man: Feminist theory and economics*, Chicago: University of Chicago Press.

Ferree, Myra Marx 1976 'Working Class Jobs: Housework and paid work as sources of satisfaction', *Social Problems* 23(4) April: 431–441.

Ferree, Myra Marx 1990 'Beyond Separate Spheres: Feminism and family research', *Journal of Marriage and the Family* 52 November: 866–884.

Festinger, L. 1957 *A Theory of Cognitive Dissonance*, Evanston, Ill.: Row Peterson.

Festinger, L. and Carlsmith, J. M. 1959 'Cognitive consequences of forced compliance', *Journal of Abnormal and Social Psychology* 58: 203–210.

Finch, L. 1993 *The Classing Gaze: Sexuality, class and surveillance*, Sydney: Allen & Unwin.

Fisher, S. R., and Ury, W. 1981 *Getting to Yes: Negotiating agreement without giving in*, Boston, Mass.: Houghton Mifflin.

Flick, B. 1990 'Colonisation and Decolonisation: An Aboriginal experience', in S. Watson (ed.), *Playing the State*, Sydney: Allen & Unwin.

Folbre, N. 1983 'Of Patriarchy Born: The political economy of fertility decisions', *Feminist Studies* 9 (2), 261–284.

Folbre, N. 1991 'The Unproductive Housewife: Her evolution in 19th century economic thought', *Signs* 16 (3): 463–484.

Foster, V. 1998 'Space Invaders: Desire and threat in the schooling of girls', *Discourse: Studies in the cultural politics of education* 17 (1): 43–63.

Foucault, M. 1978 *The History of Sexuality: Volume I*, London: Allen Lane.

Foucault, M. 1980 'Truth and Power' in *Power/Knowledge: Selected interviews and other writings, 1972–1977*, Colin Gordon (ed.), trans. Gordon et al., New York.

Four Corners, ABC television, 12 October 1992.

Fraser, N. and Gordon, L. 1994 'Dependency Demystified: Descriptions of power in a keyword of the welfare state', *Social Politics* 1 (1): 4–31.

Frazer, E. and Lacey, N. 1993 *The Politics of Community: A feminist critique of the liberal-communitarian debate*, Toronto: University of Toronto Press.

Friedman, M. 1962, *Capitalism and Freedom* [1982 edn], Chicago: University of Chicago Press.

Furniss, N. and Tilton, T. 1977 *The Case for the Welfare State*, Bloomington: Indiana University Press.

Gale, F. and Lindemann, S. 1988 'Women in the Academic Search for Excellence', *Australian Universities' Review* 32(2).

Gallop, J. 1997 *Feminist Accused of Sexual Harassment*, Durham: Duke University Press.

Game, A. and Pringle, R. 1983 *Gender At Work*, Sydney: Allen & Unwin.

Garner, H. 1995, *The First Stone: Some questions about sex and power*, Sydney: Picador.

Geerken, M. and Gove, W. R. 1983 *At Home and at Work*, Sage: Beverly Hills.

Gellner, E. 1994 *Conditions of Liberty: Civil society and its rivals*, London: Hamish Hamilton.

Gershuny, Johnathan and Robinson, J. P. 1988 'Historical Changes in the Household Division of Labor', *Demography* 25(4): 537–552.

Gibson, S. 1994 'Loose Rules and Likely Stories', in Clare Brant and Yun Lee Too (eds) *Rethinking Sexual Harassment*, London: Pluto Press.

Giddens, A. 1990 *The Consequences of Modernity*, Stanford Ca.: Stanford University Press.

Giddens, A. 1992 *The Transformation of Intimacy: Sexuality, love and eroticism in modern societies*, Cambridge: Cambridge University Press.

Goldby, J. M. (ed.) 1988 *Culture and Society in Britain 1850–1890*, London: Oxford University Press.

Goldman, L. 1986 'The Social Science Association, 1857–1886: A context for mid-Victorian liberalism', *English Historical Review* 95–134.

Goldman, L. 1987 'A Peculiarity of the English? The SSA and the absence of sociology in 19th century Britain' *Past and Present* 114: 133–171.

Goldscheider, F. K. and Waite, L. J. 1991 *New Families, No Families? The transformation of the American home*, Berkeley: University of California Press.

Goodin, R. 1982 *Political Theory and Public Policy*, Chicago: University of Chicago Press.

Goodin, R. E. (ed.) 1996 *The Theory of Institutional Design*, Cambridge: Cambridge University Press.

Goodin, R. E. 1996 'Institutions and their Design', in R. E. Goodin (ed.), *The Theory of Institutional Design*, Cambridge: Cambridge University Press.

Goodnow, Jacqueline and Bowes, Jennifer 1994 *Men, Women and Household Work*, Melbourne: Oxford University Press.

Graham Yates, G. 1985 *Harriet Martineau on Women*, New Brunswick NJ: Rutgers University Press.

Granovetter, M. S. 1973 'The Strength of Weak Ties', *American Journal of Sociology* 78: 1360–1380.

Grasmick, H. G. and Bursik, R. 1990 'Conscience, Significant Others and Rational Choice: Extending the deterrence model', *Law and Society Review* 24: 837–861.

Greenhalgh, S. (ed.) 1995 *Situating Fertility: Anthropology and demographic enquiry*, Cambridge: Cambridge University Press.

Greenhalgh, S. 1996 'The Social Construction of Population Science: An intellectual, institutional, and political history of twentieth-century demography', *Comparative Studies in Society and History* 38(1).

Grimshaw, P. 1991, 'Was Biology Destiny? Historical demography and white colonial women', *Lilith* (7).

Grimshaw, P., Lake, M., McGrath, A. and Quartly, M. 1994 *Creating a Nation: 1788–1990*, Melbourne: McPhee Gribble.

Guillemard, A-M. 1991 'International Perspectives on Early Withdrawal from the Labor Force', in J. Myles and J. Quadagno (eds.) *States Labor Markets and the Future of Old Age Policy*, Philadelphia: Temple University Press.

Gutek, B. and Morasch, B. 1982 'Sex Ratios, Sex-Role Spillover, and Sexual Harassment of Women at Work', *Journal of Social Issues* Winter (55).

Haas, Linda 1987 'Wives' Orientation Toward Breadwinning', *Journal of Family Issues* 7: 358–381.

Haraway, Donna J. 1997 'The Virtual Speculum in the New World Order', *Feminist Review* 55: 22–72.

Hardesty, C. and Bokemeier, J. 1989 'Finding Time and Making Do: Distribution of household labor in nonmetropolitan marriages', *Journal of Marriage and the Family* 51: 253–267.

Harding, A. and Mitchell, D. 1992 'The Efficiency and Effectiveness of the Tax/Transfer System in the 1980s', *Australian Tax Forum* 9 (3).

Harman, K. 1989 'Culture and Conflict in Academic Organisation: Symbolic aspects of university worlds', *Journal of Educational Administration* 27(3): 30–54.

Harrison, B. 1971 *Drink and the Victorians: The temperance question in England 1815–1872*, London: Faber & Faber.

Hartmann, Heidi 1981 'The Family as the Locus of Gender, Class and Political Struggle: The example of housework', *Signs* 6(3): 336–394.

Hartmann, Heidi 1987 'Changes in Women's Economic and Family Roles in Post-World War II United States', in Lourdes Beneria and Catharine Stimpson (eds), *Women, Households and the Economy*, New Brunswick: Rutgers, pp. 33–64.

Head, B. 1982 'The Origins of "la Science Sociale" in France 1770–1800', *Australian Journal of French Studies* 19: 115–132.

Healy, J. M. 1988 'Elderly Couples and the Division of Household Tasks', *Australian Journal of Sex, Marriage and the Family* 9(4): 203–214.

Hearn, J. and Parkin, W. 1987 *'Sex at "Work": The power and paradox of organisation sexuality'*, Brighton: Wheatsheaf.

Held V. 1990 'Mothering Versus Contract' in *Beyond Self-Interest*, Jane Mansbridge (ed.), Chicago: University of Chicago Press, pp. 287–384.

Held, V. 1993 *Feminist Morality*, Chicago: University of Chicago Press.

Heschel, S. 1995 'Feminists Gain at Cairo Population Conference', *Dissent* Winter.

Hicks, N. 1978 *'This Sin and Scandal': Australia's population debate, 1891–1911*, Canberra: Australian National University Press.

Higginson, C. 1994, 'Workplace Initiatives' in Centre for Research On Women, *Proceedings of the Feminist Research Symposium, 22 July 1994, Perth WA*: Murdoch University.

Hill, L. 1996 'The Un-Reconstructed Republic', *Australian Journal of Political Science* 30(3): 589–594.

Hobson, B. 1994 'Solo Mothers, Social Policy Regimes and the Logics of Gender', in D. Sainsbury (ed.) *Gendering Welfare States*, London: Sage.

Hochschild, Arlie 1989 *The Second Shift*, New York: Avon Books.

Hollway, W. 1989 *Subjectivity and Method in Psychology: Gender, meaning and science*, London: Sage.

Holton, S. 1988 *The Professional Development of Women Academics: A case study in South Australia*, Canberra: Australian Government Publishing Service.

Hood, J. C. 1986 'The Provider Role: Its meaning and measurement', *Journal of Marriage and the Family* 48: 349–359.

Huber, Joan and Spitze, Glenna 1983 *Sex Stratification: Children, housework and jobs*, New York: Academic Press.

Huggins, J. 1994 'A Contemporary View of Aboriginal Women's Relationship to the White Women's Movement', in N. Grieve and A. Burns (eds) *Australian Women: Contemporary feminist thought*, Melbourne: Oxford University Press.

Hugo, G. 1993 'Recent Trends in Fertility Differentials in Australia', *People and Place* 1 (2).

Hunt, M. 1994 'Degrees of Separation: Good boundaries support good relationships', *On the Issues* 3(3): 19–21.

Hunter, R. 1996 'Working the Republic: Some feminist reflections', in J. Hoorn and D. Goodman (eds.) *Vox Reipublicae: Feminism and the republic*, special edition of the *Journal of Australian Studies*, Bundoora: La Trobe University Press.

Huntington, S. P. 1968 *Political Order in Changing Societies*, New Haven, Conn.: Yale University Press.

Industry Task Force on Leadership and Management Skills (Karpin Report) 1995 *Enterprising Nation: Renewing Australia's managers to meet the challenges of the Asia-Pacific century*, Canberra: Australian Government Publishing Service.

Irving, H. 1994 'Boy's Own Republic', *Arena Magazine* Dec. 1993–Jan. 1994 (8): 24–26.

Irving, H. 1996a 'The Republic is a Feminist Issue', *Feminist Review* 52: 87–101.

Irving, H. 1996b 'Equal Opportunity, Equal Representation and Equal Rights?: What republicanism offers to Australian women', *Australian Journal of Political Science* 31(1): 37–50.

Irving, H. 1996c 'Thinking of England: Women, politics and the Queen', in J. Hoorn and D. Goodman (eds) *Vox Reipublicae: Feminism and the republic*, special edition of the *Journal of Australian Studies*, Bundoora: La Trobe University Press.

James, S. 1976 *Women, The Unions and Work*, Bristol: Falling Wall Press.

Jennings, A. 1993 'Public or Private? Institutional economics and feminism', in M. Ferber and J. Nelson, *Beyond Economic Man: Feminist theory and economics*, Chicago: University of Chicago Press.

Johansson, S. Ryan 1991 ' "Implicit" Policy and Fertility During Development', *Population and Development Review* 17(3).

Johnston, E. 1991 *Royal Commission into Aboriginal Deaths in Custody: National report*, volume 4, Canberra: Australian Government Publishing Service.

Joyce, P. 1994 *Democratic Subjects: The self and the social in nineteenth-century England*, Cambridge: Cambridge University Press.

Kalleberg, Arne and Rosenfeld, Rachel 1990 'Work in the Family and in the Labor Market: A cross-national, reciprocal analysis', *Journal of Marriage and the Family* 52: 331–346.

Kanter, R. M. 1984 *Men and Women of the Corporation*, New York: Basic Books.

Kaplan, G. 1985 'Coming Up with Bright Ideas: Women in academia', *Vestes* 28 (2): 19–22.

Keating, Hon. P. (Prime Minister) and Fatin, Hon. W. (Minister for the Arts and Territories and Minister Assisting the Prime Minister for the Status of Women) 1992 'Government Response to *Half Way to Equal* – The Report of the Inquiry into Equal Opportunity and Equal Status for Women in Australia by the House of Representatives Standing Committee on Legal and Constitutional Affairs' Australian Government, Canberra: Australian Government Publishing Service.

Kemmis, R. 1995 'Introduction', in UTS (University of Technology, Sydney) Women, Culture and Universities: A chilly climate? Conference Proceedings: 1–5.

Kendig, H., Paris, C., and Anderton, N. 1987 *Towards Fair Shares in Australian Housing: A report for the International Year of Shelter for the Homeless*, National Committee of Non-Government Organisations, Canberra: Australian Government Publishing Service.

Kenway, J. 1991 'Masculinity – Under seige, on the defensive and under reconstruction', paper presented to the Bergamo Conference, Dayton, Ohio.

Kerber, L. 1980 *Women of the Republic: intellect and ideology in Revolutionary America*, Durham, NC: University of North California Press.

Kernot, C. 1995 'Social Cohesion and the Political Process' *Bureau of Immigration, Multicultural and Population Research* 13: 19–20.

Kernot, C. 1996 'Breaking up the Boys' Club: Making the republic relevant to Australian women', in J. Hoorn and D. Goodman (eds) *Vox Reipublicae: Feminism and the Republic*, special edition of the *Journal of Australian Studies*, Bundoora: La Trobe University Press.

Knodel, J. and Jones G. W. 1996 'Post-Cairo Population Policy: Does promoting girls' schooling miss the mark?' *Population and Development Review* 22 (4).

Kolberg, J. (ed.) 1992 *The Study of Welfare State Regimes*, New York: ME Sharpe.

Kouwenberg, S. 1993 'Mary Graham: A Kumbuerri perspective' *Horizons* 2(3): 7–8.

Krygier, M. and Glass, A. 1995 'Shaky Premises: Values, attitudes and the law', *Sydney Law Review* 17: 374–385.

Kyle, N. and Wright, J. 1993 *Breaking Down Traditional Barriers: The attitude of small industry to women in non-traditional schooling and work: An Illawarra case study*, Women's Bureau, Dept of Employment, Education and Training. Canberra: Australian Government Publishing Service.

Lahey, K. A. 1987 'Feminist Theories of Inequality', in S. L. Martin and K. E. Mahoney (eds) *Equality and Judicial Neutrality*, Toronto: Caswell.

Lake, M. 1994a 'Personality, Individuality, Nationality: Feminist conceptions of citizenship 1902–1940', *Australian Feminist Studies* 19: 25–38.

Lake, M. 1994b 'A Republic for Women?', *Arena Magazine* (9): 32–33.

Lake, M. 1996 'The Republic, the Federation and the Intrusion of the Political', in J. Hoorn and D.Goodman (eds) *Vox Reipublicae: Feminism and the republic*, special edition of the *Journal of Australian Studies*, Bundoora: La Trobe University Press.

Langmore, J. and Quiggin, J. 1994 *Work for All: Full employment in the nineties*, Melbourne: Melbourne University Press.

Leech, Marie 1994 'Women, the State and Citizenship: "Are women in the building or in a separate annex?"', *Australian Feminist Studies* 19: 79–92.

Lepper, M. R. 1973 'Dissonance, Self-perception and Honesty in Children', *Journal of Personality and Social Psychology* 25: 65–74.

Lewis, J. 1984 *Women in England 1870–1950: Sexual divisions and social change*, Brighton: Wheatsheaf Books.

Lewis, J. 1992 'Gender and Welfare Regimes', *Journal of European Social Policy* 2 (3): 159–171.

Lewis, S. and J. Clout 1995 'Tough New Reforms to Protect Small Business', *Australian Financial Review*, September 22: 18.

Linder A. and Peters D. 1995 'The Two Traditions of Institutional Designing: Dialogue versus decision?', in Weimer, D. L. (ed.) *Institutional Design*, Boston Mass.: Kluwer.

Lloyd, G. 1993 'Maleness, Metaphor and the "Crisis" of Reason', in L. Antony and C. Witt (eds) *A Mind of One's Own*, Boulder, Col.: Westview.

MacFarlane, L. 1990 *Policies and Trends for Affordable Housing in Industrialised Countries: An overview*, paper prepared for the OECD/United Nations Conference on 'Sustainable Development in Industrialised Nations: The challenge of decent and affordable housing for all', New York, (Oct.).

Macintyre, S. 1985 *Winners and Losers: The pursuit of social justice in Australian history*, Sydney: Allen & Unwin.

MacKinnon, C. 1979 *Sexual Harassment of Working Women*, New Haven: Yale University Press.

MacKinnon, C. 1987 *Feminism Unmodified: Discourses on life and law*, Cambridge, Mass., Harvard University Press.

Mackinnon, A. 1990 'Awakening Women: Women, higher education and family formation in South Australia c1880–1930', unpublished Ph.D. thesis, University of Adelaide.

Mackinnon, A. 1995 'Were Women Present at the Demographic Transition?: Questions from a feminist historian to historical demographers', *Gender and History* 7(2).

Mackinnon, A. 1997 *Love and Freedom: Professional women and the reshaping of personal life*, Cambridge: Cambridge University Press.

Magarey, S. 1986 *Unbridling the Tongues of Women: A biography of Catherine Helen Spence*, Sydney: Hale and Iremonger.

Mahoney, K. 1993 'Gender Bias in Judicial Decisions', Seminar sponsored by Australian Institute of Women's Research and Policy and Women's Legal Service, Brisbane, 25 May.

Makkai, T. and Braithwaite, J. 1994 'The Dialectics of Corporate Deterrence', *Journal of Research in Crime and Delinquency* 31: 347–73.

Maley, B. 1990, 'Babies – A National Resource', paper presented to the Australian Family Conference, Sydney.

Manning, I., King, A. and Yates, J. 1988 *Housing Futures*, A Report to the Victorian State Advisory Council for International Year of Shelter for the Homeless, National Institute of Economic Industry Research, Melbourne.

Marsden, S. 1993, 'Becoming an Australian', forum organised by Susan Marsden, State Historian of South Australia, State History Centre, Old Parliament House, Adelaide, (27 June) as part of Ideas for Australia Program; materials kindly supplied by Susan Marsden.

Marshall, J. 1984 *Women Managers: Travellers in a male world*, Chichester: John Wiley and Sons.

Martin, J. 1991 'Multiculturalism and Feminism', in G. Bottomley et al. (eds), *Intersexions: Gender/class/culture/ethnicity*, Sydney: Allen & Unwin.

Martin, M. 1989, 'Sexual Harassment: The link joining gender stratification, sexuality and women's economic status', in J. Freeman (ed.) *Women: A feminist perspective*, Palo Alto, Calif.: Mayfield Publishing.

Maslen, G. 1995, 'Gender Roles Swapped: Report finds uni men "disadvantaged"', *Campus Review* 5 (12) (30 March–April 5): 5.

Mason, C. 1994 'Women's Policy in Queensland', *Social Alternatives* 12(4): 13–16.

Matthews, G. 1992 *The Rise of Public Woman*, London: Oxford University Press.

Mayer, P. and Bacchi, C. 1997 'The Two Cultures of Equal Opportunity', unpublished seminar paper available from Politics Department, University of Adelaide.

McDonald, P. 1988 'Families in the Future: The pursuit of personal autonomy', *Family Matters* (22).

McDonald, P. 1995 *Families in Australia: A socio-demographic perspective*, Melbourne: Australian Institute for Family Studies.

McDonald, P. 1997 *Gender Equity, Social Institutions and the Future of Fertility*, Working Papers in Demography, No. 69, Canberra: Australian National University.

McKenzie, D. 1996 'ALP Puts Immigration at Centre of Population Big Picture', *Australian*, January 10.

McLennan, W. and Goward P. 1997 *Australian Women's Year Book*, Canberra: Office of the Status of Women and Australian Bureau of Statistics.

McNeil, M. (ed.) 1987 *Gender and Expertise*, London: Free Association Books.

McNicholl, G. 1994 'Institutional Analysis of Fertility', in K. Lindahl-Kiessling and H. Lanberg (eds), *Population, Economic Development and the Environment*, Oxford University Press.

McNicoll, G. 1995 'Institutional Impediments to Population Policy in Australia', *Journal of the Australian Population Association* 12(5): 97–112.

Mead, J. 1995 'Sexual Harassment and Feminism', *De Republica* issue 2, Sydney: Angus and Robertson.

Meyer, T. 1994 'The German and British Welfare States as Employers: Patriarchal or emancipatory?', in D. Sainsbury (ed.) *Gendering Welfare States*, London: Sage.

Mitchell, D. 1995 'Women's Incomes', in Edwards, A and Magarey, S. (eds) *Women in a Restructuring Australia*, Sydney: Allen & Unwin: 79–94.

Mitchell, D. 1997 'Family Policy', in Galligan, B., McAllister, I. and Ravenhill, J. (eds) *Developments in Australian Politics*, Melbourne: Macmillan.

Mitchell, D. 1998 'Wages and employment: The long march to equality', in B. Caine et al. (eds), *Oxford Companion to Australian Feminism*, Melbourne: Oxford University Press.

Mitchell, D. and Dowrick, S. 1994 'Women's Increasing Participation in the Labour Force: Implications for equity and efficiency', Centre For Economic Policy Research, Discussion Paper No. 308, Australian National University, Canberra.

Mitchell, Deborah, Harding, Ann and Gruen, Fred 1994 'Targetting Welfare', *Economic Record* 70(210): 310–335.

Mitchell, S. 1995, 'The Culture of Complaint', *Weekend Australian*, 15–16 April.

Moen, Phyllis 1989 *Working Parents: Transformations in gender roles and public policies in Sweden*, London: Adamantine Press.

Moreton-Robinson, A. 1992 'Masking Gender and Exalting Race: Indigenous women and Commonwealth employment policies', *Australian Feminist Studies* 15: 5–24.

Morgan, J. 1995 'Sexual Harassment and the Public/Private Dichotomy: Equality, morality and manners', in M. Thornton (ed.) *Public and Private: Feminist legal debates*, Melbourne: Oxford University Press.

Morris, M. 1993 'The Very Idea of a Popular Debate (Or, Not Lunching with Thomas Keneally)', *Communal/Plural* 1(2): 153–167.

Munro, M. and Smith, S. 1989 'Gender and Housing: Broadening the debate', *Housing Studies* 1(4): 3–17.

Myles, J. 1990 'States, Labor Markets and Life Cycles', in R. Friedland and A. Robertson. (eds) *Beyond the Marketplace: Rethinking economy and society*, New York: Aldine de Gruyter.

Naffine, N. 1992 'Windows on the Legal Mind: The evocation of rape in legal writings', *Melbourne University Law Review* 18: 741–767.

Naffine, N. 1995 'Sexing the Subject (of Law)', Thornton, M., *Public and Private: Feminist legal debates*, Melbourne: Oxford University Press.

National Committee on Violence 1990, 'Violence: Directions for Australia', Canberra: Australian Institute of Criminology.

National Committee on Violence Against Women 1991, Position Paper 10, Canberra: Australian Government Publishing Service.

National Health and Medical Research Council 1944, Report of Eighteenth Session: Appendix 1, Interim Report on the decline of the birthrate.

National Housing Strategy 1991 *The Affordability of Australian Housing*, Issues Paper No. 2, Canberra: Australian Government Publishing Service.

National Housing Strategy 1992a *Agenda for Action*, Canberra: Australian Government Publishing Service.

National Housing Strategy 1992b *Housing Location and Access to Services*, Issues Paper No. 5, Canberra: Australian Government Publishing Service.

National Tertiary Education Union 1997 *Advocate* 4(2).

Nelson, Julie, A. 1996 *Feminism, Objectivity and Economics*, London: Routledge.

Nemy, E. 1975 'Women Begin to Speak Out Against Sexual Harassment at Work', *New York Times*, 19 August.

Nicholls, J. 1995 'Students, Academic Staff, the Personal and the Professional: A discussion paper for the National Tertiary Education Union (NTEU).

Nightingale, F. 1852 *Cassandra* (1852), Reprinted in Goldby 1988: 244–256.

Notestein, F. W. 1945 'Population – the Long View', in T. W. Schultz (ed.), *Food for the World*, Chicago: University of Chicago Press.

Oakley, Ann 1974 *The Sociology of Housework*, New York: Pantheon.

O'Brien, M. 1984 'The Commatization of Women: Patriarchal fetishism in the sociology of education', *Interchange* 15 (2): 43–60.

O'Neill, R. 1995 'After the First Stone', *Independent Monthly* October: 48–55.

O'Shane, P. 1994 'Comments on Irene Moss as Race Discrimination Commissioner' *Aboriginal Law Bulletin* 3(68): 2–4.

OECD (Organisation for Economic Cooperation and Development) 1990 *Housing Policies and Social Integration in Cities*, Group on Urban Affairs, OECD, Paris.

Offe, C. 1995 'Designing Institutions in East European Transitions', R. E. Goodin (ed.) *Theory of Institutional Design*, Cambridge: Cambridge University Press.

Office of the Status of Women 1992 Department of the Prime Minister and Cabinet, 'Women in Australia: Australia's second progress report on implementing the United Nations Convention on the Elimination of All Forms of Discrimination Against Women', Canberra: Commonwealth of Australia.

Office of the Status of Women 1995 Department of the Prime Minister and Cabinet, 'Australian National Report to the United Nations Fourth World Conference on Women', Canberra: Commonwealth of Australia.

Okin, S. M. 1989 *Justice, Gender and the Family*, New York: Basic Books.

Oldfield, A. 1992 *Woman Suffrage in Australia*, Cambridge: Cambridge University Press.

Orloff, A. 1993, 'Gender and the Social Rights of Citizenship: State policies and gender relations in comparative research', *American Sociological Review* 58(3): 303–328.

Palmieri, P. 1995 *In Adamless Eden*, New Haven: Yale University Press.

Pateman, C. 1988 *The Sexual Contract*, Cambridge: Polity Press.

Pateman, C. 1989 *The Disorder of Women*, Cambridge: Polity Press.

Pell, G. 1997 'Australia Must Populate: Pell', *Australian*, 8 November.

Perucci, C., Potter, H. R. and Rhoads, D. L. 1978 'Determinants of Male Family-role Performance', *Psychology of Women Quarterly* 3(1): 53–66.

Pettit, P. 1994 'Liberal/Communitarian: Macintyre's mesmeric dichotomy', in J. Horton and S. Mendus (eds), *After Macintyre*, London: Polity.

Pettman, J. 1992 *Living in the Margins: Racism, sexism and feminism in Australia*, Sydney: Allen & Unwin.

Phillips, A. and Taylor, B. 1980 'Sex and Skill: Notes towards a feminist economics', *Feminist Review* 5: 79–88.

Pierson, P. 1994 *Dismantling the Welfare State*, Cambridge: Cambridge University Press.

Pleck, Joseph 1985 *Working Wives, Working Husbands*, Beverly Hills: Sage.

Pocock, B. 1988 *Demanding Skill: Women and technical education in Australia*, Sydney: Allen & Unwin.

Poiner, G. and Wills, S. 1991, *The Gifthorse: A critical look at equal employment opportunity in Australia*, Sydney: Allen & Unwin.

Polanyi, K. 1944 *The Great Transformation*, Rinehart, New York.

Pollack 1990 'Sexual Harassment: Women's experience *vs* legal definitions', *Harvard Women's Law Journal* 13: 221–222.

Powell, A. and Russell, G. 1993 'Managing Affirmative Action', in E. M. Davis and V. Pratt (eds), *Making the Link 4: Affirmative action and industrial relations*, Canberra: Australian Government Publishing Service.

Pratt, V. 1993 'The Glass Ceiling: The need for debate', in C. Burton et al. (eds) *Women, Organisations and Economic Policies. Canberra Bulletin of Public Administration*, a joint publication of the Royal Institute of Public Administration of Australia and the Affirmative Action Agency, No. 76, April, pp. 46–48.

Prentice, A., Bourne P., Cuthbert Brandt, G., Light, B., Mitchinson, W. and Black, N., 1988 *Canadian Women: A history*, Toronto: Harcourt Brace Jovanovich.

Pringle, Rosemary 1983 'Women and Consumer Capitalism', in C. Baldock and B. Cass (eds), *Women, Social Welfare and the State*, Sydney: Allen & Unwin, pp. 85–103.

Pringle, R. 1994 'Ladies to Women: Women and the professions', in N. Grieve and A. Burns (eds) *Australian Women: Contemporary feminist thought*, Melbourne: Oxford University Press: 202–215.

Pringle, R. and Collings, S. 1993 'Women and Butchery: Some cultural taboos', *Australian Feminist Studies* 17 (Autumn): 29–46.

Pringle, R. and Watson, S. 1992 '"Women's Interests" and the Post-structuralist State', in M. Barrett and A. Phillips (eds) *Destabilizing Theory: Contemporary feminist debates*, London: Polity: 53–73.

Purkiss, D. 1994 'The Lecherous Professor Revisited: Plato, pedagogy and the scene of harassment', in C. Brant and Y. L. Too (eds), *Rethinking Sexual Harassment*, London: Pluto Press.

Pusey, Michael 1991 *Economic Rationalism in Canberra: A nation building state changes its mind*, Cambridge: Cambridge University Press.

Pyke, J. 1993 *Women in Building*, Women's Bureau, Department of Education, Employment and Training, Canberra.

Radio National, ABC radio, 8 August 1995.

Ramsay, E. 1995a 'Management, Gender and Language – Or who is hiding behind the glass ceiling and why can't we see them?', in B. Limerick and B. Lingard (eds) *Gender and Changing Educational Management*, Edward Arnold: forthcoming.

Ramsay, E. 1995b 'The Politics of Privilege and Resistance', in UTS (University of Technology, Sydney) *Women, Culture and Universities: A chilly climate? Conference Proceedings:* 91–97.

Raspail, J. 1973 *The Camp of the Saints*, Detroit, Mich.: Social Contract Press.

Rawls, J. 1971, *A Theory of Justice*, Cambridge, Mass.: Harvard University Press.

Reagon, B. J. 1983 'Coalition Politics: Turning the century', in B. Smith (ed.) *Home Girls: A Black Feminist Anthology*, New York: Kitchen Table, Women of Color Press.

Reiger, Kerreen 1985 *The Disenchantment of the Home*, Oxford: Oxford University Press.

Rendall, J. 1985 *The Origins of Modern Feminism: Women in Britain, France and the United States 1780–1860*, London: Macmillan.

Research School of Social Sciences (RSSS) 1994, Australian National University, Reshaping Australian Institutions: Towards and Beyond 2001. Three Year Progress Report, 1992–94.

Reskin, B. F. and Roos, P. A. (eds) 1990 *Job Queues, Gender Queues: Explaining women's inroads into male occupations*, Philadelphia: Temple University Press.

Richards, L. 1989 *Nobody's Home: Dreams and realities in a new suburb*, Melbourne: Oxford University Press.

Riley-Smith, B. 1992 'The Women's View: Market research study on women's perceptions of themselves and government programs and policies', Canberra: Office of the Status of Women, Department of Prime Minister and Cabinet.

Robinson, J. 1980 'Housework Technology and Household Work', in S. F. Berk (ed.), *Women and Household Labor*, Beverly Hills: Sage, pp. 53–67.

Ronalds, C. 1987 *Affirmative Action and Sex Discrimination: A handbook on legal rights for women*, Sydney: Pluto Press.

Ronalds, C. 1990 'Government Action Against Employment Discrimination', in S. Watson (ed.) *Playing the State: Australian feminist interventions*, Sydney: Allen & Unwin.

Roos, P. A. 1990 'Hot Metal to Electronic Composition: Gender, technology and social change', in B. F. Reskin and P. A. Roos (eds) *Job Queues, Gender Queues: Explaining women's inroads into male occupations*, Philadelphia: Temple University Press: 275–298.

Roper Renshaw, L. 1994 'Strengthening Civil Society: The role of NGOs', *Development* 4: 46–50.

Rosenman, L. 1995 'Superannuation Guarantee Charge: Benefits and risks', in A. Edwards and S. Magarey (eds) *Women in a Restructuring Australia*, Sydney: Allen & Unwin.

Ross, Catherine 1987 'The Division of Labor at Home', *Social Forces* 65(3): 816–833.

Rowley, S. 1996 '"Coming of Age" – Again', in J. Hoorn and D. Goodman (eds), *Vox Reipublicae: Feminism and the republic*, special edition of the *Journal of Australian Studies*, Bundoora: La Trobe University Press.

Royal Commission into the Decline of the Birthrate and the Mortality of Infants, (New South Wales), 1904 Report Vol. 2, Sydney.

Royal Commission into Health, 1926 Report, Melbourne: Victorian Government Printer.

Ruddick, S. 1989 *Maternal Thinking: Toward a politics of peace*, Boston: Beacon Press.

Ruggie, M. 1988, 'Gender, Work and Social Progress: Some consequences of interest aggregation in Sweden', in J. Jenson, E. Hagen and C. Reddy (eds), *Feminization of the Labour Force*, Cambridge: Polity Press, pp. 173–188.

Sainsbury, D. (ed.) 1994 *Gendering Welfare States*, London: Sage.

Sampson, S. 1991 *Dismantling the Divide: Women into non-traditional occupations*, Canberra: Australian Government Printing Service.

Sanchez, Laura 1994 'Gender, Labor Allocations, and the Psychology of Entitlement Within the Home', *Social Forces* 73(2) December: 533–553.

Sandler, B. R. and Hall, R. M. 1986 'The Campus Climate Revisited: Chilly for women faculty, administrators and graduate students', Project on the Status and Education of Women, Association of American Colleges, Washington, DC.

Saunders, C. 1996, 'Introduction', in J. Hoorn and D. Goodman (eds), *Vox Reipublicae: Feminism and the republic*, special edition of the *Journal of Australian Studies*, Bundoora: La Trobe University Press.

Saunders, P. 1994 *Welfare and Inequality*, Cambridge: Cambridge University Press.

Sawer, M. 1989 'Monitoring Social Justice' in 'Social Justice in Australia', Supplement to *Australian Society* December 1988/January 1989: 18–22.

Sawer, M. 1990 *Sisters in Suits: Women and public policy in Australia*, Sydney: Allen & Unwin.

Sawer, M. 1993 'Reclaiming Social Liberalism: The women's movement and the state', in R. Howe (ed.) *Women and the State: Australian perspectives*, special edition of *Journal of Australian Studies*, Bundoora: La Trobe University Press with the Centre for Australian Studies, Deakin University, and the Ideas for Australia Program.

Schultz, V. 1992 'Women "Before" the Law: Judicial stories about women, work and sex segregation on the job', in J. Butler and J. Scott (eds) *Feminists Theorise the Political*, New York and London: Routledge.

Scott, J. W. 1988a *Gender and the Politics of History*, New York: Columbia University Press.

Scott, J. W, 1988b 'Deconstructing Equality-versus-Difference: Or the uses of poststructuralist theory for feminism', *Feminist Studies* 14(1).

Seccombe, W. 1993 *Weathering the Storm: Working-class families from the industrial revolution to the fertility decline*, London: Verso.

Seligman, A. B. 1993 'The Fragile Ethical Vision of Civil Society', in B. S.Turner (ed.) *Citizenship and Social Theory*, London: Sage: 139–161.

Sex Discrimination Commissioner 1992 Report on Review of Permanent Exemptions Under the Sex Discrimination Act 1984, Canberra: Australian Government Publishing Service.

Shanley, M. L. 1989 *Feminism, Marriage and the Law in Victorian England*, Princeton, NJ: Princeton University Press.

Sharp, R. 1995 'Women and Superannuation: Super bargain or raw deal?', in A. Edwards and S. Magarey (eds) *Women in a Restructuring Australia*, Sydney: Allen & Unwin.

Sharpe, Sue 1984 *Double Identity: The lives of working mothers*, London: Penguin.

Shaver, S. 1988 'Sex and Money in the Welfare State', in C. Baldock, and B. Cass (eds) *Women, Social Welfare and the State*, Sydney: Allen & Unwin, 150–167.

Shaver, S. 1992 *Women and the Australian Social Security System: From difference to equality*, SPRC Discussion Paper No. 41, University of NSW.

Shaver, S. 1995 'Women, Employment and Social Security', in A. Edwards and S. Magarey (eds) *Women in a Restructuring Australia*, Sydney: Allen & Unwin.

Sheppard, D. L. 1989 'Organizations, Power and Sexuality: The image and self-image of women managers', in J. Hearn, D. L. Sheppard, P. Tancred-Sheriff and G. Burrell (eds) *The Sexuality of Organization*, London: Sage: 139–157.

Shotter, J. 1993 'Psychology and Citizenship', in B. Turner (ed.) *Citizenship and Social Theory*, London: Sage: 115–130.

Siedlecky, S. and Wyndham, D. 1990 *Populate and Perish: Australian women's fight for birth control*, Sydney: Allen & Unwin.

Smith F. B. 1982 *Florence Nightingale, Reputation and Power*, London: Croom Helm.

Smith, S. 1989, 'Gender Differences in the Attainment and Experience of Owner-Occupation in Australia', Working Paper No. 19 (Dec), Urban Research Unit, Canberra: Australian National University.

Smith, S. 1990, 'Income, Housing Wealth and Gender Inequality', *Urban Studies* 27, (1): 67–88.

Sofoulis, Z. 1993, 'Gender and Technological Rationality', in D. Baker and M. Fogarty, (eds) *A Gendered Culture: Educational management in the nineties*, Melbourne: Victoria University of Technology, 28–43.

Soloway, R. A. 1990 *Demography and Degeneration: Eugenics and the declining birthrate in twentieth-century Britain*, Chapel Hill and London: University of North Carolina Press.

Spitze, Glenna 1986 'The Division of Task Responsibility in US Households: Longitudinal adjustments to change', *Social Forces* 64(3) March: 689–701.

Stacey, Judith and Thorne, B. 1985 'The Missing Feminist Revolution in Sociology', *Social Problems* 32: 301–316.

Stafford, R., Backman, E. and Dibona, P. 1977 'The Division of Labor Among Cohabiting and Married Couples', *Journal of Marriage and the Family* 39(1): 43–57.

Standing Committee on Social Issues 1993 *Sexual Violence: The hidden crime. Inquiry into the incident of sexual offences in New South Wales, Part I*, Sydney: Legislative Council, Parliament of NSW.

Steiger, T. and Reskin, B. F. 1990, 'Baking and Baking Off: Deskilling and the changing sex make-up of bakers', in B. F. Reskin and P. A. Roos (eds) *Job Queues, Gender Queues: Explaining women's inroads into male occupations*, Philadelphia: Temple University Press: 257–274.

Still, L. 1993 *Where to From Here? The managerial woman in transition*, Sydney: Business and Professional Publishing.

Stoler, A. L. 1995 *Race and the Education of Desire: Foucault's history of sexuality and the colonial order of things*, Durham and London: Duke University Press.

Strasser, Susan 1978 'The Business of Housekeeping: The ideology of the household at the turn of the century', *The Insurgent Sociologists* 11(2 and 3): 147–163.

Strassman 1993 'Not a Free Market: The rhetoric of disciplinary authority in economics', in M. A. Ferber and J. A. Nelson (eds) *Beyond Economic Man: Feminist theory and economics*, Chicago: University of Chicago Press.

Stretton, H. 1970 *Ideas for Australian Cities*, Adelaide: Orphan Books.

Sullivan, B. 1990, 'Sex Equality and the Australian Body Politic', in S. Watson, (ed.) *Playing the State*, Sydney: Allen & Unwin.

Swedish Social Democratic Party 1993 *The Power Handbook*, reproduced and distributed by S-Kvinnor, Stockholm, Sweden: Sveriges Socialdemokratiska Kvinnoforbund.

Sykes, R. B. 1990 'Black Women and the Continuing Struggle for Resources', in D. Spender (ed.) *Heroines: A contemporary anthology of Australian women writers*, Melbourne: Penguin.

Szreter, S. 1993 'The Idea of Demographic Transition and the Study of Fertility Change: A critical intellectual history' in *Population and Development Review*, 49.

Tahi, B. 1995 'Biculturalism: The model of Te Ohu Whakatupu', in M. Wilson and A. Yeatman (eds) *Justice & Identity: Antipodean practices*, Sydney: Allen & Unwin.

Tajfel, H. 1978 *Differentiation Between Social Groups: Studies in the social psychology of intergroup relations*, London: Academic Press for the European Association of Experimental Social Psychology.

Thompson, Linda 1991 'Family Work: Women's sense of fairness', *Journal of Family Issues* 12(2) June: 181–196.

Thornton, M. 1990 *The Liberal Promise: Anti-discrimination legislation in Australia*, Melbourne: Oxford University Press.

Thornton, M. 1994 'The Seductive Allure of EEO', in N. Grieve and A. Burns (eds) *Australian Women: Contemporary feminist thought*, Melbourne: Oxford University Press.

Thornton, M. 1995 *Public and Private: Feminist legal debates*, Melbourne: Oxford University Press.

Titmuss, R. 1974 *Social Policy*, London: George Allen & Unwin.

Tittle, C. R. 1980 *Sanctions and Social Deviance*, New York: Praeger.

Turner, B. S. (ed.) 1993 *Citizenship and Social Theory*, London: Sage.

Turner, J. C. 1987 *Rediscovering the Social Group: A self-categorization theory*, Oxford: Basil Blackwell.

Tyrrell, I. 1991 *Woman's World/Woman's Empire: The WCTU in international perspective 1880–1930*, Chapel Hill: University of North California Press.

Ullmann-Margalit, E. 1977 *The Emergence of Norms*, Oxford: Oxford University Press.

Ungerson, C. (ed.) 1990 *Gender and Caring*, Hemel Hempstead: Harvester.

United Nations Development Program 1995 *Human Development Report*, London: Oxford University Press.

University of Adelaide, 1995 Sexual Harassment Policy and Sexual Harassment Complaint Resolution Procedures.

UTS (University of Technology, Sydney) 1995 'Women, Culture and Universities: A Chilly Climate?' *Conference Proceedings*.

Vanek, Joahn 1980 'Time Spent in Housework', in A. Amsden (ed.) *The Economics of Women and Work*, New York: Penguin, pp. 82–90.

Vasta, E. 1991, 'Gender, Class and Ethnic Relations: The domestic and work experiences of Italian migrant women in Australia', in G. Bottomley et al. (eds) *Intersexions: Gender/class/culture/ethnicity*, Sydney: Allen & Unwin.

Victoria University of Technology 1995 *Nexus* 5 (23) November 6.

Victorian Trades Hall Council 1993 'Making Affirmative Action Work', in E. M. Davis and V. Pratt (eds) *Making the Link 4: Affirmative action and industrial relations*, Canberra: Australian Government Publishing Service.

Wajcman, J. 1991 *Feminism Confronts Technology*, Sydney: Allen &Unwin.

Walby, Sylvia 1986 *Patriarchy at Work*, Cambridge: Polity.

Walker, Katherine and Woods, M. 1976 *Time Use: A measure of household production of family goods and services*, Washington: Center for the Family of the Home Economics Association.

Wallace, V. 1946 *Women and Children First: An outline of a population policy for Australia*, Melbourne: Geoffrey Cumberledge and Oxford University Press.

Walter, J. 1996 *Tunnel Vision: The failure of political imagination*, Sydney: Allen & Unwin.

Wanganeen, R. 1990 'The Aboriginal Struggle in the Face of Terrorism', in S. Watson (ed.), *Playing the State*, Sydney: Allen & Unwin.

Waring, M. 1985 *Women Politics and Power*, London: Unwin Paperback.

Watkins, S. C. 1993 'If All We Knew About Women Was What We Read in Demography, What Would We Know?' *Demography* 30(4): 556–558.

Watson, S. 1988 *Accommodating Inequality: Gender and housing*, Sydney: Allen & Unwin.

Watson, S. 1990 *Playing the State*, Sydney: Allen & Unwin.

Wattenberg, B. 1987 *The Birth Dearth: What happens when people in free countries don't have enough babies?* New York: Pharos Books.

Wattenberg, B. 1998 'Where Have All the People Gone?' *Age, Good Weekend* 17 January.

Webb, R. K. 1960 *Harriet Martineau: A radical Victorian*, London: Heinemann.

Weimer, D. (ed.) 1995 *Institutional Design*, Boston: Kluwer Academic.

Weiss, R. S. 1987 'Men and Their Wives' Work', in F. J. Crosby (ed.) *Spouse, Parent, Worker: On gender and multiple roles*, New Haven: Yale University Press.

West, C. and Fenstermaker, S. 1995 'Doing Difference' *Gender and Society* 9(1) February: 8–37.

West, C. and Zimmermann, D. H. 1987 'Doing Gender' *Gender and Society* 1(2) June: 125–151.

Western, M., Baxter, J. and Western J. 1993 Class Structure of Australia Project, machine-readable dataset, Brisbane: University of Queensland.

White, W. 1993 'A Systems Perspective on Sexual Exploitation of Clients by Professional Helpers', *Dulwich Centre Newsletter*, Nos. 3 & 4: 77–87.

Whiteford, P. 1994 'Income Distribution and Social Policy Under a Reformist Government: The Australian Experience', *Policy and Politics* 24(4).

Willard, F. 1879 *Home Protection Manual*, reprinted in DeSwarte Gifford 1987.

Willard, F. 1895 *Do Everything: A handbook for the world's white ribboners*, reprinted in DeSwarte Gifford 1987.

Willey, B. 1949 *Nineteenth Century Studies*, London: Chatto & Windus.

Williams, J. 1991 'Domesticity as the Dangerous Supplement of Liberalism' *Journal of Women's History* 2(3): 69–88.

Wilson, R. 1996 'Ms-leading indicators', *Australian* 28 February, p. 24.

Winter, J. and M. Teitelbaum, 1998 *A Question of Numbers: High migration, low fertility and national identity*, New York: Hill and Wang.

Wise, S. and L. Stanley 1985 *Georgie Porgie: Sexual Harassment in everyday life*, London: Pandora.

Women's Policy Unit 1992 *Stop Violence Against Women: Queensland Government statement of policy*, Brisbane: Women's Policy Unit, Office of the Cabinet.

Women's Policy Unit 1994 *Women's Budget Statement 1994–95*, Brisbane: Women's Policy Unit, Office of the Cabinet.

Woods, M. H. 1994 Australian Family Association, Address to the Liberal Party Weekend Seminar (typescript).

Wright, E. O., Shire, K., Hwang, S. L., Dolan, M. and Baxter, J. 1992 'The Non-effects of Class on the Gender Division of Labor in the Home: A comparative study of Sweden and the United States', *Gender and Society* 6(2): 252–282.

Yates, J. 1988 'Housing in the 1980s: Dream or nightmare?' *Current Affairs Bulletin* 65(1).

Yates, J. 1989a *Home Ownership: Who misses out in the private sector and why*, Background Paper No. 2, National Housing Policy Review, Canberra: Department of Community Services and Health.

Yates, J. 1989b 'Housing Policy Reform: A constructive critique', *Urban Studies* 26: 419–433.

Yates, J. 1991 *Australia's Owner-Occupied Housing Wealth and its Impact on Income Distribution*, Social Policy Research Centre Reports and Proceedings, University of New South Wales.

Yates, J. 1994 'Home ownership and Australia's Housing Finance System', *Urban Policy and Research* 12(1): 27–39.

Yates, J. and Vipond, J. 1989 *Housing and Urban Inequalities*, Department of Economics, University of Sydney.

Yeandle, S. 1984 *Women's Working Lives*, London: Tavistock.

Yeatman, A. 1990 *Bureaucrats, Technocrats, Femocrats: Essays on the contemporary Australian state*, Sydney: Allen & Unwin.

Young, G. M. 1963 *Victorian England: Portrait of an age*, London: Oxford University Press.

Young, I. M. 1990 *Justice and the Politics of Difference*, Princeton: Princeton University Press.

Young, M. and Willmott P. 1973 *The Symmetrical Family*, London: Routledge.

Zagarri, R. 1992 'Morals, Manners, and the Republican Mother', *American Quarterly* 44(2): 192–215.

Zeldin, T. 1973 *France 1848–1945*, Oxford: Clarendon Press.

Ziegert, K. A. 1995 'Judicial Decision-making, Community and Consented Values: Some remarks on Braithwaite's republican model', *Sydney Law Review* 17: 352–373.

Zschoche, S. 1989 'Dr Clarke Revisited: Science, true womanhood and female collegiate education', *History of Education Quarterly* 29(4): 545–569.

Index